The Writer's Handbook for Sociology

The Writer's Handbook for Sociology gives students the tools that they need to develop evidence-based writing skills and format academic papers in American Psychological Association (APA) and American Sociological Association (ASA) style. This book helps learners develop a reader-friendly writing style incorporating active voice, parallel structure, and conciseness. In addition, grammar and mechanics are presented in a systematic way to facilitate learning, helping students fill learning gaps.

Dona J. Young, MA, teaches professional writing at Indiana University Northwest. She earned an MA in education from The University of Chicago and a BA in sociology from Northern Illinois University. Young believes that writing is a powerful learning tool and that learning shapes our lives; she is also the author of *The Writer's Handbook: A Guide for Social Workers* (2014), *Business English: Writing for the Global Workplace* (2008), and *Foundations of Business Communication* (2006), among others.

The Writer's Handbook for Sociology

Dona J. Young

Routledge
Taylor & Francis Group

NEW YORK AND LONDON

First published 2019
by Routledge
52 Vanderbilt Avenue, New York, NY 10017

and by Routledge
2 Park Square, Milton Park, Abingdon, Oxon, OX14 4RN

Routledge is an imprint of the Taylor & Francis Group, an informa business

Library of Congress Cataloging-in-Publication Data
Names: Young, Dona J., author.
Title: The writer's handbook for sociology / Dona J. Young.
Description: New York, NY : Routledge, 2019. | Includes bibliographical
references and index. |
Identifiers: LCCN 2018034565 (print) | LCCN 2018036439 (ebook) | ISBN
9780203702949 (Master Ebook) | ISBN 9781351334853 (Web pdf) | ISBN
9781351334846 (ePub) | ISBN 9781351334839 (Mobipocket) | ISBN
9781138571266 (hardback) | ISBN 9781138571273 (pbk.)
Subjects: LCSH: Sociology--Authorship. | Sociology--Research. | Academic
writing. | Sociology--Study and teaching (Higher)
Classification: LCC HM569 (ebook) | LCC HM569 .Y68 2019 (print) | DDC
301.072--dc23
LC record available at https://lccn.loc.gov/2018034565

ISBN: 978-1-138-57126-6 (hbk)
ISBN: 978-1-138-57127-3 (pbk)
ISBN: 978-0-203-70294-9 (ebk)

Typeset in ITC Galliard and Univers by
Servis Filmsetting Ltd, Stockport, Cheshire

To the open mind in quest of truth

Contents

Part 4:
Quick Guides   **383**

Writing in Sociology

Purpose, Voice, and Viewpoint

Academic writing is challenging, even for those who have developed excellent composition skills. That's because academic writing is *scholarly writing* and embraces a unique set of demands and expectations beyond skills developed in other types of writing.

For example, academic writing is *evidence-based*: writers use research to support their claims, arguments, and outcomes and must meticulously cite their sources. In addition, academic writing applies elements of style such as *third-person viewpoint* and *active voice*, which take conscious effort to apply until you develop your academic voice. In sociology, you also have other requirements, such as applying guidelines from citation systems, such as those of the American Psychological Association (APA) and the American Sociological Association (ASA), which are briefly discussed in this chapter and in various chapters throughout the book.[1,2]

In fact, until you become familiar with writing in sociology, you may feel like a novice writer all over again, even if you have well-honed skills. By developing expertise with *purpose, voice,* and *viewpoint,* you are building core skills in evidence-based writing: these skills support you in developing a writing style that meets the expectations of any audience, including your professors, the publishers of scholarly journals, and potential employers.

This chapter reviews the types of writing in sociology and how to adapt your writing for your audience to achieve effective results. From the chapters that follow, you will gain additional understanding and skill in evidence-based writing as well as APA and ASA citation styles. Even if you do not plan to become a professional sociologist, these skills will serve you well in all areas of your studies and throughout your career.

When you have completed this chapter, you will be able to:

- Understand how *academic*, *professional*, and *reflective* writing differ.

- Analyze purpose to determine audience, voice, and viewpoint.

- Adapt your voice for an academic audience.

- Apply APA and ASA guidelines for pronoun viewpoint, voice, and verb tense.

- Understand the difference between a thesis statement and a hypothesis.

- Write a purpose statement, a thesis statement, and an introductory paragraph.

- Discuss the relationship between voice and plagiarism.

As you review this chapter, understand that adapting your writing for your audience is an element of *editing*, not composing. In Chapter 2, "Process, Strategy, and Style," you will review the writing process and the importance of separating composing from editing. Thus, as you compose, do not expect yourself to write in a specific style or from a specific viewpoint: *apply principles to shape your words when you edit.* Let us get started by exploring *purpose* as it applies to academic, professional, and reflective writing.

Purpose

When you think of writing in sociology, the challenges of writing a paper probably come to mind—writing a paper can feel like a daunting task, even if you are not doing original research or submitting your paper for publication. However, in sociology, other types of writing are also important, and you will be at an advantage if you become proficient in the style of each: *academic writing*, *professional writing*, and *reflective writing*.

Academic Writing

Academic writing is evidence-based writing, and the most formal type of writing. Academic writing involves taking ideas and concepts apart: analyzing data, decisions, positions, and actions, as well as asking questions in a dispassionate, non-adversarial way. As a professional sociologist, you learn to remove bias, such as beliefs and opinions, from your writings. When you write a paper, you base your findings on research, fact, and logic.

Evidence-based academic writing tasks in sociology include the following:

- Research papers
- Arguments and summaries
- Case studies
- Participant-observation studies
- Abstracts and synopses
- Surveys and research design

Academic writing is complex because it involves the following:

- Knowing content or subject matter well enough to summarize in your own words
- Analyzing, synthesizing, and evaluating concepts
- Applying basic writing skills such as grammar, punctuation, word usage, and more
- Applying editing skills to reshape and revise for purpose, clarity, and structure

According to the *taxonomy of educational objectives*, a learner must understand and be able to apply information before being able to analyze, synthesize, or evaluate it.[3] Thus, when you get stuck with your writing, consider if the barriers that you are facing are due to not yet understanding the content well enough to write about it. At those times, read and re-read to deepen your understanding. Then reflect on what you have read and recollect key points, jotting them down in your own words. Critical reading is a precursor to critical writing; so when your writing does not flow well, identify what is holding you back and take the action you need to fill the learning gap.[4]

This book assists you in filling learning gaps in your composing and editing skills, and gives you structure for writing academic papers. Here's how to make real progress:

- Practice principles until you can apply the new learnings to your own writing
- Throughout the process, use writing as a learning tool by summarizing key points in your own words

Whenever you feel stuck, do what you need to do so that you can move forward—if you don't know what that is, discuss your topic with a friend.

Professional Writing

When you write a message to a professor or a colleague, you provide information, pose questions, and offer your views. In contrast to evidence-based writing, professional communication may include opinions and beliefs. In addition, professional writing involves developing relationships built on respect and trust: for professional writing, context is important, and relationships help define context. Though professional writing might sound easy compared to academic writing, knowing audience expectations and applying protocol makes a difference in the results you achieve.

Professional writing tasks include the following:

- E-mail messages
- Proposals
- Letters and memos

Reflective Writing

As you work on projects and conduct research, keep track of your insights and observations as well as sources for your research. Though reflective writing can be personal, anything that you write about your professional activities has important implications beyond your personal use. The following are examples of reflective writing:

- Notes
- Work journals
- Blogs

Each of these types of writing is explored in more depth in this chapter and throughout this book. Next, let us examine voice and how viewpoint relates to each type of writing.

Your Voice and Viewpoint

Voice is a powerful element of all writing. By becoming mindful of voice, you gain the ability to control the tone of your writing: using an effective tone shows respect for your readers, and you receive a better response from them. You see, to reach your audience, you must adapt your voice to meet *their expectations.*

In fact, your writing already spans a broad spectrum from casual to formal: think of the difference between the way that you write a text message to a friend and the way that you write an e-mail message to a professor. Now think of the kind of language that you use when you write a paper. *Do you notice that you already use a different voice for each type of writing?*

A starting point for understanding voice is pronouns.

Pronouns

First-Person or "I" Viewpoint

Use the first-person viewpoint when you are speaking from your own understanding and experience. When speaking from your own perspective, using "I" is a natural part of the writing process. (Note that the personal pronoun "I" is *always* capitalized.)

Second-Person or "You" Viewpoint

Use the second-person viewpoint when you intend to speak directly to your readers (or audience); for example, "You may be asked to chair the committee."

Third-Person Viewpoint

Use third-person viewpoint to convey information from an "outside" viewpoint or another's point of view; for example, "*The research* demonstrates the need for additional funding."

Since writing in sociology involves *reflective*, *professional*, and *academic* writing, here is how pronouns are used in each type of voice:

Reflective Voice

Write from your *reflective voice* for journals, notes, and blogs. For reflective writing that is personal, write in whatever style you wish. When you are expressing your feelings and opinions, you naturally speak from the *I* **viewpoint**.

Another purpose of reflective writing is to keep track of events and record your thoughts, at times in a work journal. In fact, in some professions, notes are considered official records. Thus, when you are employed under those circumstances, be fastidious with your personal notes: adjust your voice and writing style for the possibility that they could become part of a legal case and enter the public domain.

Do you currently write online, such as on social media sites? This type of reflective writing is already part of the public domain and used by potential employers to screen applicants. A good general rule is not to say anything online or in writing that you would not mind being broadcast on the local and national news: careers have been destroyed by a single tweet or posting; text messages have also destroyed careers and been used as evidence in civil and criminal cases.

Professional Voice

Write from your *professional voice* when you write e-mail messages to professors and colleagues. Limit your use of the *I* **viewpoint**, shifting to the *you* **viewpoint** when possible; for example:

Weak: I need your assistance.

Revised: Would you be able to assist me?

Connect with your readers and show them respect through correct, clear, and concise writing. Avoid texting language, slang, colloquialisms, and clichés as well as abbreviations: spell out words, use standard rules of capitalization, and write in full sentences. Also keep in mind that any e-mail that you write is essentially a legal document because it can be used as evidence in litigation: e-mail messages never go away, even when they are deleted.[5] In fact, all electronic messages leave a "footprint."

Academic Voice

Write from your *academic voice* for formal papers. Use the **third-person viewpoint**, avoiding the *you* **viewpoint** entirely (second person). Examples of using the third-person viewpoint would be "The study included important data" or "Jones conducted the research," and so on.

- If you are the sole *author* of a paper, refer to yourself as "I"; if you coauthor a paper, you and your coauthors may refer to yourselves as "we."

- When referring to the author of a study, book, or article, introduce an author by first and last name; subsequently, use only the author's last name, for example:

  Weak: Max's findings were supported by subsequent research.

  Revised: Weber's findings were supported by subsequent research.

Thus, at times, using the *I* **viewpoint** for academic writing would be acceptable; however, only in specific ways and places, such as when you are the author of a study, or perhaps when you share insights and recommendations in concluding remarks of a paper.

> *Note*: In general, APA style does not allow the use of first names, but uses only initials.

Academic Viewpoint and Voice

In academic writing, pronouns and verbs work together to construct a viewpoint and voice. For example, in not speaking from a personal voice, writers commonly use *passive voice*. Though passive voice is necessary and accepted in academic writing, APA style and ASA style both recommend using the *active voice* when possible. Thus, when you can, use the active voice, for example:

Passive voice:	The survey was administered to 500 registered voters.
Active voice:	Five hundred registered voters completed the survey.
Passive voice:	It was concluded that . . .
Active voice:	The authors concluded that . . .

Note: See Chapter 2, "Process, Strategy, and Style," and Chapter 8, "Active Voice," for more information about active and passive voice.

When you write about someone else's work, academic writing requires the *third person*. For example, when you are summarizing an article, you are not speaking from *your* point of view; you are speaking from the viewpoint of the *article's author*. Let us say that you are summarizing an article written by sociologist Max Weber. As you discuss Weber, you would most effectively write from the *third-person point of view, singular and plural*, for example:

Weber argues that capitalism . . .

Weber further determines that . . .

He maintains . . .

The Protestant ethic is a central focus . . .

In the above, the reader is not addressed directly. Instead, the third-person viewpoint focuses on the topic and what the article's author says about it. Writing from this viewpoint, you would connect to the reader in an indirect way, not a direct way.

Once again, in academic papers avoid using first-person pronouns, such as *I* and *me*, unless you are writing about your own research or the response part of a **summary-response essay**. In addition, in academic writing you would not speak directly to your audience, so you would also not use second-person pronouns, such as *you* and *your*. On the occasions when you speak from a personal viewpoint in an academic paper, edit out your opinions unless your views are part of a response or are supported by evidence.

Academic Writing and Verb Tense

Since academic writing involves evidence, references to research are common. Thus, verb tense is used slightly differently in academic writing than writing in real time.

- You could be citing research that was conducted decades ago and still make a comment such as, "Mills *concludes* that the sociological imagination is a good thing."

- As you write a description of your paper, stay in the present tense, for example:

  Do not state: This paper *will explore* population growth and poverty.

  Do state: This paper *explores* population growth and poverty.

In a literature review, if the discussion is of past events, stay within the chosen tense. Use past tense, such as "productivity increased," to describe the results. However, report *your* conclusions in the present tense, such as "The outcomes of the pilot indicate more research is needed." Here are some points to consider:

- When summarizing, paraphrasing, or quoting from a source, use a **signal verb**: signal verbs not only signal the reader that ideas are coming from another source, they also put ideas in a context, such as *agree, analyze, conclude, demonstrate, disagree, explain, identify, introduce, observe, report, suggest, theorize,* and so on.

- When emphasizing the findings of research, use the present tense.

  Mead demonstrates that the policy results in higher retention.

- When emphasizing how the author conducted the research, use the past tense.

  Mead surveyed 20 participants in the initial stages of the study.

- When contrasting research from different periods, use the past tense for older research and present tense for current research.

  Jones (2015) supports Turner's findings that additional research was needed.

- When describing situations that are conditional (which involve modals such as *would* or *could*), use the *subjunctive mood*.

  If the pilot *were* not conducted on site, the results *would* differ.

Use verbs to create smooth transitions among past, present, and future events. When you compose, keep your focus on getting your insights on the page; when you edit, screen your use of verb tense.

Purpose Statements, Theses, and Hypotheses

Purpose is at the core of all writing, and most academic writing defines purpose through a *thesis statement*. However, when writing a research paper, a *hypothesis* would define your central purpose. In addition, you can enhance your planning process by writing a *purpose statement*.

- A **purpose statement** summarizes your purpose, providing your aim or focus and letting your reader know what to expect.

- A **thesis statement** presents the topic, problem, or argument and lets the reader know how the topic will be developed.

- A **hypothesis** is a theory that can be tested: it is an explanation between two or more variables that predicts an outcome or explains a phenomenon.

Let's briefly review each type: the *purpose statement*, the *thesis statement*, and the *hypothesis*.

Purpose Statements

Purpose is the principal element of all writing, and some writers find that a purpose statement enhances their planning process. Here are some questions to get you started:

- What is your question?

- What are your key ideas?

- What value does your topic have?

- Does it matter? If so, why?

For example, if your professor asks for a description of your project before approving it, write a brief purpose statement.

Draft Message:

> *Hi,*
>
> *My name is Giorg Simms, and my purpose for writing is to let you know about my topic for the paper that is due in your SOC 223 class.*
>
> *I have chosen to do a paper on crime rates in urban areas because the topic is relevant and of interest.*
>
> *Giorg Simms*

In your final draft of a paper or even a message, avoid using the word *purpose*. In addition, do not introduce yourself by name in writing: the reader knows your name because of your sign-off or typed signature.

Revised Message:

> *Hi Professor Jones,*
>
> *For your SOC 223 class, my topic will discuss factors contributing to crime rates in urban areas. I have noticed that in some cities the crime rate continues to rise, whereas other cities have made progress in cutting crime. Because I might major in criminology, this topic intrigues me and could contribute to my future career.*
>
> *Would this topic be acceptable?*
>
> *Giorg Simms*

For an academic paper, a purpose statement would introduce the thesis statement; for example:

> **First draft:** The purpose of this paper is to examine various theories . . .
>
> **Revised:**   This paper examines various theories of . . .

A purpose statement would lead to your thesis statement, giving your reader an overview of the problem you are discussing.

Thesis Statements

The thesis statement is often presented toward the end of the first paragraph. A thesis statement expresses a unique and specific point about your topic, unifying the content of the entire paper. For most papers, you would write a thesis that could be argued. (Thus, your thesis statement would not be a statement of "fact," as facts would not be argued.)

To identify your purpose, start by defining your problem:

What is my core question?

For example, let us say your task is to summarize Max Weber's theory of capitalism and how it relates to the Protestant ethic. Start by stating the problem as a question:

Thesis Question: How does Weber's theory of capitalism relate to the Protestant ethic?

Next, turn your question into a statement:

Weber's theory reveals that the Protestant ethic, or belief system, encouraged its members to embrace capitalism.

Finally, once you understand some of the broader implications of your question, draft a statement that reflects your response:

Thesis Statement: Weber's theory of the Protestant ethic explains how the role of religion influenced the development of capitalism.

Once again, as you write about your purpose, avoid using the word *purpose*. For example, your first draft might include a statement such as the following:

The purpose of this paper is to discuss how Max Weber's theory of the Protestant ethic has influenced the development of capitalism.

When you revise your purpose statement, remove the word *purpose*:

Max Weber's theory of the Protestant ethic influenced the development of capitalism . . .

Let us turn one more problem into a thesis statement. For example, here is how you could work through a topic addressing *poverty*.

Thesis Question: What are the implications of increased poverty in major cities as compared to rural areas?

Thesis Statement: Increased poverty in rural areas has different
                         implications from increased poverty in major
                         cities.

While the introductory paragraph discusses purpose, body paragraphs present evidence to support the thesis, and the conclusion summarizes the results, tying back to the introduction and the thesis statement. (For more on paragraphs, see Chapter 7, "Cohesive Paragraphs and Transitions.")

Hypotheses

For formal research papers, a thesis statement is not sufficient. Instead, you would develop a hypothesis that is *testable*.

> [A hypothesis is] "a statement of how variables are expected to be related to one another, often according to predictions from a theory . . . A hypothesis predicts a relationship between or among variables, factors that change, or vary, from one person or situation to another."[6]

At times, exploratory studies are used to develop hypotheses, with the purpose of gaining information that would result in a hypothesis or prediction that could be tested. Thus, an exploratory study would not have its own hypothesis but rather would be used to develop one for subsequent research. Developing a testable hypothesis is a process that starts with observation and reflection and leads to data collection, review of the literature, and so on. Chapters 2 to 5 contain more information on research in sociology; for now, here are some basics about hypotheses.

Let's say your sociology professor wants to test a new method for teaching research skills and has asked you to conduct the research. You would start with a *research question*:

Research Question: Is Method X effective in teaching research
                         skills?

To test Method X, you would need something to compare it with, such as Method Z. As the researcher, you would turn the question into a *hypothesis* theorizing the expectations from the study.

Hypothesis: Method X is more effective than Method Z in
                         teaching research skills.

Remain flexible with your writing. Your purpose is likely to change as you probe more deeply into the problem and your insights become more profound. *Writing is thinking on paper*: as your thinking evolves, so does your writing.

Introductory Paragraph

In general, in the introductory paragraph, state your purpose and give an overview of your paper. In addition, you may wish to pose questions about your topic to awaken your reader's curiosity or use a quotation to draw interest. Though the thesis statement can be presented anywhere in the introductory paragraph, generally it comes toward the end of the paragraph so that it is placed in context.

The type of introductory paragraph that you write depends largely on the type of paper that you are writing. For example, when you are summarizing an article, *give a complete reference in the introductory paragraph*: include the author's name, the name of the article or book, and its purpose. Then throughout your paper, when you refer to authors and other subjects, refer to them by *last name*. The following is one possible template to use:

> In the article entitled "Facebook Addiction," Jones argues (or *asserts* or *reveals*) that ego casting is the predominant mode of communication on social media sites.

Your introductory paragraph is a critical element of your paper or essay: first impressions make a difference. If the reader is immediately engaged, he or she will look to confirm a good impression while reading the remainder of the work. However, the opposite is also true. An unfavorable initial impression leaves the reader looking to confirm his or her original reaction.

Have you ever put off writing a paper because you didn't know how to start? Writing the introduction first is a difficult approach. Since the introduction gives an overview of your paper, an introduction is naturally easier to write once you have developed your line of thought. By writing your introduction as a last step, you can incorporate the insight that you gained as you worked through the body and conclusion. The key is to start writing what you know about: once you start putting your thoughts on paper, one idea will lead to the next. Trust the process, but first you must engage in it. In fact, make it your goal to become immersed in your project—the more you read and think about it, the more your ideas will flow.

Introductory Paragraph—Research Papers

For research papers in the social sciences, common patterns have been identified for introducing topics. One pattern identified by John Swales is known as the CARS model: creating a research space. The CARS model of research reveals three rhetorical moves made in most research introductions.[7]

Move 1: Establishing a Research Territory

What is the social significance of your research?

1   Show that the research area is important, central, interesting, problematic, or relevant

2   Introduce and review items of previous research

Move 2: Establishing a Niche

What are the limitations of previous studies?

1   Identify gaps in previous research

2   Raise questions

3   Indicate how you will extend knowledge

Move 3: Occupying the Niche

How does your work contribute? How is your paper organized?

1   Outline purposes or state the nature of the present research

2   List research questions or hypotheses

3   Announce principal findings

4   State the value of the present research

5   Indicate the structure of the research paper

Especially for a research paper, writing the introductory paragraph last is the best approach. As one graduate student revealed, she spent six months thinking about how to start her master's paper. So, in frustration, she started in the middle, which led to her conclusions. Only in retrospect did she understand that writing the introduction first wasn't even a possibility.

Voice and Plagiarism

Academic writing can be intimidating: some writers think that they need to sound smart, so their writing becomes pretentious and filled with unnecessarily complicated words and long, complex sentences. All readers— even academic audiences—are more concerned about quality of thought than complicated wording designed to impress. Thus, one measure of all writing is authenticity.

Until you gain confidence in your own writing, the words of another will often sound more appealing than your own. At any rate, that is an argument developing writers sometimes use to justify taking parts of someone else's writing—whether it be sentences, paragraphs, or even parts of sentences.

The use of the internet has made plagiarism more tempting and accessible now than in the past; however, plagiarism is a crime whenever it occurs. Though plagiarism is about stealing someone else's words and ideas, it is about more than the words on the page. When writers depend on the words of others, rather than their own, they are robbing themselves of their skill development and their self-confidence. You see, as you write, you are developing your critical thinking skills—your ability to solve problems. Plagiarism interferes with skill development, and it also has other long-term repercussions that seem subtle but are no less devastating.

Plagiarism is a form of lying, and research shows that "telling small lies causes changes in the brain that lead people down a 'slippery slope' toward increasingly large acts of dishonesty." In fact, "deceivers often recall how small acts of dishonesty snowballed over time and they suddenly found themselves committing quite large crimes."[8] In effect, each new deception becomes easier to commit than the previous one.

The way to feel confident about writing is to find your voice, and the way to find your voice is to write from your own experience about your own ideas and insights until your words flow. Make it a point never to copy any part of someone else's writing: even when you take notes, put ideas in your own words, keeping track of sources for possible citations.

You can never expect your writing to be perfect. The value of writing comes from its power as a learning tool. As you write about a topic, you are developing your thinking and enhancing your ability to solve problems. Learning can be frustrating at times, and even painful, and there are no shortcuts: *just like writing, learning is a process that takes time.*

As John Dewey once said, "You become what you learn."

Chapter 2, "Process, Strategy, and Style," reviews the process of writing: by writing freely, you develop your ability to write fluently. Then, as you edit, you can shape your writing for your audience: good writing is a result of effective editing. As you build your editing skills, you will see that it is through editing that your voice becomes clear, concise, and engaging.

Recap

Academic writing requires that you write about topics for their merit and relevance to the profession or to fulfil someone else's requirements, such as a professor's or a publisher's. If you can embrace these requirements rather than resist them, writing becomes less stressful. As you write about a variety of topics, you become a more versatile writer and thinker.

Here are some of the points stressed in this chapter:

- Understand the purpose of each type of writing task.

- Adapt your voice to the expectations of your audience.

- Develop your academic voice by writing in the third person.

- Apply APA and ASA guidelines for pronoun viewpoint and verb tense.

- For essays, summaries, and arguments, include a thesis statement in the first paragraph of the work.

- For research papers, develop a hypothesis that can be tested.

- Write from your own voice: *plagiarism is a thief.*

In the next chapter, you will learn about the writing process and more about style and how to structure papers.

Writing Workshop

Activity A: Analyzing Voice and Purpose

Instructions: Select a paper that you have written or exchange papers with a peer. Analyze the paper by answering the questions below. (Take notes as you do your analysis so that you are prepared to complete the second part of this assignment, *Part 2: Process Message*—see below.)

1   **Voice**

    1.1   For what type of audience is the paper written?

    1.2   What pronoun viewpoint(s) did the writer use throughout the paper?

    1.3   Does the writer adapt the voice of the paper for the audience?

    1.4   Does the writer need to make changes in voice or viewpoint? If so, how?

2   **Thesis Statement**

    2.1   Can you identify the thesis of the paper? What is the original question?

    2.2   Does the paper answer that question effectively? Please explain.

    2.3   Where does the thesis appear? Is the thesis placed effectively?

3   **Introductory Paragraph and Conclusion**

    3.1   Does the introductory paragraph give an overview of the paper?

    3.2   Are the authors who are cited referred to by last name?

    3.3   Is the conclusion tied to the thesis or questions posed in the introductory paragraph?

Activity B: Process Message

Instructions: Write your professor a process message describing what you learned in this chapter about voice, viewpoint, and purpose along with what you discovered from analyzing the paper in Activity A above.

This type of message is called a *process message* because you discuss your learning process by sharing insights, asking questions, and giving updates. In short, you can also think of a process message as a *progress message*. Your professor will provide details about how to send your message (see Figure 1.1).

> *Note*: For all messages, use a proper greeting such as "Hi Professor Smith." Also use an appropriate closing. Since e-mail messages are considered *informal*, do not use a *formal* closing, such as "sincerely," but instead use an informal closing, such as "All the best," "Best regards," or "Enjoy your day."

Send	From ▾	Jeremy Smith
	To...	Professor Tamburro
	Cc...	
	Subject	Process Message: Paper Analysis
	Attached	Smith.Assn 1.1 Paper Analysis.docx 12 KB

Hi Professor Tamburro,

Here is an analysis of the paper that I edited and revised; my paper is attached.

Some of the changes included stating my purpose more clearly in the introduction and then providing more evidence to support my thesis. These changes led to a stronger conclusion that tied back into my introduction. I also corrected errors in APA style, such as in the running head and references.

I look forward to receiving your feedback.

All the best,

Jeremy

Jeremy Smith
Sociology 232

Figure 1.1 A process message is a learning tool that allows you to communicate "behind-the-scenes" information about your process in completing an assignment.

References

1   APA. (2010). *Publication manual of the American Psychological Association* (6th ed). Washington, DC: American Psychological Association.

2   ASA. (2014). *American Sociological Association style guide* (5th ed). Washington, DC: American Sociological Association.

3   Bloom, B. (Ed.). (1984). *The taxonomy of educational objectives.* Boston, MA: Addison Wesley.

4   University of Leicester. (n.d.). Student Learning Development: What is critical reading? Retrieved from https://www2.le.ac.uk/offices/ld/resources/ writing/writing-resources/critical-reading

5   Young, D. J. (2006). *Foundations of business communication.* New York: McGraw-Hill/Irwin.

6   Henslin, J. M. (2012). *Sociology: A down to earth approach* (11th ed). New York: Pearson.

7   Swales, J. M., & Feak, C. B. (2008). *Academic writing for graduate students.* Ann Arbor: University of Michigan Press, pp. 242–244.

8   Garrett, N., Lazzaro, S. C., Ariela, D., & Sharot, T. (2016). The brain adapts to dishonesty. *Nature Neuroscience*, 19, 1727–1732.

CHAPTER 2

Process, Strategy, and Style

When you are assigned a fresh writing project, are your first thoughts about the finished product or about your process? For example, do you quickly become focused on the impending due date, the quality of your writing, getting it right, and your final grade? Or do you relax into the project, reflecting on first steps and getting excited about what you will learn?

If relaxing into a project is not your *modus operandi*, you are not alone. As one sociology professor shared, he had so much writing anxiety in college that he wrote "first and final drafts," often finishing a paper the morning it was due. Once a draft was completed, his anxiety would lift, "If I only had one more week . . . I didn't really understand what I was writing about until my draft was completed."

To gain maximum value of your time, acknowledge your anxiety and embrace the process: launch a project by making a plan based on *backtiming*: set *internal deadlines* starting from the due date and working backwards. Deadlines have a psychological impact, so use them to your advantage. Then do not expect the first draft of any part of your paper to be perfect—that's the purpose of editing.

- The first section, *Managing the Process*, reviews the writing process, providing a foundation for developing a writing strategy.

- The second section, *Simplifying Your Style*, reviews elements of style for academic writing, such as active voice, parallel structure, and information flow.

- The third section, *Clarifying Your Tone*, covers principles of style to shape the tone of professional writing, such as being concise, shifting to the "you" viewpoint, and focusing on the positive.

When you have completed this chapter, you will be able to:

- Develop an effective writing strategy on familiar and unfamiliar topics.

- Use prewriting techniques and planning to overcome writing blocks.

- Overcome editor's block by composing freely and editing effectively.

- Solve writing problems by applying mind mapping, page mapping, and freewriting.

- Manage aspects of style that lead to simple, clear, and concise writing.

- Apply principles of style to shape the tone of academic and professional writing.

Managing the Process

When you have a new project, do you ever get stuck before you even start? If so, you might think that you have *writer's block*. However, writer's block is more common among seasoned writers who cannot think of what to write than it is among writers who have a specific topic or task. In fact, developing writers are more likely to suffer from *editor's block* and *critic's block* than from *writer's block*. By analyzing your process, you can apply the correct remedy. Let's explore a few less well-known writing blocks, and then review process tools so that you can fine-tune your writing process.

Writing Blocks

A first step to improving your writing process is to gain insight into how you currently approach a writing task; for example:

- Do you try to figure things out in your head *before* putting words on the page?

- Do you correct grammar, punctuation, and word usage *as you compose*?

- Do your ideas dissolve before you get them down?

- Do you submit work without proofreading and editing it?

If you answered *yes* to any of the above questions, you are likely to have *editor's block.*

- **Editor's Block Type A:** You edit as you compose, and your ideas get jammed in your head or dissolve before they reach the page.

- **Editor's Block Type B:** You do not proofread or edit your work because you feel anxious about finding errors or are unsure of what to correct or revise.

You can overcome **Editor's Block Type A** by separating composing from editing: *write freely and then edit ruthlessly.* By writing freely, you will see an immediate difference in your writing, producing more in less time. To get your words on the page, use composing and planning tools such as **mind mapping**, **page mapping**, and **freewriting**, which are covered on pages 27–33.

You can overcome **Editor's Block Type B** by planning time to edit: set an *internal due date* for your first draft so that you have time for a *final copy edit.* Then work systematically to build your editing skills. (You get an entrée to some principles of style in this chapter on pages 34–43, with full chapters on major principles in Part 2 of this book, "Editing for Clarity.")

Another issue that holds writers back is *critic's block.* Starting a new project takes motivation because it involves facing the unknown, which is always uncomfortable. At those times, it takes extra strength to muster up the energy to push through doubts and fears.

- **Critic's Block:** You have a subtle, nagging anxiety about writing. When you think about writing, you remember negative feedback that you didn't understand or expect. As a result, you put off writing tasks because the writing process feels uncomfortable and even intimidating.

To overcome **Critic's Block**, turn off messages that are self-defeating: *No one writes perfectly.* In fact, fear of criticism is worse than criticism itself; that's because once you hear the actual words, you can regroup and emerge stronger. In contrast, fear is paralyzing, and the only way to combat fear is to take action: *start writing, even if you are writing about your own fears.*

Phases of Writing

To stop yourself from editing as you compose, mindfully focus on only one phase of the writing process at a time: **composing** *or* **editing** *or* **revising**. Proofreading your copy is the final step.

1   **Composing:** creating, inventing, discovering, and molding your topic.

    a   **Prewriting**: researching, reading, discussing, taking notes, mapping, and thinking reflectively.

    b   **Planning:** organizing and prioritizing key ideas; clarifying purpose and audience.

    c   **Drafting:** getting your ideas on the page in narrative form.

2   **Editing:** making stylistic changes so that writing is clear and concise.

3   **Revising:** restructuring, rethinking, or reorganizing content so that your message is effective.

4   **Proofreading:** correcting grammar, punctuation, and word usage as well as making final formatting adjustments.

Editing is the key to producing good writing: develop an obsession for editing, and you will bring your writing to higher levels. You do not need to complete an entire paper before editing or revising, but try to complete one or two pages first. Feel free to go back and forth from composing to editing or revising throughout the entire production of a document. The *key* is doing only one activity at a time.[1]

The Centipede Syndrome

Do you try to edit your words as you compose? As you read the following poem by Katherine Craster (1871), consider how it relates to the writing process:[2]

> 'The Centipede was happy quite,
> Until a Toad in fun
> Said, "Pray, which leg goes after which?"
> And worked her mind to such a pitch,
> She lay distracted in a ditch
> Considering how to run.'

British philosopher George Humphrey (1889–1966) developed a theory about hyper-reflection known as *Humphrey's Law*, which states that "consciously thinking about one's performance of a task that involves automatic processing impairs one's performance of it."[3]

Does the centipede syndrome help explain why your words get lost before they reach the page? The most important step in the writing process is to separate composing from editing: *compose freely and then edit ruthlessly.*

Composing and Prewriting

Until you compose freely, writing is more difficult than it needs to be. When you stop editing as you compose, and composing still feels difficult, you may not yet understand your topic. To jumpstart your process, focus on *prewriting* to develop the thinking behind the writing. Prewriting activities—reading, thinking, discussing, and summarizing—help you develop an understanding of your topic in a gentle, natural way:

- Reading is a form of meditation and reflection: do you notice that some of your best ideas bubble up as you read?

- Discussing your project allows you to probe more deeply and articulate your thinking more clearly.

Reflective thinking gives you insights when you least expect them; when you feel blocked, change activities—but stay engaged. As you read and discuss, jot down insights and questions in a notebook or on your computer (or an app on your phone), putting concepts *in your own words*. Writing down insights and details keeps you engaged with your topic and connected to your project. After you have done some research, get your ideas down in a quick and spontaneous way by *freewriting*.

Freewriting

Simply start writing: get your words on the page in a free-flow, stream-of-consciousness way. As you freewrite, you build your ability to compose freely as you practice blocking the compulsion to correct your writing.

■ **If you have never tried freewriting, set the clock for 10 minutes and start writing whatever comes to mind.**

Since writing is a problem-solving activity, writing freely will help clear your head, allowing you to focus and renew your energy. Once you are engaged with your topic, try *focused writing*.

Focused Writing

Focused writing helps you make good use of small amounts of time that would otherwise be lost. When you are avoiding a task, freewrite about why you might be putting it off and then transition into a focused writing on what you already know about the topic.

- ■ **Select a topic and write about only that topic for about 10 to 15 minutes or three pages. Put all ideas on the page, even if you can't yet see the connections—keep your ideas flowing without correcting them.**

According to Leonardo da Vinci, "Inaction weakens the vigors of the mind . . . action strengthens the essence of creation." Take action and you will make progress. Use writing as a learning tool: start putting your ideas on the page as soon as you begin a new project. *Write to learn.*

Planning Tools

Planning tools help you to get your ideas on the page as well as to organize and prioritize them. Though you may be familiar with the planning tools discussed here, the key is using them to develop flow with your writing.

Formal Outlines

Many people are intimidated by formal outlines because an outline is difficult to structure before you have become thoroughly familiar with the topic. Experiment using an outline in a flexible way; for example, use an outline as a brainstorming tool before you start to write or as an organizing tool after you have a draft. (Most computer software programs have a template for creating a formal outline.)

Start with your **central idea** (or thesis statement). Write a skeleton outline and then fill in your ideas. Be flexible with your outline until it is time to

Figure 2.1 Building a skeleton outline around a central idea can be a first step in creating a formal outline

Homicide[4]

I.   Introductory Paragraph
II. Body
  A. Historical Context
    1. History in the United States
      a. Colonial Times
      b. 1900s to Present
    2. History in Europe
    3. Variants of Homicide
  B. Modernity, Social Class, and Homicide
  C. Social Structure and Homicide
III. Concluding Paragraph or Section
  A. Summary of Main Points
  B. Recommendations

turn it in, at which time make sure it meets the standards of a formal outline. In terms of structure, each part of the outline should contain at least two or more points: that means for every number "I," you should also have at least a "II"; for every letter "A," you should also have at least a "B"; and so on (see Figure 2.1 above).

Scratch Outlines

Rather than using a formal structure, roughly sketch your ideas on paper before you begin to write. Many writers do this informally, thinking they are doing something wrong because they are not developing a formal outline. In fact, if your topic is unfamiliar, scratch outlines can be superior to formal outlines; they are more flexible and adaptable to change. (You can also think of a "scratch" outline as a "draft" outline: planning is a process. Your ideas will evolve as you learn more about your topic.) Let go of rigid structures so that your ideas can take shape as you gain insight.

Mind Maps

Mind mapping is an alternative to writing a formal outline. This form of brainstorming, also called *clustering*, allows you to get your ideas down in a quick, spontaneous way. First, choose your topic. Next, write your topic in the middle of the page, circling it. Finally, free-associate ideas, as in Figure 2.2 below, which is a mind map responding to the question, "What is difficult about writing?"

Page Maps

Put the key points from your scratch outline or mind map along the side of a blank page. Then fill in the details by using each key point as the topic for a *focused-writing activity* (see Coaching Tip, page 31). This technique helps eliminate the hurdle of starting with a blank page. Once you have your page map, write about what you know first. When you get stuck, do more research (see Figure 2.3, page 31).

Figure 2.2 Mind Map: *What is difficult about writing?* Use mind mapping to get your ideas on the page before they dissolve. Also use mind mapping to plan your day, or an important phone call.

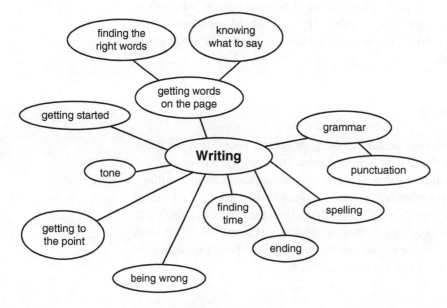

Figure 2.3 Page Map: Finding a job. After you complete a mind map, use the information to create a page map. For example, imagine that you did a mind map on *finding a job*; these could be your side headings.

FINDING A JOB

INTRODUCTION

> Thesis statement
>
> Finding a job requires skill and know-how

NETWORKING

> Associations
>
> Local organizations
>
> Online

PORTFOLIO

> Résumés
>
> Letters of reference
>
> Work samples

PAY AND BENEFITS

> Medical and dental
>
> Tuition reimbursement
>
> Training

Coaching Tip: Gain practice in applying these tools

1. Select a topic and spend 3 minutes drawing a mind map.

2. Next, turn your mind map into a page map.

3. Finally, under each side heading on your page map, compose freely for about 3 minutes.

As an alternative, after you complete the mind map, do a 10-minute focused writing on your topic.

Fishbone Diagrams

Also known as a "root-cause diagram" or "Ishikawa diagram," the fishbone diagram is a brainstorming tool used to discover root causes. In using the fishbone, start by identifying your problem, and then identify major components of it. For each component, ask "why" five separate times. (If you do an internet search on "fishbone brainstorming technique," you will find different variations of this tool.)

■ **To use the fishbone in an informal way, first turn your problem into a statement, and then work through it by asking the question "why" five times, for example:**

Problem statement: I am having difficulty with this writing task.

> Why?   I am having trouble getting started.
>
> Why?   I am feeling as if it is out of my control.
>
> Why?   I don't understand the topic well enough.
>
> Why?   I haven't done my research.
>
> Why?   I haven't taken the time to find resources.

Once you have gained insight into your problem, here is an additional step to add to your fishbone diagram process:

> **Next Step:** Do research today from 3 to 4 p.m.

Journalist's Questions

Journalists focus on the *who, what, when, where, why,* and *how* of an event. When you find yourself stuck, use these questions to tease out the dynamics of your problem.

- **Who?**   Who or what is involved or affected?

- **What?**   What problems need to be resolved? What are the desired outcomes? Which details are important, which irrelevant?

- **When?**   When did the event happen? What is the timeline? Is the time frame relevant?

- **Where?**   Is a specific location involved? Is the location significant or unique?

- **How?**   How did the events occur or the situation evolve? Who did what?

- **Why?**   Why did this happen? Why is this important? Why is my solution the best?

You can also adapt these questions to plan your task:

- **Who?**   Who is my reader? What does my reader expect?

- **What?**   What outcomes can I expect? What are some differing views?

- **When?**   What is my time frame? When is the project due? What are my internal due dates?

- **How?**   How will I complete this task? How can others assist me?

- **Why?**   Why is this issue important? What is at stake?

A difficult element of all writing is seeing beyond your own point of view: examine the problem from various angles and consider your reader's viewpoint.

Purpose: Content and Context

Writing is a problem-solving activity. For all writing, purpose is vital and drives the process; purpose starts with the question, "What is the problem?"

Once you have defined your problem, immerse yourself in the research, and start writing: the process will draw you toward answers. That's why selecting a topic that interests you is critical. If you engage deeply with the topic, you may become intrinsically motivated to ask deep questions and maintain the interest needed to chase down answers. However, when you start a project, you may try to start writing a response at the peril of not understanding the question at the root of the problem. As Gertrude Stein said:

> What is the question? If there is no question, then there is no answer.[5]

Writing in sociology goes beyond topic or content and demands that you frame your writing in the *context* of each project.

- What type of writing does your task entail:

    o   Academic? Professional? Reflective?

    o   Summary? Argument?

- What are your professor's requirements?

You can put much work into a paper; but if instructions are not followed, you are not likely to reap good results. In addition to researching your topic, also research the expectations for the assignment. For example, one graduate student was given the assignment to summarize various theories on child abuse. After doing a thorough summary, she received a C on her paper. When she asked what her summary was lacking, her professor responded, "You did not provide an argument. You're in graduate school and should know that." Her naiveté was in interpreting "summary" at face value.

While your professor will give you some details, you must dig more deeply into the type (sometimes referred to as "genre") of the assignment: certain types of writing have a history and "personality." For example, a literature review or case study follows an established pattern. The closer your paper follows the traditional pattern—or expectations in the field—the better your outcomes will be. (See Chapter 3, "Research and Evidence-Based Writing," Chapter 4, "Literature Review," and Chapter 5, "Writing in the Field.")

Once you have your topic and understand the context, focus on defining the problem until your thesis or your hypothesis becomes clear. When you can articulate your thesis, you understand your mission and are ready to convey it to your audience effectively. At that point, purpose will drive the writing process.

Writing is *thinking on paper*. When you feel stuck, write yourself clear-headed. As you write, your understanding becomes clear. Go back and forth between pre-writing and composing: read more and then discuss your ideas with a peer. After you read, summarize what you have learned *in your own words*. (Cut-and-paste plagiarism destroys careers and confidence.)

- Don't wait for the muse: schedule your writing time and show up.

- Identify a topic that you *want* to learn about.

- Be mindful of your writing blocks and manage them effectively.

- Remember that when you get stuck, you might need to read more, discuss your topic, or take a break.

- Embrace the process: stay engaged and use process tools that work for you.

Simplifying Your Style

Academic writing has a reputation for being overcomplicated and replete with long, passive sentences. At one time, complicated writing was the norm in academia. One notorious example is Talcott Parsons, a major theorist in sociology in the 1950s and 1960s. Parsons is known for his work with social systems theory and was infamous for writing "page-long sentences" that were grammatically correct.

In *The Sociological Imagination*, Charles Wright Mills categorizes social scientists on the basis of their understanding of and appreciation for Parsons' grand theory presented in *The Social System*.[6,7] One of the categories included "those who do not claim to understand it, but who like it very much." To sum up the conundrum, Mills states:

> "Now all this raises a sore point—intelligibility. . . . After all the impediments to meaning are removed from grand theory and what is intelligible becomes available, what, then, is being said?"[8]

Today academics are expected to produce intelligible work that is also accessible. However, academic writing still has a reputation for being overly complicated. In part, that is because academic writing must distance itself from the "I" viewpoint, making passive voice an easy solution. While passive voice is a necessary element of academic writing, reducing its use improves the quality of writing.

Let's review principles to shape the style of your writing so that it is clear, concise, and active.[9] You see, even professors appreciate writing that is reader friendly. Here are the concepts you will cover in this section:

- Controlling sentence length
- Using the active voice
- Using real subjects and strong verbs
- Building old to new information flow
- Cutting empty information
- Using parallel structure

While this section gives you an overview of these topics, you can gain additional practice on some principles in Part 2 of this book, "Editing for Clarity."

Control Sentence Length

Sentence length relates to the amount of information the average reader retains. Try to keep sentences between 10 and 25 words in length. Beyond

25 words, a reader may find it necessary to reread the beginning of the sentence to understand its meaning. For example:

> Writing experts suggest keeping sentences to fewer than 25 words in length because readers may have difficulty retaining information in longer sentences and may need to read the beginning of a sentence over again if the meaning of the beginning becomes lost by the time the end is reached. (49 words)

Sentences more than 25 words in length become unmanageable for the reader (as well as the writer). When you edit your writing, count the number of words in sentences that take up more than two full lines. In sentences that contain more than 25 words, either break the information into two shorter sentences or cut unnecessary information. By doing so, you improve both the quality and readability of your writing.

Use the Active Voice

Experts agree that the active voice is easier to understand than the passive voice. The active voice is direct and uses fewer words. More importantly, with the active voice, the **subject**, **verb**, and **object** perform their prescribed grammatical functions.

Here is an example:

Active: Turner submitted the paper.

The subject (*Turner*) is transferring action to the object through the verb (*submitted*). "Turner" is the **grammatical subject** based on position: in English, the grammatical subject generally precedes the verb. "Turner" is also the **real subject**. The **real subject** is the "who" or "what" that performs the action of the verb.

Passive—Version 1:   The paper was submitted by Turner.

In passive voice, the subject is acted upon. In this example, the subject (*paper*) is not performing an action. "Turner" is still performing the action, but Turner is in the object position. Thus, the verb does not transfer action from the subject to the object. The **grammatical** subject (*paper*) is different from the **real subject** (*Turner*).

Passive—Version 2:   The paper was submitted.

In this passive construction, the **grammatical subject** (*paper*) performs no action. Because the **real subject** is missing, even this simple sentence is somewhat abstract.

- In the active voice, the grammatical subject performs the action of the verb: *the grammatical subject and real subject are the same.* Active voice is clear, direct, and concise.

- In the passive voice, the grammatical subject does not perform action: *the real subject is not the grammatical subject.* Thus, the passive verb *describes*, but it does not *act*. The passive structure is abstract and wordy.

Even though the active voice is usually the preferred voice, passive voice is a grammatically correct construction. In fact, passive voice is more effective when you do not know who performed an action or do not want to call attention to that person. For example, it is more tactful to say "my phone call was not answered" than to say "you never answered my call."

Use Real Subjects and Strong Verbs

Did you know that "it is" and "there are" are considered weak constructions? (These are called **expletive forms**.) Since the subject and verb are critical elements, focus on using real subjects followed by strong verbs. Here is how to keep your subjects real and verbs strong:

- Use the active voice.

- Avoid starting sentences with *it is* or *there are*.

- Use action verbs rather than state-of-being verbs (*is, are, seem*) and weak verbs (such as *make, give, take*).

In each example below, the main subject is underlined once and the verb is underlined twice. Compare the subjects and verbs between the two groups.

There <u>are</u> many clients waiting.	Many <u>clients</u> <u>are waiting</u>.
It <u>is</u> well <u>known</u> that her preference is survey research.	<u>Everyone</u> <u>knows</u> she prefers . . .
<u>He</u> <u>made</u> everyone aware of the information.	<u>He</u> <u>informed</u> everyone.
<u>We</u> <u>will take</u> that into consideration.	<u>We</u> <u>will consider</u> that.
There <u>are</u> many policies that need to be changed.	Many <u>policies</u> <u>need</u> to be changed.
It <u>is</u> their belief that we should relocate.	<u>They</u> <u>believe</u> that we should relocate.
The <u>book</u> <u>seems</u> to discuss social contracts.	The <u>book</u> <u>discusses</u> social contracts.

Build Old to New Information Flow

To start, think of information as being broken into two types: *familiar ideas* and *unfamiliar ideas.*

- *Old information* consists of familiar ideas that provide context and anchor the reader in understanding; old information also tends to be more global than specific.

- *New information* consists of unfamiliar ideas that extend the reader's understanding; new information tends to be specific, extending the reader's knowledge.

When a sentence starts with a familiar idea (old) as a lead-in to an unfamiliar idea (new), readers have an easier time making connections. For example, suppose you are describing the topic of your next paper. As you compose, you may start with the new information. (Note that old information is presented in italics below.)

> **New to *Old*:**   Changes in rates of crime during an economic downturn will be *the topic of my next paper.*

When you edit, switch the order so that the sentence begins with the familiar, old information (presented in italics below), which would be *the topic of my next paper* or simply, *my next paper,* for example:

> ***Old* to New:**   *My next paper* will discuss changes in crime rates during an economic downturn.

While new information might sound abrupt or unexpected to the reader, familiar information provides a "cushion" and the *context*. For example, suppose you are sending a message about an upcoming meeting. As you compose, you may start with the new information.

> **Poorly worded:** Ground rules, team roles and responsibilities, and an action plan will be on *the agenda for our next meeting.*

When you edit, switch the order so that the sentence begins with "meeting," which is the familiar information that provides context for the rest of the sentence:

> **Revised:** *At our next meeting,* the agenda will include ground rules, team roles and responsibilities, and an action plan.

By beginning the sentence with the familiar concept (meeting), you ease your readers into the unfamiliar information. Here's another example (familiar information italicized):

> **Poorly worded:** New research guidelines will be developed as a result of *ongoing problems.*

> **Revised:** *Because of ongoing problems,* we will develop new research guidelines.

As the writer, you understand how new information connects to your topic before you even put your ideas on the page. When you edit, order the information into a logical flow for your reader.

Cut Empty Information

Due to insecurity or the pure challenge of composing, writers often use too many words. At times, writers are afraid that their work will not be long enough, so they fill it with empty information:

- **Empty information**: information that adds no value for the reader.

Regardless of the reason, when too many words appear on the page, cut the message: excessive words bog down the reader; the fewer words you use, the more your key points stand out.

Wordy:	When you finally decide to sit down and start working on your paper, you should try to have all necessary resources organized and available so that you do not waste precious time looking for them.
Concise:	When you start working on your paper, organize your resources so that you do not waste time.

Use Parallel Structure

Parallel structure relates to **syntax** and **clarity**. Parallel structure creates balance by presenting related words in the same grammatical form. Make sure that you present related nouns, verbs, phrases, and clauses in a consistent form.

Here are some examples (with parallel items presented in italics):

Incorrect:	The team envisioned a successful future through *strong leadership, making decisions effectively*, and *new approaches being tried.*
Corrected:	The team envisioned a successful future through *strong leadership, effective decisions*, and *new approaches.*
Incorrect:	Bob's duties are *surveying* the population, *aggregate* the data, and to *prepare* the report.
Corrected:	Bob's duties are *surveying* the population, *aggregating* the data, and *preparing* the report.
Incorrect:	The Baker study would have gone smoothly if *reports were prepared on time, we returned their calls*, and *would have included some sort of follow-up.*
Corrected:	The Baker study would have gone smoothly if *we had prepared reports on time, returned their calls*, and *included some follow-up.*

Parallel structure adds flow through consistency in form. When checking for parallel structure, look for consistent verb tense, word endings, and voice (active or passive). Correcting for parallel structure comes while you are editing your work, not composing it. (For more information, see Chapter 9, "Parallel Structure.")

Clarifying Your Tone

As a sociologist, most of your daily writing will be informal: you will write messages to colleagues and clients, and you may even keep a blog. By controlling the tone of your messages, you also have more control over managing the quality of your professional relationships and possibly your career opportunities. To shape the tone of your professional writing, apply the following principles:

- Be concise

- Shift to the "you" viewpoint

- Focus on the positive

- Choose simple language

Be Concise

Being concise relates, in part, to eliminating **redundant phrases** and **outdated expressions**. Here are some examples:

First and foremost, the plan does not work.	First, the plan does not work. (And: *Second, . . .*)
Five different organizations reviewed the study.	Five organizations reviewed the study.
The group reached a *consensus of opinion.*	The group reached consensus.
As *per* our discussion . . .	As we discussed . . .
Attached please find the requested form.	The form you requested *is attached.*
Thank you in advance for your assistance.	*Thank you* for assisting us.

Do you use any of the above in your writing?

Shift to the "You" Viewpoint

When you write professional e-mail messages, do you start many of your sentences with the personal pronoun "I"? When you can shift to the "you" viewpoint, the quality of your writing improves because your focus is on your reader. When you compose, let your words flow freely: compose for yourself and then edit for your reader. When you edit, shift from the "I" viewpoint to the "you" viewpoint.

"I" Viewpoint: *I* am writing to let you know that *I* would like to invite you to our next meeting.

"You" Viewpoint: Would *you* be interested in attending our next meeting?

By speaking directly to your reader through the "you" viewpoint, you engage your reader and tune in to your reader's needs. Here are more examples:

"I" Viewpoint: *I* am interested in the position in community research.

"You" Viewpoint: Could you please tell me about the position in community research?

"I" Viewpoint: *I* would like to know what you think about the change.

"You" Viewpoint: What do you think about the change?

"I" Viewpoint: *I* would like to encourage you to apply for the new position.

"You" Viewpoint: Are you interested in the new position? You should apply for it.

Not all writing can or should be written from the "you" point of view. At times, the "I" point of view is necessary and important to avoid sentences that sound awkward. For more information on this topic, see Chapter 10, "Pronouns and Viewpoint."

Focus on the Positive

Everyone appreciates positive words; even subtle comments add energy. In writing, you can help set a positive tone by describing situations in affirmative language. In other words, rather than saying what will go wrong if procedures are *not* followed, say what will go right if the procedures are followed. Here are some examples:

Negative: If you do not submit your proposal within 10 days, you will not be considered.

Positive:	If you submit your proposal within 10 days, you will be considered.
Negative:	By not going to the meeting, you will miss important information.
Positive:	By going to the meeting, you will learn valuable information.
Negative:	When you are not on time, our meetings do not run well.
Positive:	When everyone is on time, our meetings run well.

Writing in the affirmative takes fewer words and keeps information clear. When you can, avoid using the word "not":

George will not be on time.	George will be late.
The chair did not remember the agenda.	The chair forgot the agenda.

Once again, focus on what will go right if things are done according to plan, rather than what will go wrong if things are not done accordingly. This simple shift sounds less threatening to the listener or the reader.

Choose Simple Language

Whether you choose simple words or more complicated ones also affects the tone of your document. When possible, use a simple word instead of a complicated one. Here are a few examples:

We *utilize* the best *methodology.*	We *use* the best *methods.*
The project will *terminate* in April.	The project will *end* in April.
We *endeavor* to give the best service.	We *try* to give the best service.
The information will be *disseminated.*	We will *share* the information.
We will *institute incremental* changes.	We will *make gradual* changes.

Do you notice other complicated words in your writing that have a simpler version? For more information on using simple language, see Chapter 10, "Conciseness."

Recap

In this chapter, you first reviewed process tools and techniques and then reviewed principles of style that make writing simple, clear, and concise and thus more readable. In fact, to measure the flow of your writing, use your speech as a guide:

> If you wouldn't say it that way, don't write it that way.

When you have difficulty composing, *do more research* to develop the thinking behind your writing. Write about your topic as you learn about it. Writing, like every other skill, demands practice. The more you compose and edit, the better your skills will become. When you apply principles as you edit and revise your writing, you make writing decisions with more confidence and less effort. Here are some of the points stressed in this chapter:

- To reduce writing anxiety, work on your task.

- Compose freely and then edit ruthlessly.

- Use mind mapping, focused writing, and page maps.

- Set internal deadlines earlier than your external deadline.

- Simplify your writing: use active voice and choose simple words.

- Clarify your tone by using the *you* viewpoint and writing in the affirmative.

- Proofread your document as your last step.

To gain the practice that you need to build your skills, complete each activity of the **Writing Workshop** below.

Writing Workshop

Activity A. Manage Your Writing Process

Writing is difficult for everyone at times, even the best and most prolific authors. As Ernest Hemingway is credited as saying, "There's nothing to writing. All you do is sit down at a typewriter and bleed."

Instructions: In a small group or with a partner, explore the following, jotting down key points.

1 **What is difficult about writing?**

    1.1 What challenges you? For example, getting started, getting organized? What about grammar, punctuation, active voice, conciseness? What else?

    1.2 What do you think about your ability to write?

    1.3 What kinds of experiences have shaped your feelings about writing?

2 **What are your writing blocks?** As you can see, everyone has writing challenges and, at times, a writing block, such as editor's block or critic's block.

    2.1 What kinds of writing blocks do you have?

    2.2 How can you address your writing blocks? What tools or techniques can you use?

    2.3 When you get stuck, what can you do to move forward?

3 **What is your writing process?** Reflect on your current writing process; for example, are you able to compose freely, or do you still edit as you compose? As you review the following questions, ask yourself how you wish to modify your writing process.

    3.1 What do you want to **stop** doing?

    3.2 What do you want to **start** doing?

    3.3 What do you want to **continue** doing?

Activity B. Process Message

Instructions: Write your professor a process message summarizing what you learned from completing this exercise.

- What's difficult about writing for you?

- What kinds of writing blocks do you have and how will you resolve them?

- What changes will you make in your process?

    Note: For all messages, use a proper greeting such as "Hi Professor Smith." Also use an appropriate closing. Since e-mail messages are considered *informal,* do not use a *formal* closing, such as "sincerely," but instead use an informal closing, such as "All the best," "Best regards," or "Enjoy your day."

Activity C. Develop Your Strategy

The way you approach a writing task is unique: you know what works for you and what doesn't. By becoming mindful of your approach, you can develop a strategy to produce effective results consistently.

Instructions: Identify a writing project that you have now in any class (but sociology is preferred). Define your writing strategy by developing responses to the questions below.

1 **Purpose.** Staying focused on purpose is key to any writing strategy.

 1.1 What is your thesis?

 1.2 What type of paper are you writing: a summary, an argument, a literature review?

 1.3 What is your purpose statement?

 1.4 If the paper is for a sociology class, what is the sociological context: which sociological theories, concepts, or principles apply?

2 **Topic.** Academic writing does not always allow freedom in choosing a topic; when you can select your own topic, choose one that you are genuinely interested in.

 2.1 What would you like to learn about? What are your passions, interests, and causes?

 2.2 What problems interest you on a personal level and a global level?

 2.3 What are some issues that cause you to react or feel emotion?

3 **Time Management.** To write a plan, start with your end date, create internal due dates, and establish times to write.

 3.1 What is your due date? What is the internal due date for your first draft?

 3.2 What days and times can you plan into your schedule to write and do research?

4   **Prewriting and Drafting.** Tools and techniques for writing include freewriting, mind mapping, page mapping, and creating various types of outlines—which tools work for you?

5   **Editing and Revising.** Have you planned in time to edit, revise, and proofread your paper?

References

1   Elbow, P. (1998). *Writing with power: Techniques for mastering the writing process* (2nd ed). New York: Oxford University Press. Peter Elbow is the master of writing as process. For a deeper discussion of process, see any of Elbow's publications, including *Writing Without Teachers* (2nd ed., 1998 [1973], New York: Oxford University Press).

2   Colman, A. M. (2015). *A dictionary of psychology.* Oxford, UK: Oxford University Press, p. 119.

3   Ibid., p. 350.

4   Beeghley, L. (2003). *Homicide: A sociological explanation.* Lanham, MD: Rowman & Littlefield.

5   Gertrude Stein's last words, according to: Sprigge, E. (1957). *Gertrude Stein, her life and work.* New York: Harper & Brothers, p. 265.

6   Mills, C. W. (1961). *The sociological imagination.* New York: Oxford University Press.

7   Parsons, T. (1964). *The social system.* Toronto: Collier-Macmillan Canada.

8   Mills (1961) Op. cit., p. 27.

9   Williams, J. M. (1990). *Style: Toward clarity and grace.* Chicago, IL: University of Chicago Press. Some principles discussed in this chapter were originally learned in Joseph Williams's class, 'Academic and Professional Writing', offered at The University of Chicago in 1988. *Style* is a must-read for writers who want to learn more advanced concepts related to style, structure, and clarity.

Research and Evidence-Based Writing

Do you realize the extent to which you use research daily? For example, every day you make decisions, and each decision starts with a question. On important issues, do you evaluate past experiences or ask others what they have done in similar situations? These types of inquiries are a rudimentary form of research, which is *systematically investigating materials and resources to explain, predict, and/or control phenomena.*[1]

Research is an organized attempt to answer specific questions—an attempt to bring order to interpreting the chaos of what we see, hear, and feel in a complex world. Questions are at the core of research, and thus questions are at the core of writing in sociology: questions that are important to you, offering clarity and resolution; questions that fill a knowledge gap, giving insight into humankind; and questions that reveal unexpected truths, "turning the world upside down."

Writing in sociology is *evidence-based*: theory is used in developing arguments, and research is used in supporting and refuting claims. Theory and research are intricately intertwined: *theory reveals relationships, and research tests them.* However, as you analyze research, you must evaluate it with an especially critical eye. At times, profit, ideology, or ego can skew results at the peril of truthful outcomes. When decisions are based on faulty research, the outcomes can be disastrous. By further developing your skill in using evidence to support writing in sociology, you may even develop a *sociological imagination*—a way of thinking that can serve you well in any profession.

Since writing is *thinking on paper*, this chapter starts with a few concepts that explore the thinking behind the writing, providing a context for writing in sociology. Then basic principles for integrating evidence into writing are reviewed. Since graphics convey research in a concise and powerful way, graphics are also discussed.

When you have completed this chapter, you will be able to:

- Apply principles of evidence-based writing to an editing strategy.

- Understand how facts, beliefs, opinions, and assumptions relate to evidence.

- Identify qualities of a sociological imagination.

- Gain insight into the types of research conducted in sociology.

- Display research using charts, graphs, and tables.

Sociological Mindset

Sociology is a science which attempts to uncover truths that explain the ways individuals and groups interact within a society. In his book *The Sociological Imagination*, C. Wright Mills states that "Neither the life of an individual nor the history of a society can be understood without understanding both."[2]

Mills defines a sociological perspective as "the vivid awareness of the relationship between experience and the wider society." Life happens in social context, and social context helps define the individual. By becoming increasingly aware of the relationship between experience and context, you may also gain insight into developing new perspectives and alternative ways of thinking.

As you apply sociological principles and develop research skills, you analyze and evaluate ideas more critically and may be less likely to take "facts" at face value. You use evidence to support your ideas and anchor your thinking. You may also begin to see gaps in thinking, theory, and processes and have the inclination to develop theories (or hypotheses) and test ideas, formally and informally. In other words, you may also develop a *sociological imagination*, becoming an open-minded inquisitor about all sorts of phenomena, even beyond the sociological.

On the way to developing a *sociological imagination*, you may try to become objective, awakening to biases and making a conscious effort to look through a neutral lens. While trying to become objective is an honorable quest, it is arguably not possible for an individual to drop all bias: the lens through which each of us sees the world is unique and based on a complicated network of experiences and filters—social, political, psychological, cultural, historical, and more. Thus, when you write in sociology, an important aim is to write without bias, so let's review what that means.

Research, Beliefs, and Bias

Social constructionism is a theory in sociology that refers to the "socially created nature of social life," which is saying that, to some extent, together we construct our reality.[3] Sociologists call this the *social construction of reality*.[4]

Beliefs play a vital role in how each of us constructs our own reality. American sociologists W. I. Thomas and Dorothy S. Thomas are known for developing the *definition of the situation* or the "Thomas theorem," which states the following:[5]

> If men define situations as real, they are real in their consequences.

In other words, when people believe an idea to be true, they base their actions on the belief, and their actions have real consequences. For example, if a person believes that higher education is "a waste of time that brings little reward," that person is also less likely to commit to higher education. And while it is possible for a college or high-school dropout to become a billionaire, that's the rare exception: research shows that "workers with college degrees earn significantly more than those without . . . and lower education levels tend to correspond with higher unemployment rates."[6]

When you do research in sociology, your goal is to uncover one tiny aspect of truth that may have the potential to change irrational beliefs and thus behavior and outcomes. So when you when you write and conduct research in sociology, you must be aware of your own beliefs and how powerful beliefs are in your world—and in everyone else's.

For evidence-based writing in research, you are attempting to work with data in an unbiased way. The American Sociological Association's Code of Ethics addresses bias with the following statement:[7]

> Sociologists respect the rights, dignity, and worth of all people. They strive to eliminate bias in their professional activities, and they do not tolerate any forms of discrimination . . . . In all of their work-related

activities, sociologists acknowledge the rights of others to hold values, attitudes, and opinions that differ from their own.

Thus, mindfully avoid letting beliefs or assumptions or positions interfere with how you conduct your research and interpret your data. Think the way a physician might if treating a patient who has a contrary set of beliefs and values: physicians are considered ethical when they do not allow their own beliefs, values, or assumptions to interfere with how they treat any patient. Applied to evidence-based writing, let us see how beliefs and opinions compare with facts and theory, the primary sources of evidence.

Evidence: Facts and Theory vs. Beliefs and Opinions

In sociology, *facts* and *theory* provide evidence, while beliefs and opinions do not. However, as discussed, strong beliefs can sometimes be confused with fact or "the truth." Let's review some qualities of each of these types of information:[8]

- A **fact** is verifiable through research and evidence. Facts provide support for an argument, thesis, or hypothesis. (Established facts would not generally be argued.) When using facts, put them in context and draw conclusions to make them meaningful. An example of a fact would be, "In 2017, Chicago had 675 homicides."

- A **theory** is "a general statement about how some parts of the world fit together and how they work. It is an explanation of how two or more 'facts' are related to one another."[9] When you use theory as evidence, theory has the potential to play a broad role; for example, some theoretical perspectives in sociology have accumulated bodies of knowledge over long periods of time.

- A **belief** is a conviction based on culture, personal faith, or values. Since a belief is not based on fact, beliefs cannot be argued or serve as basis for a *thesis*. However, a belief can be an element of a *hypothesis*, or a proposition to be argued. For example, a correlation could be made between people who hold certain beliefs and then express specific social actions.

- An **opinion** is a judgement that is based on a fact or a belief. Opinions would not be considered evidence; when you include an opinion in your writing, back up the opinion with evidence. An example of an opinion would be, "The homicide rate in Chicago is high." Now, *what evidence can you provide to support that opinion?*

A *bias* or a *prejudice* is the result of belief: the word "prejudice" means "to pre-judge." Pre-judging involves forming an opinion—positive or negative—that is not based on experience, fact, or other evidence. Bias, or prejudice, is antithetical to a *sociological perspective*. However, "unlike a belief, a prejudice is testable: it can be contested and disproved on the basis of facts."[10]

While everyone has beliefs—some stronger than others—here's how beliefs have the potential to restrict academic discussion and progress:

- The failure to recognize your own belief or position as an opinion that could be mistaken.

- The refusal to acknowledge the possibility that another's opinion could be correct.[11]

The following observation puts facts and opinions in perspective:

> **Everyone is entitled to their own opinion, but not their own facts.**[12]

In addition to beliefs and opinions, be on the lookout for *assumptions*—yours and those of others. For example, as you examine research, you may see that an author bases some findings on assumptions. If research is founded on an assumption that is not acknowledged and discussed, that omission would become part of your critique of the literature. What is an "assumption?"

Assumptions

An assumption is similar to a belief in that an assumption is an idea or notion that is accepted without proof. Whereas beliefs are developed over a lifetime and are strongly held convictions based on a person's faith or world perspective, assumptions are not generally adhered to as solidly as a belief.

An assumption is similar to an *untested theory*. In fact, we all apply these untested theories to our lives daily; at times consciously, at other times unconsciously. While some untested theories may be valid, that cannot be known until they are tested. For example, a story was told about a man who was on trial for a crime, and he gave a very detailed alibi. When the verdict was given, the judge stated, "You must be guilty because your alibi is too detailed to be true."

Everyone has assumptions: some are valid, some are not. At times, assumptions seep through into a person's thinking and writing. As you evaluate research, identify assumptions that may not be logical or that may create bias. By identifying your own assumptions, you may begin to see gaps in how you are interpreting a situation, allowing you to see more options.

The Value of Uncertainty

Doubting everything or believing everything are two equally convenient solutions, both of which save us from thinking—Jules Henri Poincare[13]

Sustaining an open mind—a state of *not knowing*—is challenging but necessary to reach a depth of understanding beyond easy answers. John Dewey, a twentieth century educator, sums up the challenge of keeping an open mind:

> One can think reflectively only when one is willing to endure suspense and to undergo the trouble of searching. To many persons both suspense of judgment and intellectual search are disagreeable; they want to get them ended as soon as possible. They cultivate an over-positive and dogmatic habit of mind, or feel perhaps that a condition of doubt will be regarded as evidence of mental inferiority. . . . To be genuinely thoughtful, we must be willing to sustain and protract that state of doubt which is the stimulus to thorough inquiry . . . .

An open, inquisitive mind is an asset in sociology and will aid you significantly in your research and evidence-based writing.

Have you ever felt the discomfort of "not knowing" and then, to resolve the anxiety, accepted an "easy explanation" that later proved to be ineffective?

An Open Mind

When working with research, an important quality is remaining open to innovative and diverse ideas—thinking "outside of the box." Exploring possibilities involves suspending judgment. Your mind is open when you evaluate evidence and consider possibilities; an open mind contributes to adapting to change and giving ideas (and people) a chance before drawing a conclusion. For instance, it is easy to become overly attached to what you assume that you know, and your understanding of even the "best theories" can change as knowledge evolves. Here are two examples.

- At one time, it was believed that the world was flat. Galileo was brought to trial, publicly humiliated, and condemned for heresy because he challenged that belief.

- In 1982, two Australian physicians, Dr. Robin Warren and Dr. Barry Marshall, identified a link between *Helicobacter pylori* bacteria and peptic ulcers. Few listened to Drs. Warren and Marshall, and in 1995 most physicians in the U.S. still treated ulcers as if they were caused only by stress. Only 5 percent of ulcer patients were being treated with antibiotics. It wasn't until Dr. Barry Marshall induced ulcers in his own stomach by swallowing *H. pylori* that the theory was taken seriously. In 1997, the Centers for Disease Control launched a campaign to educate physicians and change their attitudes about ulcers.[15]

- ■ *Can you think of other examples? Are there times when you have an insight, but no one can see what you see? Are there times when you don't listen because the message doesn't fit into the way you view the world?*

- **Finding the squares:** Since reality isn't always as it appears at first glance, let's do a little experiment. In Figure 3.1 below, how many squares can you find? Are there only 16? How about 20? Can you find 22? 24? 25? 30?

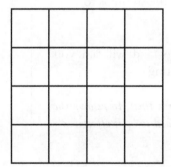

Figure 3.1 Finding the Squares

Paradigm Shift

When you listen with an open mind, you may experience a *paradigm shift*: a paradigm is the *context* in which a person holds information. Here's a more developed definition:

> A *paradigm* is a set of rules and regulations (written or unwritten) that does two things: 1) it establishes or defines boundaries; and 2) it tells you how to behave inside the boundaries in order to be successful.[16]

Paradigms, or models, help shape the way we view the world; as such, they determine how we analyze and interpret relationships. Most of us are not even aware of our own paradigms. A *paradigm shift* changes the *context* of how we perceive reality. The examples discussed above led to paradigm shifts.

- With the discovery that the world was round and not flat, people changed their perception of that reality: voyagers were no longer afraid that they would fall off the Earth into an abyss, which led to increased travel and the discovery of worlds new to them.

   (*Note*: Some people still believe the world is flat.[17])

Through discovering that the *H. pylori* bacterium caused ulcers, doctors prescribed antibiotics, a treatment that usually cures the illness; patients were no longer told that their uncontrolled stress was the sole cause of their disease.

   (*Note*: Researchers are now finding that *H. pylori* can also have beneficial effects, and "ongoing perspectives . . . have changed radically . . . Determining whether *H. pylori* is beneficial or detrimental in [the] human stomach has been a challenging area of research in gastroenterology."[18])

While the above examples may, at first glance, appear not to be related to sociology, could it be that social forces were working "behind the scenes"? For example, what qualities of the social and historical context encouraged people to resist these theories? What beliefs or assumptions contributed to discounting these theories before they were even tested?

Sociological Topics

According to the American Sociological Association (ASA), "Through Sociology [sic], we study our behavior as social beings, covering everything from the analysis of short contacts between anonymous individuals on the street to the study of global social processes." The ASA lists the following areas of study:[19]

- Application and sociological practice
- Biology and sociology
- Comparative/historical approaches
- Crime, law, and deviance
- Culture
- Economics, markets, and consumerism
- Education
- Family and life course
- Gender and sexuality
- Global issues
- Inequalities and stratification

- Medicine and health
- Place and environment
- Politics
- Race and ethnicity
- Religion and spirituality
- Research methods
- Social change
- Social psychology and interaction
- Technology
- Theory and knowledge
- Work and organizations

The Pew Research Center also studies social and demographic trends, listing additional topics (or breaking them down differently), a few of which are as follows:[20]

- Social media, social networking
- Generations and age
- Teens and technology
- Texting
- Social values

Each topic can be broken into subtopics for research. For example, here are some perspectives for exploring *social media*:

Social media and credibility:

1　Which social media sources can you trust for reporting truthful information?

2　What percentage of social media sources contain "false news"?

Social media and generational differences:

3   How does social media affect young people?

4   Facebook vs. LinkedIn: Who uses each and why?

Social media and personality disorders or deviant behavior:

5   Is using social media addictive? If so, which age groups are most affected?

6   Do harassment and bullying occur on social media? By which age groups?

7   Does social media promote narcissism, aggressive narcissism, or Machiavellianism?

Social media and networking:

8   Are social networks used to promote career opportunities? Which sites and why?

9   Can posting on social media harm career opportunities?

Evidence-Based Writing

Evidence-based writing starts with a problem that is written in the form of a *thesis* or a *hypothesis*. For example, for a summary or an argument, you would write a thesis; for a research paper, you would write a hypothesis.

Without evidence, writing is unsupported opinion. While that seems obvious, one of the biggest hurdles you are up against is learning how to incorporate evidence into your thinking and writing. Using evidence involves drawing upon your abilities to *analyze* and *evaluate*, as in the following examples.[21]

Analysis involves comparing and contrasting ideas and seeing how ideas are connected:

• Are there unstated assumptions or logical fallacies in reasoning?

• Are the data relevant? What criteria are you using?

• Are you able to distinguish between facts and opinions?

• Are you able to identify assumptions?

- What are the various "components" and their characteristics? How would you rank, prioritize, and sequence them, if applicable?

- Has a cause and effect been established, or simply a correlation?

Evaluation involves judging the value of material and methods, assessing the extent to which each meets criteria such as the following:

- How is the research organized and presented?

- Does the research demonstrate a logical consistency?

- Are the conclusions adequately supported by data?

- Can internal or external criteria establish the value of the work?

Deductive and Inductive Reasoning

Deductive and inductive reasoning are also involved in developing theories and hypotheses.

As you do research in sociology, at times you will use *inductive reasoning*, starting with a specific question and building evidence that ties it to a theory. At other times, you will use *deductive reasoning*, starting with a theory and making observations that lead to conclusions.

- *Deductive reasoning* starts with a general statement, such as a theory or a hypothesis, and then works toward a specific conclusion based on evidence. Because deductive reasoning moves from theory to conclusions, it is considered to be "top down."

- *Inductive reasoning* starts with a specific observation or question and then works its way to a theory or principle. Inductive reasoning is probabilistic: the more data you have, the stronger conclusions you can make. Look for patterns or trends in your data that might lead to generalizations. Because inductive reasoning moves from observation to theory, it is considered to be "bottom up."

By starting with a theory, deductive reasoning is considered to be narrower; by starting with an observation, inductive reasoning tends to be more exploratory. However, most research involves both, moving from one type to the other: from theory to observation and then using observation or new data to form new theories.

Primary and Secondary Sources

Evidence comes in the form of theories, facts, research, examples, data, and experiments. As you examine sources, take note of all evidence related to your thesis: *evidence that disputes your position is just as important as evidence that supports it.* Evidence is broken into two categories: primary and secondary.[22]

- A *primary source* consists of first-hand experiences, such as observations, documents, newspapers, and historical artifacts. Quantitative sources would include research, statistics, polls, surveys, and censuses. Qualitative sources would include interviews and participant observation along with diaries, memoirs, autobiographies, audio and video recordings, oral histories, and photographs. Primary sources are created at the time of an event or period; because primary sources generate original information, they remain "fresh" over time.

- A *secondary source* discusses information from other sources, such as a scholarly article in which research is critiqued along with documentaries, biographies, and textbooks. Because secondary sources are "interpretations" of original sources, they become dated in time. For example, some journal articles are considered old after about 15 years.

As you review journal articles for their content, also review and analyze their sources: would you benefit from reading some of their sources first-hand?

Summaries

Writing a summary is the foundation for writing an argument, so do not underestimate its importance. *Summarizing in your own words* what others are saying is the starting point for building critical thinking and writing skills. For example, when writers plagiarize, they are likely to have *learning gaps* and may lack the ability or confidence to summarize in their own words.

- As you do your research, stop at critical points to write key ideas *from your own recollection.* In other words, *take your eyes off of your sources and do not look at your notes.* Once you have summarized key ideas, compare them with the sources and *notate your references.*

If you stay too close to the main source or your notes are too detailed, you are more likely to let the words of others intimidate you. Even the best writers feel intimidated when they read a well-written final draft. However, what you are not seeing are the multiple iterations of the work along with the frustrations involved in getting there.

- As you read an article, take note of the journalist's questions: the *who, what, when, where, why*, and *how*. Also ask *so what?*, which may help you differentiate between what is important and what isn't. Since summaries often include too much information and information that is not relevant, when you edit your draft, again ask *so what?*

Do not confuse your inability to write about a topic with a lack of writing skills: when you cannot write fluently about a topic, develop the thinking behind your writing.

- *When you are stuck, learn more: read, reflect, and discuss.* The most difficult aspect of writing is learning the topic. Make it your goal to learn a topic well enough so that you can explain it to someone else. Discuss your topic, and continue to summarize sources in your own words along with your deepening insights about the topic. *Write to learn.*

Learning is a *cyclical process*, and no one can write sensibly about a topic until after the hard work has been done, which requires practice, repetition, reflective thinking, discussing, reading (and re-reading) until knowledge can be applied.[23] Once you develop your ability to summarize, you are less likely to plagiarize inadvertently; you are also that much closer to being able to write an argument. The only way to make the process work for you is to start early and stay engaged until you find the answers that you are looking for.

> There are some things which cannot
> be learned quickly, and time, which is all we have,
> must be paid heavily for their acquiring.
> They are the very simplest things,
> and because it takes a man's life to know them
> the little new that each man gets from life
> is very costly and the only heritage
> he has to leave.
>
> Ernest Hemingway[24]

Variables: Dependent and Independent

As you review evidence to support your thesis or hypothesis, some of the most powerful evidence will come in the form of quantitative research. Quantitative sociological studies search for a cause-and-effect relationship between two phenomena or variables: an independent variable (a "cause") and a dependent variable (its "effect").

Variables can be correlated in many ways without one variable *causing* the other, which is *correlation without causation*. Causation is based on a *necessary connection* between two variables that have an *asymmetrical* relationship. To determine the *direction of influence* (or which variable *causes* the other), consider these two factors: the time order and the fixity or alterability of the variables.[25]

The independent variable (or *cause*) would be:

- The variable that precedes in time, and/or

- The variable that is fixed or not subject to change.

Some variables that could be considered independent or causal would be sex, race, birth order, national origin, age, socio-economic status of parents; some variables that are not quite fixed would be social class, religion, and urban–rural residence.

- A *dependent variable* is the variable that is represents what is being tested, measured, or recorded for each independent variable: the result. On a chart, the dependent variable is represented on the *y*-**axis** (left side, vertical axis).

- An *independent variable* is the *causal* variable that is changed or controlled to create the conditions of the study: the input. On a chart, the independent variable is represented on the *x*-**axis** (bottom, horizontal axis).

Arguments

Writing a good argument starts with a well-defined problem: *What is your problem?* Arguments involve comparing and contrasting, taking a position, and providing evidence to support it. If you cannot articulate your argument clearly, do more reading, writing, and research to shore up your understanding.

Also note that a common mistake writers make is spending too much time summarizing details rather than using them to support their argument.

Since sociology studies the interaction between the individual and society, your argument will involve both; for example:

- Does your thesis express a position that can be argued? What is your position?

- What are you comparing? If there is no comparison, there is no argument.

  o What are your variables? How are the variables related?

  o Are the variables quantitative and measurable?

  o If the variables are not measurable, does qualitative research establish a relationship?

- What evidence are you using? Do *not* use personal anecdotes, experiences, or opinions as evidence for your argument.

  o What conclusions can you draw from the evidence?

  o Is any of your evidence confusing or lacking or unsubstantiated? Ask, *how do I know this?*

- What are the underlying *assumptions* in the articles you have chosen as resources?

  o For example, "Child neglect is bad, and children who are neglected should be removed from their parents."

- What are counter-arguments to this issue?

  o For example, "Children are more damaged by the foster-care system than in some neglectful environments."

- What are the *gaps* in the logic of arguments?

- What are your outcomes? What are the social consequences of your problem?

A good conclusion restates the arguments and evidence: do not provide new evidence in the conclusion. Also, make sure that your conclusion ties back to the introduction; once you have written your conclusion, revise your introduction.

Academic Voice and Viewpoint

As you compose, write freely. When you edit, clarify your voice and develop a consistent viewpoint. For example, when you argue a point, do not use the first person, such as *I agree* or *I disagree*, but rather use phrases such as "the argument" or "the author":

> This paper analyzes / discusses / examines / investigates . . .
>
> The thesis / premise / central issue is . . . The authors argue that . . .
>
> This study examines . . . Some findings / conclusions are . . .
>
> The data suggest . . . The authors assume that . . . Their research validates . . .
>
> Their research does not support . . . Based on research, the authors conclude . . .
>
> Consensus among the researchers includes agreement about . . .

Academic writing has its own style, which may seem intimidating until you have some practice. If you need to develop your academic voice, consider working with *sentence prompts*—using sentence prompts is a legitimate way to structure your ideas and is distinctly different from plagiarizing. Sentence prompts can help ease you into building your academic vocabulary. The following example is adapted from the University of Manchester's *Academic Phrasebank*:[26]

Jones (2011)	found observed	distinct significant considerable major only slight	differences between X and Y.

Note: The above sentence is written in the active voice, following the pattern real subject—active verb—(descriptor) object. Active voice is discussed in detail in Chapter 8, "Active Voice." The American Psychological Association (APA) and ASA citation styles both recommend using active voice over passive voice, when possible.

The PEER Model

When you start a new project, confusion is a normal starting point. Because you are learning about your topic and drawing connections between it and relevant theory, you are likely to feel discomfort until ideas take shape. As you collect research, consider organizing your ideas using the *PEER model*, which puts focus on the purpose of each part of your paper, stressing the importance of evidence.

P   What is the *purpose*?
        Which *principles* or *theories* apply?
        What are the key points and why are they relevant?

E   What *evidence* supports key points?
        What are the facts and details?

E   What *explanation* or *examples* can you provide?
        What do readers need to know about the evidence and its significance?

R   How can you *resolve* your thesis for your readers?
        What points provide a *recap*?
        What are your conclusions and *recommendations*?

By breaking down each part according to purpose, the PEER model can serve as a self-check to ensure you have developed relevant aspects of your paper. As you collect and rough out ideas, use each part of the PEER model as a *side heading*. When you are revising, evaluate whether you have developed your topic adequately with specific evidence and examples. You can also use the model for paragraph development.

Paragraphs: Topic Sentences and Topic Strings

Purpose is key in evidence-based writing: just as every paper you write has a thesis, every paragraph should have a *topic sentence*.

- Though it can appear anywhere in the paragraph, the *topic sentence* is most commonly placed as the first or second sentence.

- Every sentence in the paragraph should relate to the topic sentence, building a *topic string*.

- Any sentence that does not contain substance for the reader is *empty information* and should be cut.

While you can use the PEER model in a *macro* way as you collect and organize your research, you can also use it in a *micro* way to analyze your use of topic sentences and topic strings, for example:

Purpose: By applying research, you improve the quality
                            of your writing.

Evidence and examples: Evidence that supports your thesis gives
                            credibility to your argument.
                            For example, facts provide detail to engage the
                            reader in your line of thought, whereas opinions
                            and beliefs encourage doubt and skepticism and
                            cannot be used as evidence.

Recap: Thus, when you provide research to support
                            your claims, you add substance to your writing.

Effective paragraphs are built on well-constructed, purposefully written sentences that are strung together in a *logical order*. For more information on paragraph development, see Chapter 7, "Cohesive Paragraphs and Transitions." Next, let's review *meta discourse* and the types of information to edit out of evidence-based writing.

Meta Discourse

An important editing skill is knowing what to cut. Joseph M. Williams, author of *Style: Toward Clarity and Grace*, identifies various types of unnecessary information.[27] Williams uses the term *meta discourse* to describe the language writers use to describe their own thinking processes. Meta discourse is *empty information*. Here are some types of meta discourse to avoid:

- Background thinking

- Your opinions and beliefs

- Reader's perceptions

Background Thinking

Background thinking can be described as how you arrived at your conclusions. Explaining background thinking is different from explaining an issue or giving evidence to support a point; for example, "I reviewed many sources before selecting theory X." A reader does not need to know how many sources you reviewed before you found the one that resonated.

Your Opinions and Beliefs

As discussed, your opinions and beliefs detract from the purpose of evidence-based writing. Whenever you find yourself expressing your opinion or using phrases such as *I believe*, *I think*, and *I feel*, consider whether you can delete those statements. In fact, avoid the use of the "I" viewpoint for academic writing: most academic writing emanates from the third person. (See Chapter 1, "Purpose, Voice, and Viewpoint.")

Readers' Perceptions

Do not tell your reader how to interpret your message; these added comments are irrelevant and may give the reader the impression that you are unsure of your message or that you lack confidence. Thus, remove phrases or sentences that tell your readers how you think they will react; for example: "While you may be skeptical when you first review the data, your opinions may change as the evidence unfolds."

When you compose, you may need to include empty information on the way to discovering your message: the time to cut empty information is when you edit.

Displaying Research

Following along the lines of "a picture is worth a thousand words," a graphic display can have a significant visual impact on readers. Displaying numbers and other concepts in charts and graphs *clarifies meaning at a glance*. When you turn complicated data into charts, graphs, or tables, you not only make your research reader-friendly, you give your reader a visual to mull over and spend time to extend their understanding and draw conclusions.

As you create or analyze charts, note the following:

- The *dependent variable* is represented on the *y*-axis (left side, vertical axis).

- The *independent variable* is represented on the ***x*-axis** (bottom, horizontal axis).

The type of data that you are displaying will help determine the kind of visual to create. To create effective charts, graphs, and tables, become familiar with formatting options that your software offers. For example, with Microsoft Word, go to the *Insert* tab to find options for making various types of charts, graphs, and tables. To get assistance in creating a visual, search "how to create graphs in Word," and many informative sites will pop up. In addition, you can develop charts and graphs in Excel; tutorials on how to use Excel are also available online.

Graphics: Charts, Graphs, and Tables

At times, visual displays are more effective than descriptions: words can include excuses or explanations mixed in with the numbers, thus making it difficult to illuminate real trends. However, as you display your research, let your concepts and ideas lead the way, with displays remaining secondary to the information they support. On the next few pages, you will see examples of the following types of charts:

- Bar chart

- Pie chart

- Line graph

- Table

Bar Charts

Use a bar chart to compare and contrast up to six different items. You can show relationships over a period of time by clustering several different groups in the chart. The following guidelines apply to any type of bar chart:

- Display relationships horizontally or vertically.

- Make sure bar widths and the spaces between them are equal.

- Arrange bars in a logical order (such as length, age, or date) to make comparisons easier.

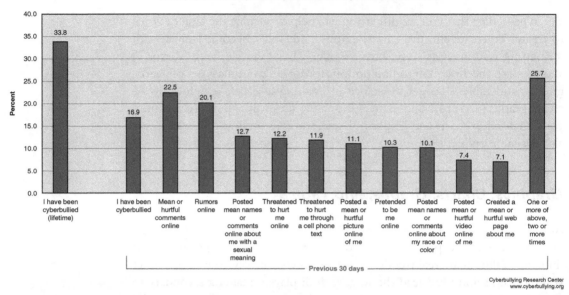

Sameer Hinduja and Justin W.Patchin (2016)

Figure 3.2 Cyberbullying Victimization[28]

In Hinduja and Patchin's (2016) study on cyberbullying, "approximately 34% of the students in [the] sample report experiencing cyberbullying in their lifetimes. When asked about specific types of cyberbullying experienced in the previous 30 days, mean or hurtful comments (22.5%) and rumors spread (20.1%) online continue to be among the most commonly-cited. Twenty-six percent of the sample reported being cyberbullied in one or more of the eleven specific types reported, two or more times over the course of the previous 30 days."[29]

Pie Charts

Use pie charts when the various components add up to 100 percent.

- Limit the number of categories to six; if you have more than six, combine them.

- Label categories directly and add percentages.

- Place the most important section at the 12 o'clock position to emphasize a point.

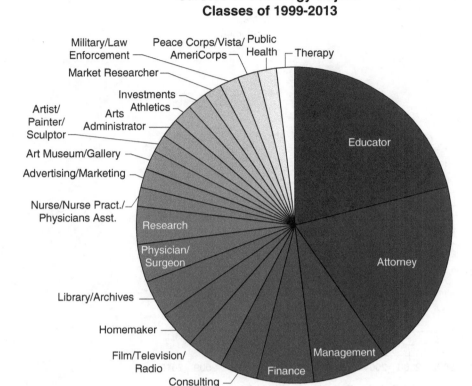

Figure 3.3 Careers of sociology majors, classes of 1999–2013[30]

In 2014, the Office of Institutional Research at Williams College did a study of the career trajectories of their sociology alums. From 1999 to 2013, Williams College graduated a total of 112 sociology majors, and Figure 3.3 shows the data from 47 of those graduates.[31]

Line Graphs

Use line graphs to show trends.

- Use left-justified, 10- or 12-point bold for line graph titles.
- State what data the graph illustrates.
- Label each axis clearly.
- In a time graph, indicate time on the horizontal axis, and display units of measurement on the vertical axis.

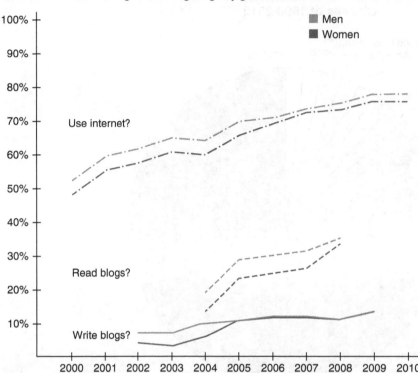

% of US adults reading and writing blogs by gender, 2000–2010 | Pew Internet

Figure 3.4 Percentage of US Adults Reading and Writing Blogs by Gender, 2000–2010[32]

> Laura Norén (2011) demonstrated that while women and men write blogs at about the same rate, they write different kinds of blogs. Food bloggers and baby bloggers are primarily women; political bloggers and tech bloggers are generally male.[33]

Tables

Include enough information on your table so that readers will be able to interpret the findings without explanation. *What conclusions are you able to draw by reviewing the table below?*

> The Bureau of Labor Statistics (2016) reported that median pay for survey researchers was $54,470 per year, or $26.19 an hour.[35] The Bureau also reported that "many research positions require a master's degree or Ph.D., although a bachelor's degree may be sufficient for some entry-level positions."

Quick Facts: Survey Researchers	
2016 Median Pay ⑦	$54,470 per year $26.19 per hour
Typical Entry-Level Education ⑦	Master's degree
Work Experience in a Related Occupation ⑦	None
On-the-job Training ⑦	None
Number of Jobs, 2014 ⑦	16,700
Job Outlook, 2014–24 ⑦	12% (Faster than average)
Employment Change, 2014–24 ⑦	1,900

Figure 3.5 Quick Facts: Survey Researchers[34]

Recap

For some people, research is the most exciting aspect of their work and life. Even if you have not yet reached that point, you may find that research adds direction and power to the way that you make decisions or form an argument.

Good research applied in the right way not only enriches life but also helps alleviate human suffering. Though those are not direct goals of sociological research, at times they are outcomes nonetheless: that's because sociological research that is effectively executed illuminates what might be a small, yet significant, glimpse of "the truth." As Maya Angelou once said, "Do the best you can until you know better. Then when you know better, do better."

Here are some of the points stressed in this chapter:

- Apply principles of evidence-based writing to an editing strategy.

- Use facts and theory for evidence, but not beliefs and opinions.

- Develop a sociological mindset to use when solving problems in a variety of professions.

- Use sociological theory as evidence in explaining social phenomena or as a basis for developing hypotheses.

- Cut meta discourse from your writing.

- Use charts, graphs, and tables to display research.

Writing Workshop

Activity A. Research

Instructions: Why is research important? How does it impact your life or your studies? Whether you realize it or not, research is all around you. From the commercials that run during your favorite TV show to the polls that track political races, the processes and products of research fill our daily lives. What type of research are you more exposed to—qualitative or quantitative?

Identify two recent encounters with research. Write a 150- to 200-word summary describing the type of research as well as the purpose and results of each.

Activity B. Process Message

Instructions: Write your professor a process message describing what you learned in this chapter about research and evidence-based writing. Be specific and include examples.

> *Note:* For all messages, use a proper greeting such as "Hi Professor Smith." Also use an appropriate closing. Since e-mail messages are considered *informal*, do not use a *formal* closing, such as "sincerely," but instead use an informal closing, such as "All the best," "Best regards," or "Enjoy your day."

Figure 3.6 Key to Activity "Finding the Squares"

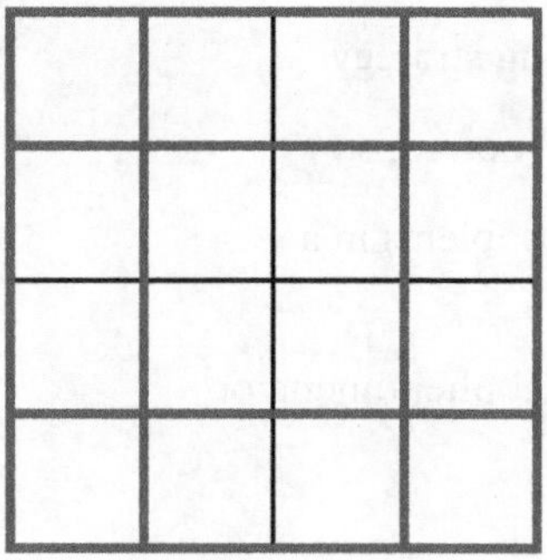

16 single squares
1 large square
4 outside squares
5 inside squares
4 3×3 squares
_____

30 squares

References

1   Gay, L. R. (1981). *Educational research, competencies for analysis and applications* (2nd ed). Columbus, OH: Charles E. Merrill.

2   Mills, C. W. (1961). *The sociological imagination.* New York: Oxford University Press, p. 3.

3   Henslin, J. M. (2012). *Sociology: A down-to-earth approach* (11th ed). Boston, MA: Pearson, p. 114.

4   Ibid.

5   Ibid.

6   Study.com. *How much more do college graduates earn than non-college graduates?* [Video file]. Retrieved from http://study.com/articles/How_Much_More_Do_College_Graduates_Earn_Than_Non-College_Graduates.html

7   ASA. (2017). *American Sociological Association Code of Ethics.* Retrieved from http://www.asanet.org/membership/code-ethics

8   Fowler, H. R. (1986). *The Little, Brown handbook.* Boston: Little, Brown. Retrieved from https://writing.colostate.edu/guides/teaching/co300man/pop12d.cfm

9   Henslin (2012) Op. cit., p. 24.

10 Fowler (1986) Op. cit.

11 Atwan, R. (2007). *America Now.* Boston, MA: Bedford/St. Martin's, p. 5.

12 This quotation is credited to Daniel Patrick Moynihan (1927–2003), a four-term U.S. Senator, ambassador, administration official, and academic.

13 Poincare, J. H. (1902). *La Science et l'hypothèse.* Paris: Ernest Flammarion.

14 Dewey, J. (1933). *How we think.* Lexington, MA: D. C. Heath and Company, p. 16.

15 Ahmed, N. (2005). 23 years of the discovery of *Helicobacter pylori*: Is the debate over? *Annals of Clinical Microbiology and Antimicrobials*, 4, 17. doi:10.1186/1476-0711-4-17

16 Barker, J. A. Paradigm. *Whole systems glossary.* Retrieved from http://www.worldtrans.org/whole/wholedefs.html

17 Wolchover, N. and Live Science Staff (2017, May 30). Are flat-earthers being serious? *Live Science.* Retrieved from https://www.livescience.com/24310-flat-earth-belief.html

18 Talebi Bezmin Abadi, A. (2014). *Helicobacter pylori*: A beneficial gastric pathogen. *Frontiers in Medicine (Lausanne)*, 1, 26. doi:10.3389/fmed.2014.00026

19   American Sociological Association. *Topics.* Retrieved from http://www.asanet.
        org/topics

20   Pew Research Center. *Topics.* Retrieved from http://www.pewresearch.org/
        topics

21   Bloom, B. (Ed.). (1984). *The taxonomy of educational objectives.* Boston, MA:
        Addison Wesley.

22   University of Guelph. *Using evidence effectively.* Retrieved from http://
        www.lib.uoguelph.ca/get-assistance/writing/writing-disciplines/using-
        evidence-effectively

23   Whitehead, A. N. (1929). *The aims of education.* Toronto: Macmillan.

24   Hotchner, A. E. (1966) Papa Hemingway. New York: Random House, p. vii.

25   Rosenberg, M. (1968). *The logic of survey analysis.* New York: Basic Books, p. 11.

26   The University of Manchester. *Academic phrasebank.* Retrieved from http://
        www.phrasebank.manchester.ac.uk

27   Williams, J. M. (1990). *Style: Toward clarity and grace.* Chicago, IL: University
        of Chicago Press.

28   Hinduja, S. and Patchin, J. W. (2016). Cyberbullying Research Center.
        Cyberbullying victimization. Retrieved from https://cyberbullying.
        org/2016-cyberbullying-data

29   Ibid.

30   Williams College. *ANSO alumni careers.* Retrieved from https://anso.williams.
        edu/student-resources/anso-alumni-careers/

31   Ibid.

32   Norén, L. (2011, July 29) US adult blog reading and writing by gender,
        2000–2010. *Graphic Sociology.* Retrieved from https://thesocietypages.
        org/graphicsociology/2011/07/29/us-adult-blog-reading-and-writing-
        by-gender-2000-2010-pew/

33   Ibid.

34   United States Department of Labor, Bureau of Labor Statistics. (2016).
        Occupational outlook handbook: *Survey researchers.* Retrieved from https://
        www.bls.gov/ooh/life-physical-and-social-science/survey-researchers.htm

35   Ibid.

Literature Review

So you must write a literature review, and suddenly the inclination to complete every other task feels like a priority: a natural response, but not a constructive one. To ease your way into the project, break it into manageable parts. This chapter assists you in this process, providing structure for getting started and staying focused.

A literature review involves collecting, synthesizing, and critiquing what others have already written on a topic, allowing you to define your problem and put it in context. Your literature review will reveal the strengths, weaknesses, gaps, and inaccuracies in the current literature. As you collect and conduct research, you may even fill knowledge gaps or identify research or theory that resolves conflicts among studies that previously seemed contradictory.

As you complete your literature review, include newer research but do not overlook older research that is relevant and substantial. For example, you may choose to track the intellectual progression of the topic or identify new ways to interpret older research. A thorough and balanced review of the literature includes *all types* of academic sources, such as books, juried journal articles, and online sources found through credible websites and databases. By establishing a credible base of evidence, you create a springboard for your thesis.

As you review potential sources, keep in mind Ockham's Razor, a scientific and philosophical maxim that states that "in explaining phenomena, do not multiply entities beyond necessity"; in other words, "the simplest explanation is usually the best."

- For competing theories, select the simpler over the more complex.

- To get to the best explanation, get unnecessary information out of the way.

- When faced with competing hypotheses, select the one that makes the fewest assumptions.

When you have completed this chapter, you will be able to:

- Identify a topic and write a research question that is clear, focused, and complex.

- Write a purpose statement describing why your research question is important.

- Complete an annotated bibliography of 10 articles.

- Analyze and critique 10 articles for a literature review.

- Write an abstract.

Literature Review: The Process

Are you writing a literature review as a stepping stone to a research project? Or are you writing a literature review to summarize and synthesize the latest findings on a topic without tying it to a broader project?

When you write a literature review for a potential research project, you have a well-defined context, problem, and purpose. For example, when you are working with a larger project, the literature review part of it will seem small in comparison to the rest of the task. In addition, you have intrinsic motivation to move forward on it. However, when you write a literature review as a stand-alone project, defining the problem and purpose takes focus without the support of a broader context.

Writing a literature review is a process, and this chapter breaks it down into incremental steps, a method known as *project-based learning* or *scaffolding*.[1] At the end of this chapter, the various steps in completing a literature review are outlined, giving you structure throughout the process (see pages 106–111). Similar to other types of writing, a literature review starts with basic questions that lead to substantial inquiry. Most of this chapter consists of questions to support you in your journey. Let's start by looking at how to develop a research question.

Getting Started

What are your professor's requirements? Use those requirements as a checklist throughout your process, for example:

- Are you required to review quantitative research articles, qualitative research articles, or both?

- Which citation style are you required to apply—*APA* or *ASA*?

- How many different *types of sources* are you required to use, such as *books*, *juried articles*, or *online sources*? Should resources be published during a specific time frame, such as within the last 15 years?

- What is your due date for the final project? Have you mapped out internal due dates for each part of the assignment?

Integrative Review

The most common type of literature review in the social sciences is an integrative review, which involves reviewing, critiquing, and synthesizing literature on a topic, generating new frameworks and perspectives.[2] That's the type of literature review discussed in this chapter. However, other types of literature reviews include the following: argumentative review, historical review, methodological review, and theoretical review.

What Is Your Topic?

Do you have a strong interest in or opinion on a current social issue? Selecting a topic that interests you is key to attaining value from your hard work and to sustaining motivation throughout the process. If you are unsure of your interests, visit a few topically-oriented research sites, such as the Pew Research Center or the American Sociological Association. Also, review your course readings and browse through some current journals.

- Select a topic that is manageable: a topic that is too broad can be over-whelming, and a topic that is too narrow may not provide sufficient resources.

- Make a list of concepts and terms; use these keywords to search online data bases.

If at any time you need guidance, speak to a librarian: librarians are incredible founts of knowledge, and helping you is an important part of their purpose for being there.

What Is the Problem?

Rather than focusing on a topic, is there a sociological *problem* that intrigues you or draws you to it? For example, academic writing involves argument, and research involves testing hypotheses. If there is no "problem," then there is no reason to argue or no hypothesis to test.

Also, identifying the problem that you would like to explore brings you closer to developing your thesis question and a possible hypothesis. When you find your problem, let your problem lead you to your question. In addition, depending on the quality of the problem, it will help validate the *why*, the motivation to find answers, which also helps answer the question "*So what?*"[3] These are questions that you will develop in your introduction and your purpose statement, if you write one.

What Is Your Question?

Next, define your topic or problem as a question, developing a *clear*, *focused*, and *complex* research question.[4]

- **Clarity**: Include enough detail so that your question expresses the concrete elements of your inquiry.

  Unclear: Why is human trafficking harmful?

  Clear: What harmful effects does human trafficking have on individuals and society?

- **Focus**: Narrow your focus so that it is specific rather than too broad to be explored in a meaningful way.

  Unfocused: Why is crime higher in impoverished areas?

  Focused: What factors contribute to increased crime in impoverished areas?

- **Complexity**: Write your question so that it needs analysis rather than having a simple "yes/no" answer.

Too simple:	Are serial murderers different from other types of murderers?
Appropriately complex:	What are the psycho-social characteristics of serial murderers?

Your question is the basis for your *thesis statement* or *hypothesis*. Read more about your topic and discuss it with peers, your professor, and your librarian. Once you understand the broader implications of your question and related variables, turn your question into a thesis statement. Here are some "draft" thesis statements:

> *Human trafficking has profound consequences and serious implications for society . . .*

> *Crime is higher in impoverished areas due to various factors such as . . .*

> *Serial murderers demonstrate psychopathic behaviors that include . . .*

However, don't jump straight into writing a thesis statement until you have explored the research, gaining knowledge and insight into your topic. For more information about thesis statements and hypotheses, see Chapter 1, "Purpose, Viewpoint, and Voice," and Chapter 5, "Writing in the Field."

Why Is Your Question Important?

While academic writing is generally done out of necessity rather than for pleasure, having a purpose that ties to your interests will help fuel your motivation. If your professor needs to approve your topic, write a *purpose statement* in which you discuss why you selected your topic and why it is important, answering the following questions:

- What purpose does your question serve?

- What social value does your question have? What benefits will result?

- Is your topic controversial: are there debates about it? What are the various viewpoints?

- Is your topic important at the local, national, or international level?

- Is your topic a current issue? Does it have historical relevance?

- *Does it matter?*

Writing a brief purpose statement will also help you clarify your thinking and ensure that your time and energy are well spent. When your writing has value beyond your interests, it may serve a broader purpose and may even contribute to filling a knowledge gap in the field.

What Makes an Article Scholarly?

Your first step will be to select a few well-written examples of literature reviews that are published in academic journals. Articles published in academic journals are distinctly different from articles published in popular magazines.

Articles published in academic journals are *scholarly* because they are written by experts in the field for other experts: faculty, researchers, subject specialists, and other scholars. In addition, they have generally been *juried*, which means that they have been *peer-reviewed* or *refereed* prior to being approved for publication.

- The *peer-review process* consists of sending the article to other researchers to analyze and assess its academic merit to the field. When an article does not meet standards, the author receives feedback and may be given the option to upgrade the article and resubmit it. However, academic journals generally put a limit on the number of times an article can be resubmitted.

  Note: At times, articles are *not* accepted because the writing is unclear, even though the research has merit: readers need access to ideas to evaluate them fairly. Thus, effective editing makes a difference, especially as it relates to publishing research.

- A *refereed article* is sent out for peer review "blind": the reviewers do not know the name of the author, and the author is not told the names of the reviewers. This anonymity ensures that a work is judged on its merit rather than the author's reputation.

In contrast, articles that you find in *popular magazines* may be informative and interesting, but their credibility cannot be compared with that of juried articles. Articles in popular magazines are often written with a slant to promote an idea, product, person, or theory. One critical standard of scholarly articles is that they present findings in an unbiased way.

Literature Review Pre-Work

Examine a sociological journal article. Read the introduction and the conclusion; identify the thesis statement and consider how the article is summarized:

- How do the authors structure their literature review?

- In the literature review section, how are the various authors introduced?

- What evidence is provided and how do the authors present it?

- How are the data presented and analyzed?

What Is Your Selection Strategy?

When you start to examine articles, develop a plan to identify the most relevant articles efficiently. Reading the *abstract, introduction*, and *conclusion* lets you know if the article applies to your question. In addition, know when to *skim*, when to *scan*, and when to read an article thoroughly.

- *Scan* an article to find if it contains relevant information: when you scan, focus on keywords and phrases; when you find a keyword, read the text before and after it carefully.

- *Skim* an article to get a quick overview: when you skim, read rapidly through key parts to evaluate if an article has worth for your purpose; key parts include the abstract, headings, introductory paragraph, topic sentences, and summaries.

- *Read* an article thoroughly applying your *critical reading skills* when you are including it in your analysis.

Once you have selected several well-written juried journal articles, the next step is reviewing them individually. As part of the process, you will create an annotated bibliography in preparation for doing a comparative analysis or critique of the literature.

What Is an Annotated Bibliography?

As you select scholarly articles, books, and other documents, also begin your annotated bibliography. To start, your annotated bibliography will include basic citation information such as author, title, publisher, year of publication, and so on.

- A *descriptive* or an *informative* annotated bibliography includes a paragraph that describes the source and summarizes the content.

- An *analytical* or a *critical* annotated bibliography goes beyond summarizing the content by also analyzing each source for *purpose*, *relevance*, and *quality*, for example:[5]

  o Who are the authors and what are their credentials?

  o What type of article is it and for what type of audience?

  o What is its purpose or relevance?

  o What are the strengths, weaknesses, and possible biases?

  o Is the article useful for your project?

For your analytical annotated bibliography, you can organize each article using these three categories: *summary*, *assessment*, and *reflection*. You can use these categories as subheadings under each source in your annotated bibliography (unless your professor requires an alternative structure). (See Writing Workshop, Step 2, page 106.)

As you review each source, you are starting the comparative analysis of your literature review. Aim for your critical annotated bibliography to be between 100 and 200 words in length, or longer depending on your purpose.

Annotated Bibliography

Below is a sample extract from an annotated bibliography written by Megan Gilliam, the author of the literature review "Beliefs Behind Behavior: Social Attitudes That Combat Male-on-Female Sexual Assault" that appears on pages 93–105. The extract is formatted in ASA citation style.

Murnen, S. K. (2015). A social constructionist approach to understanding the relationship between masculinity and sexual aggression. *Psychology of Men & Masculinity, 16*(4), 370–373.

Murnen's study aims to understand the relationship between masculinity and sexual aggression. Murnen finds that the social constructs of hostile masculinity and hypermasculinity, both of which are operationalized in Murnen's study, were most highly correlated with sexual aggression. Both constructs measure negative attitudes towards women and level of acceptance of male dominance and/or violence. This study will help me draw a connection between negative attitudes about women and normalization of violence because of the relationships Murnen found between the attitudes she studied. They are all intertwined but can also be viewed independently.

Journal Article Review

As you review articles, you are applying critical reading and thinking skills.[6] Reading critically involves critiquing the structure of an article as well as analyzing its content.

When you read one article critically, you engage in an active process that involves questioning and interpreting. When you synthesize information from multiple articles, you apply critical thinking skills to categorize and group information, compare and contrast methods and results, and identify gaps and omissions in the literature.[7] (See Figure 4.3 on page 108.)

Step 1: Select an Article

While you want to keep your search up to date, you also do not want to overlook older studies that contain substance and relevance. *Before you read an article, ask yourself*:

- What is the title and who is the author or authors? What are their credentials?

- What is the research problem? What is the central question or hypothesis?

- Does the article contain original research?

- How is the article organized? What are the headings and subheadings?

- How does this article fit into my understanding of sociology?

Read the abstract, introduction, and conclusion of the article to see if it informs your thesis or other themes and topics in your literature review. Next, look at the references. Who do the authors reference: *Do they reference their own work? Do they cite articles from other mainstream academic journals?*

While checking out the references, see if any of the other articles relate to your question; if you find an article that is a good fit for your research, you could also review that article.

Step 2: Analyze the Literature Review

All articles contain a review of the literature, which provides the context for the thesis of the paper or the hypothesis of the research. *As you read the review of the literature, ask yourself:*

- Did they use headings to identify each theme?

- How did they integrate the literature within each theme?

- How did they present points of agreement and points of conflict or disagreement?

Operational Definition

An operational definition is *the way a researcher measures a variable.*[8] For example, research in sociology involves concepts and abstractions, which must be made concrete to make observation and measurement possible.

> Operational definitions specify *what to do* and *what to observe* in order to render a social phenomenon both perceivable and communicable. Operational definitions thus make it possible to "see" particular manifestations of concepts in the real world without reifying the concepts of interest.[9]

For example, what is *social class, homelessness,* or *alienation?* How can *social class* be defined so that the abstraction becomes concrete, allowing a common understanding for observation and measurement? In fact, because operational definitions themselves are not concrete or absolute, they can also be controversial.

Step 3: Analyze the Research

As you analyze the content of an article, also pay attention to its structure and flow: good examples provide excellent models. *As you read each article, ask yourself:*

- If it is an empirical article, what are the independent and dependent variables?

- Is the research quantitative, qualitative, or both?

- Is the research exploratory, explanatory, or descriptive?

- What methods are used to collect and analyze the data?

- What are the theoretical assumptions?

- What evidence is being presented?

- What important concepts and terms are used? What are the *operational definitions*?

- How are the definitions similar to or different from those used by other authors?

- What is the sample size? Were the samples an accurate representation of the questions being studied?

- What are the sources for the data?

- What conclusions do the authors reach?

Variables: Independent, Dependent, and *Others*

A variable is any factor that can exist in differing amounts or categories.

- An *independent variable* is the variable that is changed or controlled to create the conditions of the study; the input.

- A *dependent variable* is the variable that is represents what is being tested, measured, or recorded for each independent variable; the result.

Since sociological studies are not performed in a petri dish, other factors or variables can influence the outcomes. Here are a few types of variables that you may encounter:[10]

- **Extraneous variable**—one that you are not intentionally studying and that influences the relationship between the independent and dependent variables.

- **Component variable**—part of a broader variable. When defining the independent variable, a mistake is made by identifying only a component of a broader independent variable; the broader concept would actually be the independent variable.

- **Intervening variable**—a factor intervening between the independent and dependent variable: independent variable → test factor → dependent variable.

- **Antecedent variable**—a variable that comes before the independent variable and is the true effective influence. An antecedent variable may not change the relationship between the independent and dependent variable, but it clarifies and adds depth in understanding the relationship.

- **Suppressor variable**—one that intrudes on the independent–dependent variable relationship and causes it to appear that there is no relationship, when a relationship does in fact exist.

- **Distorter variable**—one that converts a positive relationship into a negative relationship.

Understanding other variables or test factors beyond independent and dependent variables enables you "to achieve sounder, more precise, and more meaningful interpretations of two-variable relationships."[11]

Step 4. Define the Outcomes

While all studies have limitations and biases, good studies discuss their own limitations and possible sources of bias. *When you have finished reading the article, ask yourself:*

- Have the authors analyzed and interpreted their data correctly?

- What results were reported: are their conclusions justified?

- Could intervening variables (people, things, or events) have interfered with the research, leading to inaccurate results?

- What are the strengths and weaknesses of the methodology? Did the researcher identify strengths and weaknesses of the research as well as gaps?

- Were the samples (people surveyed or items examined) an accurate representation for the study?

- Could the research be biased: did personal ideology influence the methodology or outcomes?

- Could a profit motive be involved? For example, who paid for or benefited from the research?

- Did the authors identify areas for further research?

Finally, what could the authors have done differently? Did the article answer the questions it set out to explore? If not, why?

What are the Patterns, Themes, or Common Threads?

Common threads are considered objective data and can more readily be generalized. As you review various theories, look for common themes or characteristics. Ask yourself, *what information does everyone seem to hold in common?*

Step 5: Recap Your Findings

For each article, write a brief summary of your findings that you can use for your critique of the literature (as well as your annotated bibliography). *As you summarize your findings, ask yourself*:

- How did the authors integrate or synthesize the various articles into themes?

- How does the literature reviewed in the article connect to *my thesis*? Are there original articles in the review that merit reading?

- What have I learned about sociology from this article?

As you review each article, take special note of *common themes* and *patterns*, as these will be a focus of your comparative analysis.

Critique of the Literature

Once you have reviewed credible articles relating to your topic, the next step is to critique the content and do a comparative analysis:

1   Divide the articles into *themes* or *topics*.

2   Identify the strengths and weaknesses of each document, including research methods, characteristics of participants, methods of data analysis, outcomes, and conclusions.

3   Categorize and group information from various articles, compare and contrast methods and results, and identify gaps and omissions in the literature.

4   Use an analytic chart (see Figure 4.1 below) to help you identify which articles address key topics or themes in your literature review. You can also use a spreadsheet, if that works for you.

When you begin to write the review, make each topic a heading in your document to help you organize the articles. Now you are ready to integrate the literature.

*   Which articles agree on the topic?

*   Which articles provide new insights or multiple perspectives that are worth considering?

*   Which articles contradict the findings of other articles, and why?

When you write your literature review, be sure to use the *thesis statement* or *question* in your *introduction* and *conclusion*. When you describe your findings, support your topics with evidence from the literature.

■   **Using the example in Figure 4.2, assume that you are interested in child neglect. You have found four articles so far and have put the content into a grid to analyze the content and keep the articles organized.**

Note: The articles discussed in this example are fictitious.

Figure 4.1 Analytic Chart

Name of article	Topic 1	Topic 2	Topic 3	Topic 4	Topic 5

■ **Examine the similarities and differences. How does Thigpen's (2010) definition fit in? If you find disagreement among authors (and you will), go to an established source, such as the American Sociological Association's website, which has a glossary of terms.[12] You can also check other authoritative references at your library.**

Figure 4.2 Analytic chart for articles on child neglect

Article	Topic 1	Topic 2	Topic 3	Topic 4	Topic 5
	Define neglect	Ways to identify neglect	Reasons for neglect	Interventions for neglect	Outcomes
Smith (2008)	X – agree		X	X	
Jones (2010)	X – disagree	X			
Johnson (2013)	X – agree		X	X	X
Thigpen (2012)	X brief		X	X	X

Note: Smith (2008) and Johnson (2013) used similar definitions of neglect. However, Jones's (2010) definition was from a U.S. Department of Health and Human Services website and is used nationally by social service agencies. If you search "child neglect" online, you are likely to find information from sources that are not academic. However, the Child Welfare Information Gateway through the U.S. Department of Health and Human Services provides useful and relevant information and can be included in an academic literature review.

What Are Credible Online Sources?

A goal of all research, quantitative or qualitative, is an attempt to obtain clear outcomes that are supported by the data.

Credible sources are sources that you can trust because they are evidence-based. As you know, some online sources are not credible; for the most part, anyone can post anything on the web. Readers must use discretion and be selective. To start, look for university-affiliated sites, government sites such as the U.S. Bureau of Labor Statistics, and credible institutions.

When you use other online sources, consider the following:

• Does the site appear professional and current?

• What is its purpose? Is the purpose to *inform* or to *persuade*?

• Is it a personal blog or professional organization?

- How long has the site been in operation? How often is it updated?

- Is the site linked to other sites that you consider reputable?

- Does the site provide information to answer your questions accurately and objectively?

- Can you identify any bias?

- Does the site contain advertising? Is it profit-driven?

- Who is the audience: is it for experts in the field or a general audience?

- Is the site tied to a private corporation or non-profit organization? If so, have you checked the accuracy of the information through academic sites?

When you evaluate any source, consider the following:

- Who is the author? What are the author's credentials?

- Has the author written other publications on the topic? Other topics? (Do an online search.)

- Is the author associated with a group or does the author have a specific gender, sexual, racial, political, social, or cultural orientation?

- Who is the intended audience: is it for scholars or a general audience?

- Have others referenced this source?

- Are the data verifiable and accurate?

- Who published the article and when? Do the publishers have an editorial position?

- Was it peer reviewed? If self-published, were there outside editors or reviewers?

- What are the research citations? When was the research published?

- Are the sources *primary* or *secondary*?

Primary sources include autobiographies, letters, diary entries, photographs, public records, news film footage, and speeches. Secondary sources provide interpretation and analysis of primary sources, such as biographies, analyses, or critiques. While primary sources stay fresh, secondary sources may become dated; use the most relevant and most recent sources and evaluate each source on a case-by-case basis.[13]

Here are some tips:

- If you use a site such as Wikipedia, which can be helpful as an overview, also examine and read the original documentation that supports what is stated; cite original documentation in your research, not Wikipedia. (Note that anyone can update a Wikipedia entry.)

- Avoid blogs, opinion sites, and for-profit sites (many of which end in ".com"). Also avoid self-authored sites.

- Use sources your library has already screened *before* you put your topic into an outside search engine. (Your library has screened many sources through online subscriptions, data bases, and CD-ROMs.)

- Compare how information on a website meshes with the print materials in your research. (Since print materials are scrutinized heavily during the publishing process, online sources that validate those sources can be considered more seriously.)

- If you have a question, discuss your source with your local librarian.

Though you may start your research online, use your online sampling as an entrée to books and periodicals that provide substance and balance. What your library does not carry in hard copy or online subscriptions, it may carry in the form of microfilm or microfiche. Libraries can also request material for you through inter-library loan—one more reason to start your research early.

Abstract

As a final step, write an abstract that describes your literature review. Now that you have spent time scoping out effective articles, you see the value that a well-written abstract has for the research community. By succinctly summarizing the purpose of your literature review along with your findings, you become a link in expanding the knowledge of humankind.

For APA and ASA citation style, the abstract appears on page 2 of the paper. A general guideline for an abstract is that it should be a 150- to 250-word paragraph that includes the following:

- Purpose or problem

- Methods (if applicable)

- Conclusions and recommendations

The use of accurate, informative *keywords* is a critical element of your abstract. Though you will provide a *keyword summary*, also make a conscious effort to intertwine keywords throughout your abstract as well: that's how the research community will find your work, and the quality of your abstract will determine if they become enticed to read it.

However, before you write your abstract, check with your professor to make sure that you mold it for the required purpose. For example, just as there are various types of literature review, there are also various types of abstract. For example, an *informative abstract* "presents and explains all the main arguments and the important results and evidence in the paper."[14] A *critical abstract* would be an evaluative summary that also describes the strengths and weaknesses of the work, comparing it with other works in the field.

Recap

Once you become involved with research, you may find it to be exciting. Though research can illuminate even the most difficult and controversial issues, a key to making research relevant is applying it.

The project-based learning process presented in the Writing Workshop below gives you a step-by-step process to follow. Start early and stay engaged so that you meet all deadlines. Anytime you feel the anxiety of an impending deadline, take action: according to Leonardo da Vinci, "*stagnant water loses its purity and in cold weather becomes frozen; even so does inaction sap the vigor of the mind.*"[16]

Here are some of the points stressed in this chapter:

- Focus on the process, not the final product.

- Get started quickly doing prework to identify your problem.

- Work on your project in incremental steps, knowing that small steps lead to big progress.

- When you get stuck, read about your topic or talk to a colleague about it.

- Keep a notebook with you so that you can collect ideas, even in off times.

4.1 SAMPLE LITERATURE REVIEW

The following literature review was written by Megan Gilliam as part of a larger research paper entitled "Beliefs Behind Behavior: Social Attitudes to Combat Male-on-Female Sexual Assault." Gilliam wrote the paper for SOC 493, Senior Seminar, and her professor was Dr. Andrew Raridon.

(*Note*: The paper is formatted in ASA style.)

Running Head = SOCIAL ATTITUDES THAT COMBAT SEXUAL ASSAULT   1

Beliefs Behind Behavior:

Social Attitudes That Combat Male-on-Female Sexual Assault

Megan Gilliam

Valparaiso University[15]

continued. . .

SOCIAL ATTITUDES THAT COMBAT SEXUAL ASSAULT   2

ABSTRACT

This literature examines the links between individual beliefs and male-on-female sexual assault, exploring the reasons for the disproportionate rates of violence against women. Beyond each complex, individual encounter are social constructions and cultural factors that contribute to its persistence, such as gender constructs, victim-blaming, adherence to strict ideas regarding masculinity/femininity, and shame. These factors may influence a person's beliefs about sexual assault, including their own victim-blaming attitudes and rape-supportive attitudes. Importantly, the research reveals that rape-supportive and victim-blaming attitudes are held by both men and women, despite men disproportionately representing the perpetrators of sexual assault.

Keyword summary: sexual assault, violence against women, victim-blaming attitudes, rape-supportive attitudes, social constructs

continued. . .

SOCIAL ATTITUDES THAT COMBAT SEXUAL ASSAULT   3

SOCIAL ATTITUDES THAT COMBAT MALE-ON-FEMALE SEXUAL ASSAULT

Sexual assault in the United States is still largely a woman's problem. While sexual assault can happen to anyone of any gender, there is still an overwhelmingly disproportionate prevalence of male-on-female sexual assault. As with any social problem, we ask ourselves why it persists. If so many people are abhorred at sexual violence, then how does it occur at such alarming rates against women? You would be hard-pressed to find someone who says sexual assault is not a bad thing, or that perpetrators of sexual assault should keep up the behavior—unless, of course, you are conducting research on internet trolling. While people typically do not overtly state or hold those views, there are attitudes and implicit biases that people do hold that may contribute to the persistence of sexual violence.

These underlying beliefs contribute to the normalization of violence against women, a concept utilized in this study which refers to the complicit acceptance of sexual violence by removing responsibility from the perpetrator while often simultaneously placing blame on the victim. Attitudes that may influence this normalization are attitudes that shame female sexuality (i.e., holding double standards regarding the social acceptability of one gender acting on/expressing sexual desires over another). Shaming women's sexualities can make it easier to victim-blame or deny their victimhood in instances of sexual assault, especially those that occur on dates, at bars or parties, and so on. If these negative attitudes toward women do influence people's normalization of sexual violence against them, then efforts to reduce sexual assault prevalence should address them.

continued. . .

SOCIAL ATTITUDES THAT COMBAT SEXUAL ASSAULT   4

In order to measure the impact of one belief on another, it is important to recognize the larger sociological framework in which beliefs and norms are understood. Personal beliefs often stem from various socialization processes in which a person develops an understanding of society's expectations, norms, and how their own identity is situated within those social structures. Symbolic interactionism posits that the way we perceive ourselves, society, and our social interactions is how we establish meaning among ourselves and society. Thus, people's perceptions of social interactions and assessment of norm adherence partially determine the meaning they assign to people and situations. Additionally, Goffman's dramaturgical theory posits that people perform their social identities like scripts, specifically including gender as a performative social process. While this may appear general, it is directly applicable to attitudes that deal with sexual assault and the victimization of women.

There is research, which informed the present study, that examines the effects of strict gender roles on sexual assault rates, demonstrating both Goffman's theory and social interactionism as a whole. Research also shows that, depending on situational factors and personal beliefs, individuals' ideas about victim-worthiness, victim responsibility (often leading to victim-blaming), and gender roles can influence their attitudes regarding sexual violence against women. Research has even gone so far as to suggest that, under the right circumstances, those attitudes can translate into sexually aggressive behavior.

continued. . .

SOCIAL ATTITUDES THAT COMBAT SEXUAL ASSAULT   5

Interestingly, these negative attitudes are not solely held by men; women hold beliefs that contribute to the normalization of sexual assault against women, too, no matter how counterproductive it appears in theory. Shaming female sexuality can be viewed as pushback to deviation from traditional gender roles and expectations; women are expected to be more innocent and sexually reserved, and acting against this can be viewed negatively across genders. Because these problematic attitudes are not limited in beholders, it is apparent the attitudes themselves should be at the forefront of discussion on sexual assault. If we continue to address sexual assault as merely the physical act itself, we ignore ideological foundations that, knowingly or otherwise, support the continuance of sexual violence against women. Working to eliminate specific behavior does nothing to combat the beliefs and attitudes that allow that behavior to occur; those beliefs and their potential impact is what the present research aims to address.

LITERATURE REVIEW

When considering the prevalence of sexual assault in our society, the disproportionate rate of violence against women perpetrated by men is alarming, yet not surprising. Because of this gendered difference in sexual assault victimization, the present study is concerned with sexual assault committed specifically against women. The persistence of female victimization is likely the combination of many complex, intricate factors that vary in both minor and significant ways in each individual instance. However, it is possible to identify some elements of our culture that may perpetuate the problem,

continued. . .

SOCIAL ATTITUDES THAT COMBAT SEXUAL ASSAULT   6

including individual attitudes toward women, rape-supportive attitudes, and acceptance of rape myths (Abbey et al. 2001; Adams-Curtis and Forbes 2004; Bouffard and Bouffard 2011; Cowan 2000; Forbes and Adams-Curtis 2001; Frese et. al 2004; Murnen 2015; Parkinson 2017; Russell and Trigg 2017; Willan and Pollard 2003).

SOCIAL CONSTRUCTS AS CONTRIBUTORS

Social constructs such as gender contribute significantly; as well, this is likely due to the social expectations and norms which make up our society's construction of the gender categories. Thus, significance is placed both in the norms and in society's response to deviance from those norms. Negative social reactions that may affect the persistence of sexual assault include things such as victim-blaming, adherence to strict ideas regarding masculinity/femininity, and shame (Adams-Curtis and Forbes 2004; Cassidy and Hurrell 1995; Cowan 2000; Forbes and Adams-Curtis 2001; Frese et. al 2004; Murnen 2015; Parkinson 2017; Russell and Trigg 2004; Sanday 1981; Schneider 2005; Weiss 2010).

Research on the preceding factors has yielded some very interesting things regarding the role of gender in attitudes toward women. While the sexual violence in our society is disproportionately committed against women by males, the contributing factors previously identified are neither produced nor maintained solely by men. A study conducted by Cowan (2000) found that both rape-supportive and victim-blaming attitudes are held by women, too. Cowan argues women perpetuate violence against women in a similar way in that respect, maintaining attitudes which correlate with

continued. . .

SOCIAL ATTITUDES THAT COMBAT SEXUAL ASSAULT   7

the sexual victimization of women. Similarly, Cassidy and Hurrell (1995) conducted an experiment in which they found that social perception of a woman's "victim-worthiness," as it is sometimes called, affected whether or not the participants victim-blamed, and also whether the participants were willing to classify identical scenarios as rape. The victim-blaming attitudes and scenario-classifications were held regardless of the participant's gender and were significantly affected by the visual representation of the victim (specifically her clothing), not by individual characteristics of the participant (Cassidy and Hurrell 1995).

Social Environments: College Campuses

The combination of those factors, which exist across genders, results in environments that directly influence women's experiences with sexual assault, such as college campuses. Adams-Curtis and Forbes (2004) conducted a study which examined college women's experiences with sexual coercion. Again, they found that attitudes toward women, ideas about gender roles, and rape-supportive beliefs all played a role in their experiences of sexual coercion. Adams-Curtis and Forbes also found that campus values influenced sexual coercion, which in a way demonstrates the tangible effects of such commonly held shame-favoring and rape-supportive attitudes. These studies illustrate the importance of social attitudes and narratives perpetuated by society at large that influence the determination of victim-worthiness, level of victim's responsibility in their assault, and the validity in classifying the experience as assault. The sheer fact that these attitudes are not merely held

continued. . .

SOCIAL ATTITUDES THAT COMBAT SEXUAL ASSAULT   8

by men, the statistical majority of perpetrators of sexual assault, suggests that women play an important role in maintaining social values and doling out social punishments that allow sexual assault against women to persist.

Although attitudes that shame women and aid in normalizing sexual violence against them are not gender-specific in who holds them, those attitudes present in men may contribute to their willingness to commit sexual assault against women. Abbey et. al (2001) conducted a study intended to identify variables that could discriminate between men who have committed sexual assault and those who have not; two of the variables the authors found as being significant indicators of males who have committed sexual assault are attitudes and situational factors.

Attitudinal and Situational Factors

Additionally, Bouffard and Bouffard (2011) look at how rape-supportive attitudes affect men's willingness to commit date-rape using a rational choice framework; the authors attempt to understand the cost-benefit analyses present in date-rape scenarios, and ultimately to understand how these attitudes translate into actual sexually-aggressive behavior. Willan and Pollard's (2003) work explored similar concepts, examining the predictive value of attitudinal and situational factors on men's likelihood of committing sexual assault against acquaintances. Thus, the research supports the idea that attitudes toward women and sexual assault both perpetuate acceptance of violence and can translate into sexually aggressive behavior in scenarios which do not explicitly prevent it.

continued. . .

SOCIAL ATTITUDES THAT COMBAT SEXUAL ASSAULT   9

GENDER ROLES

Looking more broadly at social expectations, there is evidence to support that a society's and/or individual's strict adherence to and enforcement of gender roles can have an effect on sexual assault perpetration. Sanday (1981) conducted a cross-cultural study in which she compared what she termed "rape-prone" and "rape-free" tribes to ascertain the cultural/social factors which influence a tribe to have higher rates of sexual assault against women. Interestingly, she found that rape-prone tribes' values are rooted in more traditional gender stereotypes and expectations, showing more gender segregation and less respect for women's roles. Conversely, rape-free tribes had more respect for women's societal roles and did not strictly enforce gender roles. Murnen (2015) was inspired by the work of Sanday and conducted a study in order to expand on the attitudes which are linked with sexism and contribute to the persistence of sexual assault. She found that the social constructs of hostile masculinity and hypermasculinity were most highly correlated with sexual aggression. Both constructs measure negative attitudes toward women and level of acceptance of male dominance and/or violence.

Strict Gender Role Adherence and Sexual Violence

To see how these social constructions translate into individual-level assault, Parkinson (2017) interviewed women who had experienced sexual assault within heterosexual relationships. She found similar results to that

continued. . .

SOCIAL ATTITUDES THAT COMBAT SEXUAL ASSAULT   10

of Murnen and Sanday, stating, "Women described partners variously using sexual violence to assert some definition of 'masculinity'" (2017:45).

Parkinson also found that women often experienced sexual assault as a consequence of their role as "wife." Thus, perpetuating attitudes which are sexist and negative toward women, coupled with attitudes that support sexual aggression in males as desirable in proving masculinity, has concrete consequences for women. The preceding research suggests that strict gender role adherence in societies and individual relationships has an effect on the acceptance and prevalence of sexual violence against women. Thus, attitudinal factors play a large role in the perpetuation and normalization of male-on-female sexual assault.

Sexual Shame and Sexual Aggression

Research has also been conducted on the effects of sexual shame on sexual aggression, shame being a concept closely related to victim-blaming explored above. When comparing the United States and Germany, Schneider (2005) utilizes Scheff's theory claiming shame causes violence to argue that "sexually emancipated" societies, such as Germany, have less sexual violence than societies that attach shame to sex, such as the United States. Essentially, Schneider argues that less shame attached to sexual behaviors would lead to less sexual violence because shame causes individuals to engage in more violent behaviors that are hidden from the public.

Shame also plays a large role in victimization; Weiss (2010) found that shame connected with experiencing sexual assault affects a victim's

continued...

SOCIAL ATTITUDES THAT COMBAT SEXUAL ASSAULT   11

willingness to report it. According to Weiss, there is a gendered component to shame, and women experience shame as a result of many of the social expectations previously explored. Thus, sexually shaming women affects perpetrators' willingness to assault them and women's willingness to report their attack.

SUMMARY

The present research aims to contribute to and expand on the existing research linking attitudinal factors to male-on-female sexual assault. While it is currently known that attitudes such as victim-blaming and gender role adherence affect sexual assault prevalence, the correlation between attitudes is less clear. Because attitudes influence social environments that affect sexual assault prevalence, it is important to better understand the relationships among those attitudes. Therefore, this present research aims to explore whether individuals' attitudes that favor the sexual shaming of women influences their attitudes that normalize sexual violence against women.

continued. . .

SOCIAL ATTITUDES THAT COMBAT SEXUAL ASSAULT   12

REFERENCES

Abbey, Antonia, Pam McAuslan, A. M. Clinton, Philip O. Buck and Tina
    Zawacki. 2001. "Attitudinal, Experiential, and Situational Predictors
    of Sexual Assault Perpetration." *Journal of Interpersonal Violence*
    16(8):784–807.

Adams-Curtis, Leah and Gordon B. Forbes. 2004. "College Women's
    Experiences of Sexual Coercion: A Review of Cultural, Perpetrator, Victim,
    and Situational Variables." *Trauma, Violence, & Abuse: A Review Journal*
    5(2):91–122.

Bouffard, Leana A. and Jeffrey A. Bouffard. 2011. "Understanding Men's
    Perceptions of Risks and Rewards in a Date Rape Scenario." *International
    Journal of Offender Therapy and Comparative Criminology* 55(4):626–645.

Cassidy, Linda and Rose Marie Hurrell. 1995. "The Influence of Victim's Attire
    on Adolescents' Judgments of Date Rape." *Adolescence* 30(118):319–323.

Cowan, Gloria. 2000. "Women's Hostility Toward Women and Rape and
    Sexual Harassment Myths." *Violence Against Women* 6(3):238–246.

Forbes, Gordon B. and Leah Adams-Curtis. 2001. "Experiences with Sexual
    Coercion in College Males and Females: Role of Family Conflict, Sexist
    Attitudes, Acceptance of Rape Myths, Self-Esteem, and the Big-Five
    Personality Factors." *Journal of Interpersonal Violence* 16(9):865–889.

Frese, Bettina, Miguel Moya and Jesus L. Megias. 2004. "Social Perception of
    Rape: How Rape Myth Acceptance Modulates the Influence of Situational
    Factors." *Journal of Interpersonal Violence* 19(2):143–161.

continued...

cont.

SOCIAL ATTITUDES THAT COMBAT SEXUAL ASSAULT   13

Murnen, Sarah K. 2015. "A Social Constructionist Approach to Understanding
the Relationship between Masculinity and Sexual Aggression."
Psychology of Men & Masculinity 16(4):370–3.

Pager, Devah, and Lincoln Quillian. 2005. "Walking the Talk? What Employers
Say Versus What They Do." *American Sociological Review* 70(3):355–80.

Parkinson, Debra. 2017. "Intimate Partner Sexual Violence Perpetrators
and Entitlement." pp. 44–54 in *Perpetrators of Intimate Partner Sexual
Violence: A Multidisciplinary Approach to Prevention, Recognition, and
Intervention*, edited by L. McOrmond-Plummer, J. Y. Levy-Peck, and
P. Easteal. Routledge: The Taylor & Francis Group.

Russell, Brenda L. and Kristin Y. Trigg. 2004. "Tolerance of Sexual Harassment: An
Examination of Gender Differences, Ambivalent Sexism, Social Dominance,
and Gender Roles." *Sex Roles: A Journal of Research* 50(7):565–73.

Sanday, Peggy R. 1981. "The Socio-Cultural Context of Rape: A Cross-Cultural
Study." *Journal of Social Issues* 37(4):5–27.

Schneider, Andreas. 2005. "A Model of Sexual Constraint and Sexual
Emancipation." *Sociological Perspectives* 48(2):255–70.

Weiss, Karen G. 2010. "Too Ashamed to Report: Deconstructing the Shame of
Sexual Victimization." *Feminist Criminology* 5(3):286–310.

Willan, V. J. and Paul Pollard. 2003. "Likelihood of Acquaintance Rape
as a Function of Males' Sexual Expectations, Disappointment, and
Adherence to Rape-Conducive Attitudes." *Journal of Social and Personal
Relationships* 20(5):637–661.

Writing Workshop

Work on your literature review one step at a time, with each assignment leading to the next. Receiving feedback as you complete each step enhances the process: if you can discuss this process with your peers in class or online, you will increase your learning, incorporating various perspectives.

Step 1: Thesis Statement and Process Message

Purpose: Write a thesis statement and a purpose statement.

Instructions: Write your instructor a process message that includes a brief purpose statement.

- What is your topic or problem? What is your working thesis?

- Why did you select that topic? Why is it important?

As you write your thesis statement, keep in mind that you need to support it with evidence. You may also modify your thesis statement or question as your research progresses: research is a process, and your original ideas may change as new data emerges. (Make sure to format your message correctly by using a greeting and closing.)

Step 2: Introduction and Review of Two Articles

Purpose: Complete a *draft* review of two articles in preparation for your paper; in the process, you will discover if enough literature is available for a comprehensive review of your topic.

Instructions: Select two sociology articles. Organize information for each article using these three categories: *summary*, *assessment*, and *reflection*. These categories should appear as subheadings under each source in your annotated bibliography.

- The **summary** describes the main points presented in the article.

- The **assessment** is your evaluation of the article. Is the information trustworthy? Why or why not?

- The **reflection** identifies how you intend to apply the information to your work or your review. You can also use the reflection to make personal notes to yourself, such as how an article compares or contrasts with other articles, books, or documents.

Format your paper in APA or ASA style (see Chapter 6), whichever citation system your professor requires. After receiving feedback on this step, you are ready to complete subsequent steps.

Summary, Assessment, and Reflection

Summary: Be as objective as possible, giving a brief overview: you do not need to restate detailed information.

- What are the basic details of the article, including the *purpose, methods,* and *conclusions?*

- What information does the article provide?

- Who is the article about?

- What do the authors do? How do they do it? Why do they do it?

Assessment and Critique:

- How do I know that I can trust the information in the article?

- What is it about the article that suggests the information is reliable? (Look for evidence in Figure 4.3 or go to www.criticalthinking.org and select the tab "Universal Intellectual Standards.")

- Which critical thinking standards do the authors demonstrate?

- Which critical thinking standards are missing or are not fully implemented?

Reflection:

- Is the article useful to my study? If so, how?

- What themes does this article inform?

- How does information in the article compare, support, or contrast with information in other scholarly articles or books?

Figure 4.3 Universal Intellectual Standards

Critical thinking standard	Description	Questions to check for building your critical thinking skills
Relevance	Are all my statements relevant to the question at hand? Does what I'm saying connect to my central point?	How does this relate to the issue being discussed? How does this help me deal with this issue?
Accuracy	Are all my statements and all my information factually correct and/ or supported with evidence?	How do I know this? Is this true? How could I validate this?
Precision	Are all my statements discussed in adequate detail? Do my examples include enough specifics?	Could I be more specific? Could I give more details?
Clarity	Do I expand on ideas, express ideas in another way, and provide examples or illustrations where appropriate?	Did I give an example? Is it clear what I mean by this? Could I elaborate further?
Depth	Do I explain the reasons behind my conclusions, anticipate and answer the questions my reasoning raises, and/or acknowledge the complexity of the issue?	Why is this so? What are some of the complexities here? What would it take for this to happen?
Breadth	Am I considering alternative points of view? Have I thought about how someone else might have interpreted the situation?	Would this look the same from someone else's perspective? Is there another way to interpret this?
Logic	Does my line of reasoning make sense? Do my conclusions follow from the facts and/or my earlier statements?	Does what I said at the beginning fit with what I concluded at the end? Do my conclusions match the evidence?
Significance	Do my conclusions or goals represent a major issue raised by my reflection on experience?	Is this the most important issue on which to focus? Is this the most significant problem?
Fairness	Do I have a vested interest in this issue? Am I sympathetic to others' viewpoints?	Do I use inclusive language? Do I consider power differential?

Step 3: Complete an Annotated Bibliography of 10 Articles

Purpose: Analyze articles and summarize key information.

Instructions: As a continuation of Step 2, organize information for eight additional articles using the three categories: *summary, assessment,* and *reflection*. These three categories should appear as subheadings under each source in your bibliography.

Step 4: Synthesis of 10 Articles

Purpose: Enhance synthesis and integration skills.

Instructions: Now that you have identified and annotated (summarized and analyzed) 10 sociology articles, synthesize the articles by doing the following:

1   Integrate the articles by theme. (Keep in mind the themes must support the thesis statement or question.) For example, "Several authors support *Theme A* (citation here)."

2   Use an analytic chart (see Figures 4.1 and 4.2) to analyze and condense the data that you have found. Modify the chart as needed; an analytic chart is an analysis tool and would not be included in your final paper.

3   As you review the articles, also notice how the authors synthesize the literature. What can you learn from the approach these authors take?

4   Edit and proofread your work thoroughly.

At this point in the process, *can you see the bigger picture and how the steps are integrated?*

Step 5: First Draft—Focus on Conclusions

Purpose: Focus on the outcomes and meaning of the literature.

Instructions: Write the first draft of your conclusions; include the following:

•   Your thesis statement or question and how the literature addressed your topic.

- Your conclusions based on data from the research: statements supported by data.

- Your recommendations for actions needed.

- What you have learned.

When your first draft is complete, visit your college's writing center or have a peer read your work for clarity, correctness, and logic.

Step 6: Second Draft—Rethink, Revisit, and Revise

Purpose: Rethink your problem, support conclusions with data, incorporate feedback, and revisit your introduction.

Instructions: Based on feedback, revise your literature review; compare your conclusion with your introduction.

- Does your conclusion include your thesis statement or question and how the literature addressed your topic?

- Are your conclusions based on and supported by data?

- Can you describe your findings more clearly?

- What actions are needed based on your research?

- What have you learned?

Step 7: Presentation of Your Literature Review

Purpose: By developing a presentation of the review and findings to a group of peers, you solidify arguments. Questions from the group provide alternative perspectives as well as identifying strengths, weaknesses, and gaps in rationale.

Instructions: Develop a 10-minute presentation of your literature review; include a PowerPoint, if instructed (See Chapter 20, "Making a Presentation.") In the review, include the following:

1   Introduction that includes thesis statement

2   Synthesis of your review

3   Conclusion

After your presentation, immediately write a reflection that includes new questions and insights for your final paper.

Step 8: Literature Review

Purpose: Integrate the various pieces of the literature review that you have completed in previous steps.

Instructions: Now you are ready to write a literature review that includes at least 10 peer-reviewed sociology journal articles; you may include one or two scholarly books. Your literature review should be approximately 28–34 pages long, including the title page and references. Here is an outline to follow:

1   Title Page

2   Abstract, including a keyword summary

3   Introduction, including thesis statement or question

4   Annotated bibliography for each article, including the following:

    a   Summary

    b   Assessment and critique

    c   Reflection

5   Synthesis

6   Conclusion

7   References

Check with your instructor for additional formatting guidelines; for example, should you format your literature review in APA style or ASA style? For information on formatting, see Chapter 6, "Citation Styles: APA and ASA."

References

1   Dr. Andrea Tamburro developed the project-based literature review process presented in this chapter, breaking it into an eight-step project for The Writing Workshop.

2   Fink, A. (2005). *Conducting research literature reviews: from the internet to paper* (2nd ed). Thousand Oaks, CA: Sage.

3   University of Southern California. *Organizing your social science research paper: the research problem/question.* Retrieved from http://libguides.usc.edu/writingguide/introduction/Researchproblem

4   Indiana University. *Develop a research question.* Retrieved from https://libraries.indiana.edu/sites/default/files/Develop_a_ Research_Question.pdf

5   Cornell University. *How to prepare an annotated bibliography.* Retrieved from guides.library.cornell.edu/annotatedbibliography

6   Kain, E. L. (2017). *Sample handout to help students read professional articles.* Paper presented at the American Sociological Association, August 2017.

7   Elder, L., & Paul, R. (2010). *Foundation for critical thinking.* Retrieved from http://www.criticalthinking.org/pages/ universal-intellectual-standards/527

8   Henslin, J. M. (2012). *Sociology: A down-to-earth approach.* Boston, MA: Pearson, p. 123.

9   Frankfort-Nachmias, C., Nachimias, D. and De Waard, J. (2015). *Research methods in the social sciences* (8th ed). New York: Worth, p. 27.

10 Rosenberg, M. (1968). *The logic of survey analysis.* New York: Basic Books.

11 Ibid., p. 27.

12 American Sociological Association. *Glossary.* Retrieved from http://www.asanet.org/sites/default/files/savvy/introtosociology/Documents/Glossary.html.

13 Lee, C. (2015). *The myth of the off-limits source.* American Psychological Association. Retrieved from http://blog.apastyle.org/apastyle/2015/10/the-myth-of-the-off-limits-source.html

14 University of Southern California. *Research guides: Organizing your social sciences research paper: 3. The Abstract.* Retrieved from http://libguides.usc.edu/writingguide/abstract

15 Gilliam, M. (2018). "Beliefs behind behavior: A look at social attitudes to combat male-on-female sexual assault," unpublished paper, Valparaiso University, Sociology Department.

16 Da Vinci, L. Notebook I.

17 Elder & Paul (2010) Op. cit.

CHAPTER 5

Writing in the Field

In any field that you choose, your *sociological imagination* will prove to be an asset. To some extent, sociology has relevance for a broad range of professions: sociology can help you make unique contributions in fields as varied as education, business, and criminal justice as well as health care and journalism. By developing expert writing and editing skills, you further support your work and your opportunities.

Sociology helps you understand people in *context*—their cultures, beliefs, values, and expectations as well as their social groups, networks, and institutions—enabling you to frame situations and see things that are not visible on the surface. In part, you learn to search for truths: separating reality from wishful thinking and gaining insight into solving problems in a broad and meaningful way—thinking *outside of the box.*

This chapter provides basics in the types of writing done in sociology, such as quantitative and qualitative research papers as well as surveys and polling; but first, you review how writing from a sociological perspective can be applied to diverse fields for a variety of purposes.

When you have completed this chapter, you will be able to:

- Appreciate the contribution of a sociological imagination to a variety of professions.

- Understand basic parts of quantitative and qualitative research papers.

- Explore the process of writing a research question.

- Gain insight into the process of writing a testable hypothesis.

- Develop surveys to use in conducting quantitative and qualitative research.

The sociological skills that you are developing will serve you well throughout your career.

Sociology in Context

One way to put sociology in context is to hear first-hand from a sociologist who has applied sociological theory and research to various facets of his career, such as teaching, journalism, political analysis, and the media. The article "If I Had a Hammer" by sociologist Wayne A. Youngquist (Box 5.1) was originally given as a keynote address at the 2013 Annual Conference of Association of Applied and Clinical Sociology.[1] For a quarter century, Youngquist worked in TV news as a political analyst and pollster, projecting winners on election nights and interviewing public figures on his Sunday morning show in Milwaukee. Before and after his television career, Youngquist taught sociology at several universities and was quoted frequently in the media, especially *Time* and *Newsweek*.

5.1 **"IF I HAD A HAMMER"**

As you read Youngquist's article, notice the value he ascribes to writing in a clear and concise style. Also note how sociology intertwines with journalism.

If I Had a Hammer

Wayne A. Youngquist

In the 1960s, there was a song popular among those who wanted to change society. In part, the song said, "If I had a hammer, I'd hammer in the morning, I'd hammer in the evening . . . I'd hammer out justice . . . ." It is my argument that we have a hammer. It is the news media.

The knowledge and skills we have as sociologists can make us very valuable to the news media. The news media offer us a chance to put our professional skills to use, to display our knowledge to a wide audience, and perhaps offer us career options.

It is, of course, important to recognize that the news media are different from academia. They are market driven and cannot force their audience to watch or read what they do

---

Continued . . .

cont.   not want to; they also have a great need for clarity and simplicity. That is especially
true for local, commercial television, where time is limited. The TV "clicker" gives
the viewer immediate power of censorship—"click," and the station is changed. And
the clock rules: we once had a candidate for Congress (who went on to a distinguished
career) with an announcement we wanted to cover. It took him three minutes to make
his point; our story could only be 80 seconds. He lost his chance for a key sound bite.

Albert Einstein, however, shows that a lot can be said in a short time. After all, how
much time does it take to say *e equals m c squared*? There were many times that I was
asked to contribute a bite to a story, then asked "Can you keep it to 15 seconds?" It is
amazing how one can change from an academic mindset of giving long answers to one
where students must learn to give short answers that listeners/viewers/readers will not
tune out.

Along these lines, some "purists" feel that adapting to commercial media is "selling
out" and that concerns for profit have destroyed the independent role of the news media
in civil society. I agree that nonprofit news organizations such as U.S. Public Television
and the BBC are key parts of any news source mix. However, historically in America,
I argue that the profitability of news organizations permitted the rise of independent,
professional journalism that challenged existing, institutional powers. Watergate and the
Washington Post is only the most high-profile instance.

Another difference between academia and news media is that the latter are event driven
and action oriented. Academic social science strives generally for generalizable theories,
backed by extensive hypothesis and data testing. In news, one wants to make sense for
viewers/readers of relevant events. As a result, journalists chase events. But over time,
most working journalists acquire a significantly large "database" of sense making from
the events that they cover. At that point, journalists and academics in principle have a
natural rapport. (One remembers that when C. Wright Mills spoke of those who had and
used the *sociological imagination*, he specifically included the best journalists.)

Academics can speed up the process of journalistic learning by sharing what they
know about group patterns. As well, journalists can aid academics by sharing their
understanding of events independent of theories.

From this line of reasoning, it would seem that there is much value in the view of Robert
Park, who worked as a journalist and who saw sociology as almost a form of advanced
journalism.[2] It also follows that the news media provide great learning and employment
opportunities for our students. Good examples of sociology students in journalism
include Jim Brady, press secretary to Ronald Reagan, and George Reedy, press secretary
to Lyndon Johnson. Both studied sociology as undergraduates. I believe it was Brady
who told me he studied with Park.

Continued . . .

cont.   Our students learn certain skills that the news media need, even at a basic level. Those with a strong methods course can understand and report on public opinion polls (more study is really needed to do polling) and what is called "precision journalism"—statistical analysis and the ransacking of databases. An undergraduate level of knowledge in a number of our subfields, such as race and ethnic relations, demography, politics, urbanism and the like, provide a valuable knowledge base for news. By the same token, it would be wise for sociology students to take [journalism]-school courses or even minor/joint major in journalism. Journalism students especially learn how to write—something sociologists often find problematic—and they learn the culture of news.

I must acknowledge the recent weakening of the journalism job market; likewise, academia. And while the "old media" retrench because of declining profitability, the new media of communication offer new possibilities with new market models. In this regard, today is similar to the 1920s and 1930s as radio searched for markets. What is clearly evident is that there is a large market for news *per se*. In traditional capitalist fashion, demand will create its own supply, and with it, jobs for prepared college graduates.

Beyond all this, however, is the fact that the news media are a hammer for those who take the time and make the effort to put it to use. We have seen this with a variety of conservative individuals and groups who learned the ways of the news media and adapted the media to their own goals. One does not have to be employed by a news organization to have input.

Sociologists can bring the unique insights of the sociological imagination into news. We live today in a time of crisis. Sociology was born of social crisis and flourishes in times of crisis. The sociological imagination, which is always part of the best journalism, sees the link between biography and history, personal troubles and social issues. This adds depth, a deeper dimension to news coverage. If sociologists can get the attention of those in the news media, they can aid in defining the situations of our time.

The news media have the unique power to call public attention to issues and to confer legitimacy on issue positions, candidates, social and political groups, and causes. Think of how the perception of the Vietnam War radically changed when Walter Cronkite—the most trusted man in America—turned against the Johnson Administration. When telling their stories, news organizations bring frames to the events they cover.

A frame is sometimes unfortunately confused with a bias. As sociologists know, to make sense out of events, people must define their situations. If people define a situation as real, it is real in its consequences. A frame is a definition that a journalist brings to a situation, and which provides the lead for his or her story. Journalists frame quickly in chaotic situations. Both sociologists and journalists know that situations do not define themselves. Every news story is an act of social reality construction. The sociological

Continued . . .

> | cont. | imagination provides needed insight and depth when journalists frame news stories. This is where sociologists can offer the greatest impact in journalism.
>
> The news media are our hammer. We can use it to hammer out justice by framing social issues, relating them to personal troubles (as Mills wanted), and laying the groundwork for action. When people come to see issues as social issues, they are more likely to accept the actions that address it. In our time, the news media of mass communication are a hammer that applied sociologists need to grasp to profoundly impact our world.
>
> ■ **After reading "If I Had a Hammer," what are your takeaways, for example:**
>
> - *How do effective writing skills contribute to a sociologist's career?*
>
> - *What are some ways journalism and sociology are related?*
>
> - *What are some ways sociologists can effect social change?*
>
> - *What are some career paths in which to apply a sociological imagination?*
>
> - *Which points in the article resonate with you? Which can you apply?*

Writing in Sociology

Sociologists apply a variety of methods to study social behavior, such as *quantitative* and *qualitative* research studies, which include case studies, surveys, and observations, among other methods. Because of the human element, research in sociology comes with more challenges than research in the physical sciences. For example, the physical sciences study substances and organisms that can be controlled and manipulated; the same cannot be said for human research participants (or any sentient being, for that matter). As one sociology professor said, "A rock can't talk back to you."

Quantitative Research

Quantitative research assesses predictability through the **scientific method**, testing a **working hypothesis**: did an event happen by *chance* or is there a *causal relationship?*

At the core of every hypothesis is a research question, and finding—or discovering—*the question* is a creative process for which *there is no magic formula*. Once you have your research question, however, you have the elements that you need for writing a clear and testable hypothesis.

The process of identifying the question is not something that you can learn readily from a textbook. For example, when you read about the scientific method and papers that present research findings, you are reading the *end result*: you are being given a sterilized view of the process. The researcher—the writer—has taken the important findings from the process and turned them into pieces of a puzzle, fitting them into a standard formula for presentation, with the final result generally following this pattern: hypothesis, review of the literature, methods, results, discussion, conclusions.

While consistency of presentation is needed in the field, translating the development of a hypothesis into a *tidy package* does not give adequate understanding of the *messy side* of science: the experience of being immersed in not knowing, of chasing down ideas, of having insights in the middle of the night, of being consumed by pursuing research at the expense of other obligations . . . and more.

The process of developing a specific hypothesis generally starts with a baffling issue or problem to which a researcher becomes intimately connected, developing a passion for finding an authentic answer. For some questions, finding "the why" may help bring order and understanding to a small corner of the universe, resulting in insight that leads to changes in thinking and behavior and possibly even a paradigm shift.

Finding a question worth pursuing is not a superficial quest, and the ability to write a hypothesis that has depth starts years earlier: the researcher—the learner—must first develop expertise in the field or with the topic, assimilating and digesting theory, facts, and the body of knowledge that has been developed. All of this is itself research, sifting through and identifying what is important and what is not, what has been the outcomes of other research and what still needs to be explored.

This process involves analyzing, synthesizing, and evaluating information, which can only occur once a writer knows a topic well. For example, The taxonomy of educational objectives,[3] often referred to as Bloom's taxonomy, identifies these six levels of learning: *knowledge, comprehension, application, analysis, synthesis,* and *evaluation.* According to the taxonomy, higher-level critical thinking can occur only after a solid base of knowledge and comprehension with a topic has been established along with the ability to apply what was learned.

Thus, if you find yourself lost and unable to make progress, take time to fill knowledge gaps; by doing so, you will build a base for your ability to analyze and synthesize information. Immerse yourself in the problem/topic by steeping your mind in it: read about it, discuss it, and reflect upon it. Your answers may then come when you least expect it, such as when you are taking a walk or waking from a nap.

Some of the most important research you do will be in preparation for writing your hypothesis and forming your null hypothesis. As you read, research, and reflect, some ideas will come up, and you will want to test them. Once you develop your question, turn it into a statement that can be tested.

- What is the problem? What is the research question?

- How can you turn your question into a statement?

- What is the "opposite" of your question or statement?

Often *deductive reasoning* is applied to quantitative research: deductive reasoning starts with a general statement, such as a theory or a hypothesis, and then works toward a specific conclusion based on evidence.

Research Question

As you get started with your research question, here are some questions to consider.[4]

1   Are you choosing a quantitative research question that is descriptive, comparative, or relationship-based?

    a   For **descriptive research questions**, starting phrases would involve amounts, such as *how many, how often, what percentage, what proportion, to what extent,* and so on.

    b   For **comparative research questions**, starting phrases would focus on differences, such as "What is the difference between X and Y?"

2   What are the different types of variables that you are trying to measure, manipulate, and/or control?

    a   What is the dependent variable?

    b   What is the independent variable?

3   Are there any groups that you are interested in?

4   Based on the variables and/or groups involved, *how will you structure your quantitative research question?*

a   Should the dependent variable or group(s) be included first, last, or
     in two parts?

b   Are there words or phrases to add that provide a broader context
     to your question?

Let's apply the above questions to an example (see Box 5.2 below).

5.2 SOCIAL MEDIA STUDY: GENERATIONAL DIFFERENCES

Let's say that you decide to learn more about how different generations use social
media. Let us say your research includes surveying 1,000 people who include an equal
number from each of the following groups: the Silent Generation (born 1945 and before),
Baby Boomers (born 1946 to 1964), Generation X (born 1965 to 1980), Generation Y or
Millennials (born 1981 to 2000), and Generation Z or Centennials (born after 2001 to 2012).[5]
(Note that sources vary for the dates for Gen X, Gen Y, and Gen Z.)

Each study participant would fill out a questionnaire indicating which types of social media
they use, how much time they spend on each in a given time period, and which venue they
prefer. You would then have numerical data indicating how often each group used social
media and which types of social media they preferred. From these data, you could carry out a
statistical analysis, comparing and contrasting groups to deduce some findings.

1. Are you choosing a quantitative research question that is descriptive, comparative, or
    relationship-based?

    Social Media Study: What are the differences in the ways that various
                                   generations use social media? (comparative)

2. What are the different types of variables that you are trying to measure, manipulate, and/
    or control?

    Social Media Study: The dependent variable is social media use; the
                                   independent variable is age or generational grouping.

3. Are there any groups that you are interested in?

    Since the social-media study researches multiple groups, let us simplify our first question
    by analyzing only two groups, branching off into "Social Media Study 1":

    Social Media Study 1:   Millennials and Generation Z

Continued . . .

cont. 4. Based on the variables and/or groups involved, *how will you structure your quantitative research question*?

- Should the dependent variable or group(s) be included first, last, or in two parts?

- Are there words or phrases to add that provide a greater context to your question?

Social Media Study 1:

- What are the differences in the ways that Millennials and Generation Z use Instagram?

- Do people in Generation Z use Instagram more frequently than Millennials?

5. **Possible Hypothesis:** Generation Z uses Instagram more frequently than Millennials.

6. **Null Hypothesis:** Generation Z and Millennials use Instagram at the same frequency.

After you develop your research question into a hypothesis and null hypothesis, it may give the impression that it was a simple process to develop it. Only you will know the various iterations, self-doubt, study, reflection, reading, and discussion that it took to arrive at it.

Quantitative Research Paper

Here is a structure along with some questions to answer as you write a quantitative research paper:

1 Review of the Literature (see Chapter 4, "Literature Review")

   a What sociological question needs to be addressed?

   b How was it addressed in past studies?

   c What is your hypothesis?

For example, in the study in Box 5.2, you may hypothesize that there is a difference among the generations when it comes to the amount of time and the types of media preferred. *What is the null hypothesis?* In this example, the null hypothesis would be that there are no differences among the groups.

2 Methods

   a Procedure: What method did you use to try to answer your question or questions?

b   Sample: Why sample the population? What purpose did it serve? How was your sample selected?

c   Measures: What measures did you use?

3   Results

a   What patterns of numerical data did you find?

b   Based on your sampling, are the results generalizable?

4   Discussion

a   Do the data support or not support your null hypotheses?

b   What do the data mean?

c   How do your results relate to theory and previous empirical research?

5   Conclusions

a   What are your key findings?

b   What are the implications for future research?

Variables: Independent and Dependent

A *variable* is any factor that can exist in differing amounts or categories. In a scientific hypothesis, the hypothesis states what changes are expected to happen to the dependent variable when the independent variable is manipulated. In a sociological study, here are examples of possible variables:

- A trait, such as gender, level of education, age, race, religion, nationality.

- A condition, such as socio-economic status, poverty, crime, alcoholism, corruption.

- Feelings, such as anger, happiness, sadness, conflict, depression.

- A time period, such as the Great Depression, the nineteenth century, the 1960s, the Information Age, multimedia age, modern age, and so on.

In fact, a variable can be *any type of category* that you are trying to measure. Your research will be developed from an independent and a dependent variable, and your hypothesis will determine what the independent or dependent variable should be.

- An *independent variable* is the variable that is changed or controlled to create the conditions of the study. (Also called the *experimental* or *predictor* variable.)

  o   The independent variable is manipulated to determine if it influences or changes the dependent variable. (For example, in the previous example of how certain populations interacted on social media, age was the independent variable.)

  o   The independent variable is "the input."

- A *dependent variable* is the variable that is being tested, measured, or recorded based on changes in the independent variable.

  o   The dependent variable is measured to determine if it changes based on changes in the independent variable.

  o   The dependent variable is "the result."

Independent variable: **Possible dependent variables:**
Age   Changes in behavior, such as voting, dating habits, criminal activity, use of social media, and so on

In a research study, you are testing *correlation* between the independent and dependent variables; however, your research may in fact reveal causal links between the independent and dependent variable. Correlation is a necessary but not sufficient condition to establish causation; further testing would be needed.

Qualitative Research

Qualitative research involves gathering in-depth information, often through case studies and observation, such as participant-observation studies. Unlike quantitative research, qualitative research does not necessarily seek a cause–effect relationship. Qualitative research identifies beliefs, opinions, and behavior, providing insight into patterns of social behavior. Qualitative research identifies the current state of a specific topic.

Often *inductive reasoning* is applied in qualitative research in the interpretation of narrative data. For example, after you have completed your survey on social media (see Box 5.2 above), you realize that the numerical outcomes provide an overview but have not answered all of your questions. In applying qualitative research, you interview 25 people from different groups in the study to explore in more detail, to better understand their use of social media.

5.3 WHAT IS A *TESTABLE* HYPOTHESIS?

Karl Popper, a highly regarded philosopher of science of the twentieth century, argues that hypotheses that do not have the potential to be proven false may represent an element of "pseudo-science."[6] Popper discussed this aspect of the empirical method because he noticed some hypotheses that were being promoted and "tested" were impossible to "prove wrong." In his paper, "Science as Falsification," Popper used examples from theories of psychoanalysis in which explanations for possible behavior could not be disproved. (A loose example of this might be if someone developed a hypothesis stating that "people who use social media excessively are narcissists"; how could it be proven that they were not?)

In his own words, here are some of Popper's conclusions:[7]

- It is easy to obtain confirmations, or verifications, for nearly every theory—if we look for confirmations.

- Confirmations should count only if they are the result of risky predictions; that is to say, if unenlightened by the theory in question, we should have expected an event which was incompatible with the theory—an event which would have refuted the theory.

- Every "good" scientific theory is a prohibition: it forbids certain things to happen. The more a theory forbids, the better it is.

- A theory which is not refutable by any conceivable event is non-scientific. Irrefutability is not a virtue of a theory (as people often think) but a vice.

- Every genuine test of a theory is an attempt to falsify it, or to refute it. Testability is falsifiability; but there are degrees of testability: some theories are more testable, more exposed to refutation, than others; they take, as it were, greater risks.

- Confirming evidence should not count except when it is the result of a genuine test of the theory; and this means that it can be presented as a serious but unsuccessful attempt to falsify the theory. (I now speak in such cases of "corroborating evidence.")

- Some genuinely testable theories, when found to be false, are still upheld by their admirers—for example by introducing ad hoc some auxiliary assumption, or by reinterpreting the theory ad hoc in such a way that it escapes refutation. Such a procedure is always possible, but it rescues the theory from refutation only at the price of destroying, or at least lowering, its scientific status.

Popper's theory of refutability opens researchers to the understanding that if their theories cannot be shown to be false, they are unscientific. Popper's theory applies to quantitative and qualitative research.

5.4 SAMPLE QUANTITATIVE RESEARCH PAPER

Below is a short excerpt, "Methods," from Megan Gilliam's quantitative research paper, "Beliefs Behind Behavior: A Look at Social Attitudes to Combat Male-on-Female Sexual Assault." (To read Gilliam's literature review for this paper, see Chapter 4, "Literature Review.")[8]

First, here is how Gilliam described this project and her process:

> This was a capstone sociology project, so we were expected to produce a paper that was at least 20 pages and to include the following sections: *introduction, literature review, methods, data and results,* and *discussion,* followed by references and an appendix. This was all original research, from start to finish.
>
> This is a quantitative paper measuring social attitudes. Since the results do not include any real statistical tests, the results are not statistically significant. Those tests were not required because of unrepresentative and small samples, which is explained in the full paper.
>
> The process was non-linear; there was a lot of back-and-forth between writing, collecting data, analyzing data, and writing about it some more. Research and professional writing are far from clean-cut or chronological, so I had to write a little, erase even more, review and re-evaluate the data, write about it, then start all over again. It's hard to feel as if you're ever really finished or that you've truly made progress until it all comes together!
>
> I learned that writing individual sections as you go is much easier when the sections are straight-forward and specific. It makes it much less daunting and demystifies it a little if you're scared of such a bulky paper. While any writing is still creative in some ways, it was nice to have clear lines when one subject within the research ended and another began. Also, I learned data can be super exciting . . . which is a little funny to admit!

METHODS

The aim of this study is to examine the relationship between two distinct yet related attitudes about women: attitudes regarding shaming female sexuality and attitudes regarding the normalization of sexual violence against women. The dependent variable in this study is attitudes that normalize sexual assault against women. The principal independent variable is attitudes that favor shaming of female sexuality. Although many demographic variables were collected and measured in the study, only education level and gender were treated as focal independent variables. Those independent variables were chosen after three hypotheses

Continued . . .

cont.   were developed. Hypothesis one: there will be a positive correlation between shame attitudes and normalization attitudes; hypothesis two: education level will affect whether someone holds shame-favoring or shame-opposing attitudes; hypothesis three: gender will have no significant effect on shame-favoring or shame-opposing attitudes.

A survey was designed to measure these social attitudes. The survey questions were broken up into four sections: demographic questions, statements measuring shame attitudes on a 7-point Likert scale, statements measuring normalization attitudes on a 7-point Likert scale, and open-ended questions to end the survey with thoughts on sexual consent. Statements such as "Women who dress provocatively when they go out probably sleep around" were presented to measure shame attitudes; statements such as "If a woman drinks too much to consent to sex, she only has herself to blame if she sleeps with someone" were presented to measure normalization attitudes. Both shame and normalization attitudes were broken down into three categories: shame-/normalization-favoring, shame-/normalization-opposing, and shame-/normalization-neutral attitudes. If a participant indicated they agreed with a statement in which agreement would indicate a shame-favoring attitude, they were scored as shame-favoring; this process is applicable to each category and both attitude sections. The survey is included in an appendix of this paper.

The sample population consisted of males and females between the ages of 18 and 26. Men and women were included because research suggests both men and women hold negative attitudes towards women. The age range of the sample was decided to represent college-aged participants in the hopes of representing participants who have chosen to pursue different levels of education, and for those participants to either still be in their educational environment or to be very recently out of it.

As is the case with research, obtaining a representative sample and receiving an ample amount of responses was the most difficult part of the present study. As evidenced in the "Data and Results" section of this paper, the sample was not representative in terms of gender, race, or education level. Additionally, the respondents were not diverse in attitudes; the majority of respondents held consistently shame-opposed and normalization-opposed attitudes. This made it difficult to address hypothesis one, while the lack of diversity in demographic variables made it difficult to test hypotheses two and three. The small number of eligible responses (N=36) rendered the research ungeneralizable and statistical tests ineffective.

Here are some questions to answer as you write your qualitative paper.[9]

Background

What is the context for your analysis? What does the existing data indicate?

Methodology

What is your specific research design:

- How were the qualitative data gathered?
- What is the time frame for data gathering?
- Who are the respondents? How were they chosen?

Measurement

- What specific open-ended questions were your respondents asked?
- Did you use software to analyze your data, such as NVivo? If so, how did you use it to operationalize the themes, patterns, and notes in your qualitative data?

Data Analysis

- What are the main themes/patterns that emerge from the qualitative analysis of your data?
- Are there responses conducive for comparing and contrasting?
- To add richness, what are some exact quotes to illustrate your themes/ patterns?
- Which themes/patterns are more prominent and which less prominent?

Discussion and Implications

- What are the limitations or errors associated with your research?
- What additional research should be undertaken in the future to better understand this problem?
- What recommendations do you have?

Reliability and Validity

Reliability and validity are basic to understanding the quality of research.

- *Reliability* relates to consistency of measure; for example, if the same study is repeated several times and the outcomes are the same, then it is reliable.

- *Validity* refers to whether the study examines what it is intended to examine.

Let us say that a researcher was exploring how older adults, a defined population born between 1946 and 1966 (Baby Boomers), interacted on social media. A random sample of 100 respondents found that 80 percent had Facebook accounts, 15 percent had an account on LinkedIn, and the average time spent online per week was 20 hours. Then the same study was repeated two, three, or more times on other random samples of the same group. If the results were similar, the results would be *reliable*. In social research, factors such as time, location, and culture can vary the outcomes of a study. For example, a more affluent group of people from this age group might have behaviors that are different from people who are less affluent because of access to computers, tablets, or the internet. It does not mean that there was a flaw in the study, it means that the outcomes cannot be generalized to all people in that age group.

To assess validity, questions on the survey would be tested to verify if the questions actually revealed whether those surveyed had accounts and spent the amount of reported time on social media. Validity might also be tested by measuring the information using a different method and comparing the results. For example, the survey might be used in conjunction with participants keeping a journal that included the time that they spent on each form of media. Since the participants might forget details when filling in a survey, they would describe their behavior in detail in the journal. If the outcomes from the journal were similar to the outcomes of the survey, then the survey would be *valid*.

Here are examples of how these two terms are used:

- Our research results are *reliable*: we are confident that you can test another larger population and get similar results.

- The questions on our survey have been tested extensively and have been shown to be *valid*.

- When research results are *reliable* and *valid*, they can be reproduced and used with confidence.

- Our qualitative research has *reliability* due to the rigorous methods applied.

In addition to reliability and validity, another critical factor is *credibility*, which is discussed briefly below and more extensively in Chapter 4, "Literature Review."

Surveys and Polls

Surveys and polls are primary research tools, and they are also important listening tools. Any scientifically produced sample enables you to generalize those results to the population from which the sample came.

The internet abounds with examples of surveys and polls, most of which are not scientific in their development and use. For example, when public opinion is solicited, it is not representative of a random sample that can be used to generalize or project outcomes.

Corporations also use these tools for *planned organizational change*. Rather than design changes in benefits and training and then inform their employees, human resource departments and organizational development consultants solicit input from employees to find out what they need or want. They use employee feedback to shape policies, procedures, benefits, training, and even management style. Using these types of tools can help create a productive corporate culture.

Even if you do not become a professional sociologist, developing expertise in sociological research methods can be an asset in any profession you choose. By expanding your understanding and vision of social change and cultural trends, you expand your thinking and flexibility in solving problems.

Survey Design

Beyond sociology, surveys are used in fields as varied as marketing research, psychology, and health care. Survey design is both an art and a science, with computer software enabling ever more complex survey designs. The discussion here gives you a brief overview with courses in research design and survey methods providing in-depth knowledge and experience. According to the Pew Research Center:

> Questionnaire design is a multistage process that requires attention to many details at once. Designing the questionnaire is complicated because surveys can ask about topics in varying degrees of detail, questions can be asked in different ways, and questions asked earlier in a survey may influence how people respond to later questions. Researchers also are often interested in measuring change over time and therefore must be attentive to how opinions or behaviors have been measured in prior surveys.[10]

Creating an unbiased survey that is valid and reliable requires the expertise of a professional trained in survey design. Even then, surveys have their limitations; for example, the research you discover through surveys is *time sensitive.* What you learn today can change tomorrow depending on circumstances. In addition, what you learn with one group may be invalid with another.

Since there is a "science" to survey development, many professionals avoid creating their own, fearing they do not have the expertise to create a valid tool. However, for *limited purposes,* an effective survey can be constructed to collect current information.

Here are some questions to test the items in your questionnaire:[11]

- Does the question ask for only one piece of information?

- Does the question presuppose a certain state of affairs and, if so, is this supposition justified?

- Does the question's wording bias responses?

- Are any of the question's words emotionally loaded, vaguely defined, or overly general?

- Do any of the question's words have a double meaning that may cause misunderstanding?

- Does the question use abbreviations or jargon that may be unfamiliar to respondents?

- Are the question's response options mutually exclusive and sufficient to cover each conceivable answer?

According to research scientist David Vannette, here are 10 best practices for constructing surveys:[12]

1   Make sure that every question is necessary.

2   Keep the survey short and simple, staying focused on one topic.

3   Ask direct questions using clear and precise language.

    Don't ask: How often are you likely to avoid going to class?

    Do ask: How often do you miss class?

    Options: Never, Rarely, Sometimes, Often, All the time

4. Ask one question at a time: the word "and" is a clue that you might be asking more than one question.

    Don't ask: Which sport is the most entertaining and fun?

    Do ask: What is your favorite sport?

5. Avoid leading and biased questions: edit out unnecessary adjectives and adverbs.

    Don't ask: Social Media Network is ranked highest for innovative and appealing options. Are you likely to become a member?

    Do ask: Do you plan to become a member of Social Media Network?

6. Speak your respondent's language: keep words and sentences simple.

    Don't ask: Consider the geographic area within which you live. Which of the following outdoor sports do you participate in?

    Do ask: What is your favorite outdoor sport?

7. Use response scales whenever possible (avoid categorical or binary options such as true/false, yes/no, or agree/disagree).

    Don't ask: True or False? Spending time on social media encourages self-reflection.

    Do ask: To what degree does spending time on social media encourage self-reflection?

    Options: Not at all, Slightly, Moderately, Very much, Extremely

8. Rephrase yes/no questions if possible: instead include phrases such as "how much," "how often," or "how likely," using a response scale for richer data.

Don't ask:	Does the wait time for our call center frustrate you?
Do ask:	How pleased are you with our call center's response time?
Options:	Not at all, Slightly, Moderately, Very, Extremely

9. Avoid using grids or matrices for responses: separate questions with grid responses into multiple questions.

10. Test your survey: ask a minimum of five people to take your survey before you distribute it.

Even as you build your expertise, when you need information, consider a simple survey as a viable option. In the meantime, take survey design classes, do research on the topic, and experiment. Online sources are available for support; and when results are needed to make critical decisions, consult a professional.

Online Surveys

Many websites specialize in survey analysis. While some are free, others charge a fee to assist you in creating your survey, giving you options for the types of questions you will include. Such services distribute your survey, collect and tabulate the results (in real time), and then analyze your data. These online services also provide you with graphs and charts, so you have statistical analysis along with visuals to represent your findings.

Go online and do a search on "online surveys." Visit a few of these sites and consider what they offer. If you ever need a professionally done survey, you may want to consider this option.

Open Questions vs. Closed Questions

Depending on the survey you are constructing, you will want to ask the right type of question to solicit the information you seek.

Closed questions provide simple options such as *yes* or *no*, *true* or *false*, *agree* or *disagree*. *Multiple-choice* questions give options, but they are also closed questions.

Open questions allow flexibility by allowing respondents to reply in their own words.

Select the type of question based on the circumstances. If large numbers of people are to be surveyed, results can be tabulated and compared more efficiently using closed questions. With open questions, data are detailed and can be impossible to decipher in large numbers.

You can always design a questionnaire that has both types of questions. In fact, mixed questionnaires are common; for example, many questionnaires include the following instructions: *To any question you answer "yes," please explain.*

5.5 THE LIKERT SCALE

An *affective test*, such as the Likert Scale, assesses feelings, values, and attitudes toward self, others, and environments. These tools measure opinions and are generally based on self-reports.

	Strongly disagree	Disagree	Undecided	Agree	Strongly agree
Question 1	1	2	3	4	5
Question 2	1	2	3	4	5

Other types of scales would be a semantic differential scale and rating scales.

A **semantic differential scale** gives a quantitative rating along a continuum. The scale measures a respondent's attitude about a specific topic, for example:

Necessary	___ ___ ___ ___ ___ ___ ___ ___	Unnecessary
Fair	___ ___ ___ ___ ___ ___ ___ ___	Unfair
Better	___ ___ ___ ___ ___ ___ ___ ___	Worse

A **rating** scale gives respondents an opportunity to measure attitudes toward others; for example:

On a scale of 1 to 5, please indicate how often you are satisfied with our approach.

1	2	3	4	5
Never	Rarely	Sometimes	Often	Always

Conducting Focus Groups and Interviews

Focus groups and individual interviews consume more time than other types of qualitative research and provide specific feedback. A focus group could consist of a sampling from a large target population, but it could also consist of a small group from a defined population, such as employees of an organization. Interviews provide detailed information when working with a small population.

For example, if there were a total of 20 people in a study, individual interviews would be feasible and would give a total picture. In a small study at an organization, data gathered in a focus group could be less reliable because individuals generally express more candor when their anonymity is guaranteed. To provide valid information in a large population, a random sampling would be required.

Effective listening skills are at the core of interviewing. An interview is not a two-way conversation; interviewers use scripted, open-ended questions that are tailored to the research question; for example:

Don't ask: What do you think is wrong with the climate in the company?

Do ask: Describe the climate within the company.

Here are some questions to answer as you summarize your focus group discussion:[13]

Introduction

Develop an argument to introduce and support your topic:

- What is your topic? What are you exploring in your qualitative research product?

- Why is it important to know more about this topic?

- Why would anyone care?

Methodology

- How were your qualitative data gathered? What was your method?

- When were your data gathered?

- Who are your focus group participants? (Do not give names but do give their social characteristics.)

- What was your role in the focus group: participant, notetaker, backup facilitator?

- What was positive/negative about your experience?

- What are the advantages of a focus group for the topic in question?

- What were the strengths and weaknesses of the facilitator of your focus group?

Measurement

- What issues did you explore?

- What is a summary of the main issues?

Data Analysis

- What themes/patterns emerge from your analysis of the qualitative data?

- To add richness to your analysis, can you provide exact quotes to illustrate your themes/patterns?

Discussion and Implications

- What are the limitations or errors associated with the research?

- What would you do differently if you were able to do the research over again?

- What additional research should be undertaken in the future about your research topic?

Field Work Observations

- What are your big questions?

- What is your sampling unit?

- What are your field sites?

- Who is being observed?

- Who is being excluded?

- What are the operational definitions of key variables?

Chart:

Variables	Attributes	Indicators
_____	_____	_____
_____	_____	_____
_____	_____	_____

Describe in detail each person/interaction you have observed, including demographic information:

• Who is interacting?

• Where are people located in space? (Standing, sitting, and so on.)

• What are people doing? Are they using physical objects?

• How do people interact? Who is interacting with whom? Or, are people not interacting?

Note the following:

• Length of interaction

• Facial expressions and body language

• Tone of voice

• Distance between people

• Type of physical contact (if at all)

• Volume of conversational/interaction

Informed Consent

Research is also designed to protect the rights of interviewees. Before participating in research studies, participants must give their informed consent, which involves explaining the nature of the research and of their participation.

Many options are available to learn about developing a form for informed consent. For example, The University of Chicago provides consent form templates and examples, which you can access at their website.[14] In addition, the American Sociological Association (ASA) has a code of ethics, which you can also access at their website.[15] (More information about the ASA Code of Ethics is included in Chapter 4, "Literature Review.")

Sociology and Journalism

Sociologists and journalists have much in common, such as reporting about important social issues, getting to the truth of the matter, and presenting it in an unbiased way. Though journalists do not develop hypotheses and conduct the kind of research that sociologists do, journalists learn other important skills that are not part of a sociology curriculum.

American sociologist Robert Ezra Park, who played a leading role in developing the Chicago School of Sociology, started his career as a journalist, and journalism influenced his interest in sociology.[16] Park believed that the press was powerful because it affected public opinion, and he believed that sociologists and journalists had much in common. In fact, "the methods of observation and analysis [Park] learned as a reporter are credited with providing the foundations for his later work in the social sciences."[17]

As an adjunct to your studies in sociology, consider how journalism might support your mission by helping you acquire a diverse set of skills to complement and enhance your sociological imagination. For example, at a minimum, explore how to write an effective press release so that you can announce your findings to the public effectively. At those times, you want to think like a journalist, writing in a clear and concise style that grabs the reader's attention (which is likely to be distinctly different from the voice that you have developed through academic writing). To highlight your lead, compose a headline for your press release that captures the essence of "your story" at a glance.

As you write your draft, focus on the journalist's questions (see Chapter 2, "Process, Strategy, and Style"): *who, what, when, where, why,* and *how.* In your first paragraph, also answer *so what?* In other words, what value does your piece have for the reader? Why is it relevant? Use hard numbers and quotes to support the significance of your announcement. As you know, evidence adds credibility. As you complete your final draft, edit your writing meticulously so that it is correct, clear, and concise. And as a final touch, make sure to include your contact information. As your story takes flight, expect questions and other types of inquiries.

As a sociologist, you are more likely than most to be involved in controversial topics, and having "journalist" as part of your credentials could offer significant benefits. For example, sociologists collect socially valuable information about all sorts of topics, some of which involves criminal behavior, such as street gangs, sex trafficking, fringe political movements, child abuse, and so on. For some types of sociological research, keeping your sources confidential could benefit both the research and the source. For example, for some research, revealing a source might put lives at risk.

While the constitution provides protection for journalists, sociological researchers and other academics have no protection. For example, shield laws protect journalists from sharing their privacy notebooks, rough drafts, and computers as well as from divulging their sources. If you are a sociologist carrying a press card, you can claim protection through shield laws. So, depending on the type of research that you conduct, you might consider the advantages of becoming a part-time journalist so that you are officially a member of the press as well as a sociological researcher.

Here are some of the points stressed in this chapter:

- Understand that developing a research question is a messy process that takes time.

- Develop a hypothesis that is not only testable but also refutable.

- Be flexible in how you apply sociology in your life and the world around you.

- Develop your vocabulary with common sociological terms, especially those that apply to research.

- Experiment with writing open and closed research questions about topics that interest you.

- Select a topic and practice writing a press release.

Writing Workshop

Activity A. Descriptive Writing

Instructions: Qualitative research is descriptive. To practice your descriptive writing skills, select a space—possibly the room you are in right now—and describe every detail of the room. If possible, work with a partner so that both of you do the activity at the same time; then when you are finished, you can compare notes.

1   Keep track of the time: spend 20 minutes writing without speaking. Put
    your phone away along with any other distractions.

2   Start by simply observing before you start to write.

3   As you write, do not add any opinions or feelings or value
    judgements—simply describe the objects, shapes, colors, sizes, lighting,
    and so on. Are there people in the room? What are they doing? What
    are they wearing?

4   When you are finished, exchange papers with your partner. Read your
    partner's paper out loud and then switch roles.

5   After you have both listened to each other's descriptions, discuss the
    activity.

    a   How do the descriptions differ?

    b   How are they similar?

    c   Did you feel inclined to judge or evaluate the people or
        environment? Did any judgement seep through into your writing?

Activity B. Process Message

Instructions: The ASA's Code of Ethics articulates a common set of values
upon which sociologists build their professional and scientific work. Read a
full copy of the ASA's Code of Ethics.[18]

Next, write your professor a process message discussing a few of the points
that you learned. For example, the ethical standards set out enforceable rules
for conduct by sociologists. How does the ASA Code of Ethics relate to any
research you might do?

Remember, for all professional messages—and that includes process
messages—use a greeting that includes the recipient's name, end with a
closing, and sign off with your name.

References

1   Youngquist, W. A. (2014). "If I had a Hammer." *Journal of Applied Social
    Science*, 8(2), 96–99.

2　Robert Ezra Park was an American urban sociologist who is considered to be one of the most influential figures in early U.S. sociology, playing a leading role in developing the Chicago School of sociology.

3　Bloom, B. (Ed.). (1984). *The taxonomy of educational objectives*. Boston, MA: Addison Wesley.

4　Laerd Dissertation. How to structure quantitative research questions. Retrieved from http://dissertation.laerd.com/how-to-structure-quantitative-research-questions.php

5　Novak, J. The six living generations in America. Marketing Teacher Ltd. Retrieved from http://www.marketingteacher.com/the-six-living-generations-in-america

6　Stanford Encyclopedia of Philosophy. Karl Popper. Retrieved from https://plato.stanford.edu/entries/popper/

7　Popper, K. R. (1963). Science as falsification. In *Conjectures and refutations*. London: Routledge and Keagan Paul. Retrieved from http://www.stephenjaygould.org/ctrl/popper_falsification.html

8　Gilliam, M. (2018). "Beliefs behind behavior: A look at social attitudes to combat male-on-female sexual assault," unpublished paper, Valparaiso University, Sociology Department.

9　Senter, M. S. (2017, August 12). "Integrating 'real' research into programs for undergraduates: Suggestions from practice and practical suggestions," Annual Meeting of the American Sociological Association, Montreal.

10　Pew Research Center. Questionnaire design. Retrieved from http://www.pewresearch.org/methodology/u-s-survey-research/questionnaire-design

11　Anderson, Niebuhr & Associates, Inc. Questionnaire design and use workshop, St. Paul, MN.

12　Vannette, D. Ten tips for building effective surveys. Retrieved from https://www.qualtrics.com/research-best-practices/survey-design

13　Senter (2017) Op. cit.

14　The University of Chicago, Social & Behavioral Sciences Institutional Review Board. Consent Form Templates and Examples. Retrieved from https://sbsirb.uchicago.edu/page/consent-form-templates-and-examples

15　ASA. (2017). American Sociological Association Code of Ethics. Retrieved from http://www.asanet.org/membership/code-ethics

16　New World Encyclopaedia. Robert E. Park. Retrieved from http://www.newworldencyclopedia.org/entry/Robert_E._Park

17　Grundy, B., Hirst, M., Little, J., Hayes, M., & Treadwell, G. (2012). *So you want to be a journalist? Unplugged* (2nd ed). Cambridge, UK: Cambridge University Press, p. 69.

18　ASA (2017) Op. cit.

Citation Styles: APA and ASA

In sociology, two citation systems are used, one published by the American Psychological Association (APA) and the other by the American Sociological Association (ASA). These citation systems apply the author-date method of in-text citation. Basic information for both of these systems is explained and illustrated, and differences between the two are highlighted. The formatting guidelines presented here are APA and ASA requirements for manuscript publication. Since your professors might have different requirements, always check with individual professors to make sure that you are adapting your formatting for your specific audience.

While the basics for APA style are discussed here, for more detail see the *Publication Manual of the American Psychological Association* (6th edition).[1] The *American Sociological Association Style Guide* (5th edition) is based on *The Chicago Manual of Style* (CMOS), 16th edition.[2,3] Though working on this chapter gives you a foundation, see both the ASA and the CMOS for detailed information not covered here.

A consistent citation system conveys a shared language or code so that professionals have a common understanding, enabling them to review literature effectively. Since citation is a *code* that you are sending to your reader, using it correctly is important. For example, readers can see *at a glance* if you are applying APA or ASA style correctly: when your style and formatting are correct, you gain credibility; when they are not, you lose credibility *instantly*.

This chapter covers basic elements of each style, giving you a quick guide for formatting each. In addition, other chapters provide critical support, such as Chapter 12, "Formatting," and Chapter 15, "Quotation and Citation."

- The first section, *Documentation Guidelines*, contains general information about citation.

- The second section, *APA Citation Style*, gives you details for formatting papers in APA style and provides an example.

- The third section, *ASA Citation System*, gives you details for formatting papers in ASA style and also provides an example.

When you have completed this chapter, you will be able to:

- Apply APA and ASA citation styles to academic papers.

- Understand the costs of plagiarism.

- Know which types of information to document.

- Create a working bibliography.

- Apply correct formatting to the running head, title page, abstract, body, reference page, and headings for APA and ASA styles.

Even if you have used these citation styles for some classes, do not assume that you have used them correctly; for example, most professors focus on giving feedback about the content of your work, not "writing errors." Thus, you may *not* have received detailed feedback on your formatting and stylistic errors in the past, so now is a good time to refresh your understanding.

Documentation Guidelines

The information in this section applies to all citation systems. Citing research validates your findings and provides information so that others can find your source and read it in its entirety. While correct citation adds credibility to your work, it also allows you to avoid the most egregious type of academic failure—plagiarism.

Plagiarism

One reason why writers plagiarize relates to poor writing skills and the anxiety that goes along with it. Another reason could be that writers are unsure of what to cite, or perhaps they are unaware that their summary was actually a paraphrase needing citation.

The dilemma is that plagiarism feeds the dynamic that keeps developing writers from improving their writing skills, robbing potential as it pulls down confidence and self-esteem. When novice writers cut and paste another's words into their work, they are giving themselves a message: *Good writing and insightful thinking are out of my reach.* The irony is that effective writing is a skill that is within reach for anyone who does the work.

Writing effectively is critical for all professions today. Technology has fueled the importance of writing and, at the same time, made plagiarism easier to accomplish. While instructors do not always take the time to screen for plagiarism, when they do, it is easy to spot. A writer's grammar, spelling, vocabulary, and syntax create a profile that has unique qualities. And just a single phrase can instantly reveal the real source. *Along with everything else that is being lost, is it worth the risk?*

Incorporating other writers' ideas is a critical element of academic writing. The only requirement is that you cite your source when you quote, summarize, or paraphrase.

What to Credit

Not all information needs to be documented. For example, you do not need to cite information that is considered common knowledge or facts that are available from a wide variety of sources. Here is a list of information that *does* need to be documented:

- Direct quotation and paraphrase.

- Information that is not widely known or claims that are not agreed upon.

- Judgments, opinions, and claims of others.

- Statistics, charts, tables, and graphs from any source.

- Help provided by friends, instructors, or others.

In academic settings, you must also cite your own work from another course or article. When turning in group projects, credit the writing of other group participants; for example, identify who provided information on each presentation slide.

The two most common types of reference are *direct quotation* and *paraphrase*.

- **Direct quotation**: *Quoting* is using someone else's exact words and requires that the words be set off. For short quotes, use quotation marks; for quotes of 40 or more words, set off the quotation by indenting the left margin 0.5 inches. Use an in-text reference along with a citation on the reference page.

- **Paraphrase**: *Paraphrasing* is putting someone else's ideas in your own words so that you can explain how their ideas support or oppose your topic. When you paraphrase and cite your source, you add credibility to your work.

When first beginning scholarly writing, many writers have difficulty with paraphrasing. True paraphrasing occurs when you read material, assimilate it, write about the concepts in your own words, and credit the original author. If you have trouble paraphrasing, try explaining to someone what you think the writer means and then write it in your own words.

- When you *paraphrase*, you are "translating" an original piece of writing but not copying any parts word for word.

- When you *summarize*, you are putting elements of the original writing into your own words.

Making a few changes in word order, leaving out a word or two, or substituting similar words is *not* paraphrasing or summarizing—it is plagiarism. Until you are confident about your writing, you may be tempted to copy or quote much material into your writing. Instead, speak with your own voice, interpreting information in your own words.

- To paraphrase or summarize, first read the original source.

- Write a few notes *in your own words* about what the author is saying.

- Next, put away the original source and write your summary.

After you write your summary, look back at the original source: *Did you capture the original concepts and integrate your own interpretation into your writing?* Even when you summarize someone's ideas in your own words, you need to cite the original source.

Academic standards require you to provide evidence to support a position, and outside sources add credibility. However, *use quotations selectively*: just as a quote in exactly the right place enhances your work, too many quotes or unnecessary ones distract readers and give the impression that you may not fully understand the topic. Aim for flow, and be selective.

Working Bibliography

Citing research can be challenging because it involves details. Therefore, as you collect and use what others have discovered, compile a *working bibliography*.

Use note cards, a small notebook, or a special file on your computer as you collect your research. You can also use a bibliographic database to organize resources. Microsoft Word, EndNote, and RefWorks software allow you to cite while you write. EndNote also allows you to save electronic documents, your comment notes, and keywords to enable searches. Also learn how to insert page and paragraph numbers into the citation for citing quotations. Because electronic sources are ever-changing, print a hard copy of the material you are referencing or download the accessed information.

> *Note*: If you use these aids, ASA style is not listed on the toolbar as an option; the closest style for your software setting would be "Chicago Sixteenth Edition." However, APA is listed.

Here is the kind of information you need to collect:

For books:

- Author, title, and page number
- Publisher, location, and year of publication

For periodicals:

- Author, title of article
- Journal title, date of publication, volume and issue number

For websites:

- Author (if known) and title
- Uniform Resource Locator (URL) network address, which includes path and file names, and which are sometimes enclosed in angle brackets
- Date website was established (if available, located at the bottom of the home page)

- Date the source was published in print (if previously published)

- Date on which you accessed the information

APA and ASA have unique formatting styles, which may present challenges the first few times you use them. After you have formatted a few papers you will reach a comfort level in how you set margins, tabs, and spacing as well as how you format headings, citations, and resource lists.

APA Citation System

All citation systems, including APA style, require that sources be cited in the text and referenced at the end of the work. Citation and reference together provide the reader with complete information through cross-referencing.

- APA citation style requires **author-date** in-text citation and references.

If you are writing a document in which you want to comment or provide parenthetical information related indirectly to your text, APA allows that through *footnotes* and *endnotes*.

You may cite one resource several times in your manuscript; however, you only need to include identifying information about the book (author, publisher, location, and date) one time in your reference list. Though you may refer to a variety of sources as you do your research, for APA style, list only references on your *reference page* that you cite in your work.

Box 6.1 below provides a quick guide to APA style and can be used as a checklist. Then Figure 6.1 walks you through key information about APA style as it displays APA formatting.

- For the fine details of citation not covered in this book, make use of the many excellent resources online.

- Before submitting any sociological paper, check with your professor or department to identify special requirements.

- Before submitting a paper to a journal for possible publication, obtain the author guidelines that describe the journal's specific requirements for submission.

   Note: To set paragraph controls and create a header, see Chapter 12, "Formatting."

6.1 QUICK GUIDE TO APA STYLE

Sections	**Title page:** title of paper, author name, running head/page number **Abstract:** between 150 and 250 words, keyword summary **Main body:** Introduction, Methods, Results, and Discussion **Reference page:** title "References"
Authors/editors	Use last name and first initial (do not use first names) List all authors on the reference page
Titles	On title page and in text, use **title style** (upper and lower case) On the reference page, use **sentence style** (capitalize first word only)
Publisher	Use full name; list city names and state abbreviations
Format: General	Use 1-inch margins (top, bottom, left, and right) Double-space entire document, including block quotes Indent paragraphs 0.5 inches Leave margins unjustified (use "left align") Insert a *running head* in a header that contains the following: • On the title page, at left margin: "Running head: YOUR TITLE IN 50 CHARACTERS OR LESS"; at the right margin, the page number 1 • On second pages, format the running head with the *title only* in all capital letters in the upper left corner and the page number in the upper right corner Use a serif font such as **Times New Roman, 12-point** Use up to five heading levels Integrate short visuals within the text but put large visuals on separate pages Use two spaces after a period, one space after other punctuation marks
Format: Title Page	Center the title and byline on the upper half of the page Use up to 12 words for the title (also include other information that your professor may require)
Format: Reference Page	Alphabetize by last name of authors; use last name and first initial; list all authors If you cite two articles by the same authors, list the oldest one first Block the first line of an entry at the left margin; indent second lines 0.5 inches Italicize titles of books and journals Capitalize only the first word of titles

Quick Guide to

American Psychological Association (APA) Citation Style

Dina Studentessa

Best University

Author Note

An author's note is typically used for papers that will be published and would include

acknowledgments, departmental affiliations, disclaimers, and contact information.

However, an author's note is not required, even for theses and dissertations. If you

include an *author's note*, place it on your title page, as demonstrated here.

continued. . .

cont.

QUICK GUIDE TO APA STYLE   2

Abstract

An abstract is a one-paragraph summary of your paper that is between 150 to 250 words in length. An abstract summarizes the key ideas of your paper and may be the single most important paragraph of your paper. However, an abstract is *not* your introduction. Place the abstract on the second page, right after your title page. Notice that the section title, *Abstract*, is not presented in boldface type; section titles are different from headings. Also, though paragraphs throughout your paper are indented one half inch, *do not indent the first line of your abstract*. This paper also gives other tips about formatting APA style; however, when you have a detailed question about style, go right to the source and consult the *Publication Manual of the American Psychological Association, Sixth Edition* (2010) or visit the APA's website at www.apastyle.org.

Keywords: apa style, apa formatting, running head, apa example, apa title page, abstract, reference page

continued. . .

QUICK GUIDE TO APA STYLE   3

Quick Guide to APA Citation Style

Since APA style is used extensively for papers in sociology, this guide introduces you to common elements of APA style, providing some formatting guidelines. Your paper will include five main sections: the *title page, abstract, introduction, body,* and *reference page.* Start the abstract, introduction, and reference page each on a new page.

The introduction is the first section of your paper; start it on page 3, and include the title of your paper (not in boldface because the title of your introduction is a section title, not a heading). However, you can start the body of your paper on the same page as the introduction.

In your introduction, discuss the problem and its importance as well as your process or research strategy, presenting your thesis or hypothesis.

General Guidelines

On the upper half of the title page, double space and center the title of your paper and your name. Use up to two lines for the title of the paper. Also, ask your professor for specifics about other information to include on the title page. If your title contains more than 50 characters, abbreviate your title for your *running head.*

Following the title page, write an abstract in one paragraph between 150 and 250 words. Do not indent in your abstract but do indent your keyword summary: Type "*Keywords:*" and follow it with several words in lower case that would identify your paper in a search.

continued. . .

QUICK GUIDE TO APA STYLE   4

Formatting

For your entire document, use 1-inch top, bottom, and side margins. Use a 12 point serif font, such as 12-point Times New Roman. Also double space your entire document, including your title page and reference pages.

However, for your spacing to be correct, you also must first set your *paragraph spacing* at 0 for spacing *before* and *after*. Therefore, when you set your *line spacing* on *double spacing*, also set *spacing* for *before* and *after* at 0; all of these controls are at the *Paragraph* tab.

Indent each paragraph 0.5 inches, and block your lines at the left margin. In other words, your right margins should have ragged edges (as shown here). Space one time after all punctuation marks except the period: Space two times after the period. On the reference page, however, space only one time. Number all pages of your document, starting with the title page.

Headings and Subheadings

APA guidelines provide five levels of headings. For example, the heading at the top of this page (Formatting) is a Level 1 heading; Level 1 headings are centered and presented in bold typeface. The heading immediately above this paragraph is a Level 2 heading; Level 2 headings are flush with the left margin and in bold typeface. Table 1 below displays the various headings, describing whether each is centered, blocked at the left, indented, or presented in boldface type or italics. Note that Levels 3 through 5 are paragraph headings, with the text following the period after the heading.

continued...

QUICK GUIDE TO APA STYLE   5

APA Style: Five Heading Levels
Level 1 Centered, Boldface, Upper and Lower Case
Level 2 Blocked at Left Margin, Boldface, Upper and Lower Case
Level 3 Indented, boldface, lower case. (Start text on same line.)
Level 4 indented, italicized, boldface, and lowercase. (Start text on same line.)
Level 5 indented, italicized, and lowercase. (Start text on same line.)

Also note that *headings* are different from *section titles*. Levels 1 through 4 are in boldface type; however, the following section titles are not in boldface type: *title of your paper, title of your introduction, abstract* and *references.*

In-Text Citations

Use the author-date citation system to identify your sources, crediting authors whether you quote them directly or put their ideas and research in your own words. For indirect references (paraphrased statements), cite the author's last name and the publication year; for direct quotes, include the page number. Put this information in parentheses at the end of the quotation. However, if you use the author's name in your text, do not repeat the author's name in the parentheses.

For signal verbs, APA style recommends using the past tense (such as, "stated") or present perfect tense (such as, "has stated"), for example: "Tyler (1988) stated, '[a]ll students can learn what the schools teach if they can find an interest in it' (p. 45)."

For a citation that has only one author, list the author's last name and the year of the publication. If you are giving an exact quote, also list the page number, as shown above. For a citation with two authors, list both authors for all citations; for example: "Winger and Ginther (1992) developed the method."

continued. . .

QUICK GUIDE TO APA STYLE   6

For citations with three to five authors, list all authors for the first citation, as follows: "Ginther, Tyler, and Winger (2001) supported their research." For the second citation of the same work, cite the first author's surname and add *et al.* (the Latin abbreviation for *and others*). Put the year of publication in parentheses; for example: "Ginther et al. (2001) broke down the groups based on level of experience."

For in-text citations using signal phrases, use the word *and*; for in-text citations that do not use signal phrases, use the ampersand (&), for example:

Jones and Smith (2007) agree that research is important.

Research is important (Smith & Jones, 2007).

For your reference list, use the ampersand instead of the word *and*, for example:

Jones, R., & Smith, C. (2007). *Research is important: Do your research now.* Chicago, IL:

Action Research Publishers.

Reference List

Place the reference list at the end of the paper on a separate page. Begin the page with the word "References" centered at the top in bold typeface. Double space your reference page, but do not indent the first line: instead, indent second lines 0.5 inches, which is called "hanging indentation."

List only those works that you cite in the text (APA, 2009). References include the following: author name (or names), publication date, title of work, and publication data. Arrange the citations in alphabetical order by surname.

Each kind of reference requires a specific form, so refer directly to the rule that discusses the type of source that you are citing.

continued...

QUICK GUIDE TO APA STYLE   5

Resources

Doing anything new for the first time is difficult. After you have formatted
your first few papers in APA citation style, you will feel much more confident. In the
meantime, refer to the latest publication and website provided by the APA. Also refer
to other websites and even YouTube videos; find resources by doing a search on "APA
citation style."

Every detail makes a difference. In fact, most professors can tell *at a glance* if a
paper is formatted correctly, and any type of error could affect your grade. Proofread
and edit your papers thoroughly, then compare your paper side by side with a model
based on APA's latest guidelines. In other words, if you are using an outdated source,
your formatting will be incorrect no matter how vigilant you are when you format your
text.

continued...

cont.

QUICK GUIDE TO APA STYLE 6

References

American Psychological Association [APA]. (2009). *Concise rules of APA style.*

Washington, DC: American Psychological Association.

APA. (2010). *Publication manual of the American Psychological Association.* (6th ed.).

Washington, DC: American Psychological Association.

continued. . .

ASA Citation System

All citation systems, including ASA style, require that sources be cited in the text and referenced at the end of the work. Citation and reference together provide the reader with complete information through cross-referencing.

• **ASA citation style** requires **author-date** in-text citation and references.

If you are writing a document in which you want to comment or provide parenthetical information related indirectly to your text, ASA allows that through *footnotes* and *endnotes.*

You may cite one resource several times in your manuscript; however, you need to include identifying information about the book (author, publisher, location, and date) only one time in your reference list. Make sure that every source that you cite is on your reference list.

The following page contains a summary of major points about ASA style, which you can use somewhat like a checklist. Then on pages 157 through 166, Figure 6.2, "Quick Guide to ASA Style," walks you through key information about ASA style as it displays ASA formatting.

• ASA requires these formatting guidelines, in part, because your original manuscript will be used to typeset your article if it is approved for publication.

• For other types of submissions, such as sociological papers or dissertations, check with your professor or department to identify special requirements.

Note: To do some pre-work with setting paragraph controls and creating a header, see pages 264–267 in Chapter 12, "Formatting."

6.2 QUICK GUIDE TO ASA STYLE

Sections	**Title page**: full title, name of institution, author or authors (listed vertically), running head, page number, word count, and title footnote **Abstract**: a summary no longer than 200 words; a three- to five-word keyword summary **Main body**: introduction, literature review, methods, results, discussion, and conclusion **Reference page**: title "References"
Authors/editors	For references, use first and last name of authors
Titles	For titles, use **title case** (upper and lower case)
Publisher	Use full name; list city names and state abbreviations
Format: General	Use 1.25-inch margins on all sides (top, bottom, left, and right) Space one time after a period Double-space entire text: abstract, body, references, footnotes, and acknowledgments Block quotations may be single-spaced Create block quotations using the word-processing feature; use one hard return after a quotation block Indent paragraphs 0.5 inches; to indent, use tab stops (do not use the space bar to indent) Use "Align Left": do not right-justify text Insert a *running head* in a header that contains the following: • On title page, at left margin: "Running head = YOUR TITLE IN 50 CHARACTERS OR LESS"; at the right margin, the page number 1 • In running head on second pages, put title only in all capital letters at the left with page number in the right corner Number all pages sequentially, beginning on the title page Use a font such as Arial, 12-point. Use up to three heading levels Number tables throughout the text, and put each table on a separate page at the end
Format: Title Page	Center the title and byline on the upper half of the page; use up to 12 words for the title (also include other information that your professor may require)
Format: Reference Page	Alphabetize by last name of authors; list all authors using first and last names If you cite two articles by the same authors, list the oldest article first Block the first line of an entry at the left margin; indent second lines 0.5 inches; italicize titles of books and journals

Running Head = ASA CITATION STYLE   1

Quick Guide to

American Sociological Association (ASA) Citation Style*

Jane Doe Jones

Best University

Word Count = 1274

*Jane Doe Jones can be reached at jdjones@bu.edu. Doe Jones would like to express her appreciation to Dr. Doris Bookings, learning resource manager, Best University Library, for her research assistance. (*Note: Title footnote includes name, address, and e-mail address of the corresponding author as well as any acknowledgments, credits, and grant numbers.*)

continued. . .

cont.

ASA CITATION STYLE   2

QUICK GUIDE TO ASA CITATION STYLE

An abstract summarizes the key ideas of your paper and may be the single most important paragraph of your paper. An abstract is a one-paragraph summary of your paper that is no longer than 200 words in length. However, an abstract is *not* your introduction. Place the abstract on the second page, right after your title page, and title the abstract with the title of your paper (ASA 2014). Also, though paragraphs throughout your paper are indented one-half inch, *do not indent the first line of your abstract*. When you have a detailed question about style, go right to the source and consult the *American Sociological Association Style Guide, 5th Edition* (2014).

   Keywords: ASA style, ASA formatting, ASA title page

continued. . .

cont.

ASA CITATION STYLE   3

QUICK GUIDE TO ASA CITATION STYLE

In your introduction, which starts on page 3, discuss the problem and its importance as well as your process or research strategy, presenting your thesis or hypothesis. For ASA style, use the title of your paper as the heading for your introduction; however, do not use the word "introduction" for the heading. While you do not need to indent the first paragraph after a heading; regardless of the style that you choose, be consistent throughout your document.

GENERAL GUIDELINES

ASA citation style is based on *The Chicago Manual of Style* (CMOS), 17th edition (The University of Chicago, 2017). If you are using citation support provided in Microsoft Word, under the "reference" tab, select "Chicago Sixteenth Edition" for "style."

Your paper will include five main sections: the *title page, abstract, introduction, body*, and *reference page*. Start the abstract, introduction, and reference page each on a new page.

Title page. To format your title page, use single spacing. Include the following information: the full title of the article or paper, your name and institution, the word count (including footnotes and references), and a title footnote in which you list your name and contact information.

Abstract. Following the title page, write a one-paragraph abstract that is no longer than 200 words. Do not indent in your abstract but do indent your keyword summary: type "*Keywords:*" and follow it with several words in lower case that would identify your paper in a search.

continued. . .

cont.

ASA CITATION STYLE   4

Introduction. Start the introduction on a new page. As stated, you can title your introduction with the title of your paper, but do not title your introduction with the word "introduction." Use a level-one heading.

Body. You can start your body on the same page as the introduction. So that your writing is reader friendly, break your writing into cohesive paragraphs and apply headings. The body could include the following: a literature review, methods, results, and discussion.

Conclusion. You can title the conclusion of your paper using the word "conclusion," or you can create a title. Use a level-one heading.

Reference page. For your reference page, use the title "References," formatting it in level-one heading.

FORMATTING

For your entire document, use 1.25-inch side margins and Arial font, size 12. Also, other than the title page, double space your entire document, including the reference page.

Running head. Type a running head in the header. The running head on the title page is different from the running head on second pages; on the title page, type "Running Head =" and then follow it with your title (or an abbreviated version) in all capital letters, 50 characters maximum.

Paragraph settings. Under the "paragraph" tab, set *spacing* at 0 for spacing *before* and *after*. Then set *line spacing* on *double spacing*. To set paragraph indentation for the body, under "Special," select "First line" and then set it at 0.5". When you type the reference page, under "Special," select "Hanging" and set "By" at 0.5."

continued. . .

cont.

ASA CITATION STYLE   5

Align Left. In your toolbar, select "Align Left" for all parts of your document except the title page, which should be centered. In other words, your right margins should have ragged edges (as shown here).

Header and Page numbers. Number all pages of your document, starting with the title page. Start by clicking on your "header." Then select "different first page" before inserting page numbers.

Headings and Subheadings

ASA guidelines provide three levels of heading. First-level headings are blocked at the left margin and presented in all-capital letters. Second-level headings are blocked at the left margin, typed in title case and italics, with the text starting on the next line. Third-level headings are paragraph headings that are indented, typed in sentence case and italics, with the text immediately following.

Below is an example of how the three level headings would be typed:

FIRST-LEVEL HEAD

Second-Level Head

　　Third-level head. Start text here.
The heading immediately below this text is a first-level head, starting a new section of the body.

IN-TEXT CITATIONS

Use the author-date citation system to identify your sources, crediting authors whether you quote them directly or put their ideas and research in your own words. For indirect references (paraphrased statements), cite the

continued. . .

cont.

ASA CITATION STYLE   6

author's last name and the publication year; for direct quotes, include the page number. Put this information in parentheses at the end of the quotation. However, if you use the author's name in your text, do not repeat the author's name in the parentheses.

For signal verbs, ASA style recommends using the past tense (such as, "stated") or present perfect tense (such as, "has stated"), for example: "Tyler stated, '[a]ll students can learn what the schools teach if they can find an interest in it' (1988:45)."

For a citation that has only one author, list the author's last name and the year of the publication. If you are giving an exact quote, also list the page number, as shown above. For a citation with two authors, list both authors for all citations; for example: "Winger and Ginther (1992) developed the method."

For citations with three to five authors, list all authors for the first citation, as follows: "Ginther, Tyler, and Winger (2001) supported their research." For the second citation of the same work, cite the first author's surname and add "et al." (the Latin abbreviation for *and others*). Put the year of publication in parentheses; for example: "Ginther et al. broke down the groups based on level of experience (2001:231)."

REFERENCE LIST

Place the reference list at the end of the paper on a separate page. Begin the page with the word "References" centered at the top using a first-level head. For each reference, double space and do not indent the first line; however, indent the second lines 0.5 inches (hanging indent).

continued. . .

ASA CITATION STYLE   7

List all works that you cite in the text. References include the following: author name (or names), publication date, title of work, and publication data. Arrange the citations in alphabetical order by surname.

Each kind of reference requires a specific form, so refer directly to the rule that discusses the type of source that you are citing.

RESOURCES

Doing anything new for the first time is difficult. After you have formatted your first few papers in ASA citation style, you will feel much more confident. In the meantime, refer to the latest publication and website provided by the ASA.

Every detail makes a difference. In fact, most professors can tell *at a glance* if a paper is formatted correctly, and any type of error could affect the credibility of your work. Proofread and edit your papers thoroughly, then compare your paper side by side with a model based on ASA's latest guidelines. In other words, if you are using an outdated source, your formatting will be incorrect no matter how vigilant you are when you format your text.

continued. . .

cont.

ASA CITATION STYLE   8

REFERENCES

American Sociological Association. (2014). *American Sociological Association Style Guide*. 5th ed. Washington, DC: American Sociological Association.

The University of Chicago. (2017). *The Chicago Manual of Style, 17th ed.* Chicago: The University of Chicago Press.

continued. . .

cont.

ASA CITATION STYLE   9

Below is a table that illustrates ASA style headings.

ASA Style: Three Heading Levels
LEVEL 1 BLOCKED AT LEFT MARGIN, ALL CAPITALS
Level 2 Blocked at Left Margin, Title Case, Italics
Level 3 indented, sentence case, italics. Start text on the same line.

Recap

Differences in Style

APA

- Use 1-inch margins (top, bottom, left, and right)

- Use a serif font such as **Times New Roman, 12-point (or Courier, 12 point)**

- Space twice after a period and once after other punctuation marks

- Double-space the entire document, including block quotes

- In the header on the title page, type the following at the left margin: Running head: YOUR TITLE IN 50 CHARACTERS OR LESS

- Use up to five heading levels

- Integrate short visuals with the text, but put large visuals on separate pages

- On the *reference page*:

  o Alphabetize by last name of authors; use last name and first initial; list all authors

  o If you cite two articles by the same authors, list the oldest article first

  o Block the first line of an entry at the left margin; indent second lines

  o Italicize titles of books and journals, capitalizing only the first word of titles

ASA

- Use 1.25-inch margins on all sides (top, bottom, left, and right)

- Use a nonserif font such as **Arial, 12-point**

- Space once after all punctuation, including a period

- Double-space the entire text; block quotations may be single spaced

- In the header on the title page, type the following at the left margin: "Running Head = YOUR TITLE IN 50 CHARACTERS OR LESS"

- Use up to three heading levels

- Number tables throughout the text, and put each table on a separate page at the end

- On the *reference page*:

  o Alphabetize by last name of authors; list all authors using first and last names

  o Italicize titles of books and journals

Similarities in Style

APA and ASA

- On the title page, center the title and byline on the upper half of the page; use up to 12 words for the title (also include other information that your professor may require)

- Begin numbering on the title page

- Indent paragraphs 0.5 inches

- Avoid using the space bar to indent: for the body, set a 0.5 inch paragraph or indentation or set a tab stop; for the reference page, set a 0.5 inch hanging indentation

- Use "Align Left": do not right-justify text (right margin should appear uneven)

- Number all pages sequentially, beginning on the title page

- On all pages, insert a *running head* in a header

- On second pages, format the running head with the title *only* in all capital letters in the upper left corner and the page number in the upper right corner

- Create block quotations using the word-processing feature; use one hard return after a block quotation

- On the reference page:

  o If you cite two articles by the same authors, list the oldest article first

  o Block the first line of an entry at the left margin; indent second lines

A key element of citation is detail. The more you work with author-date in-text citation styles, the better your skills become. Now that you know the basics of APA and ASA citation styles, you can readily use online journal databases that provide citation formats. You can find a wealth of information online, including sites that format references in APA and ASA styles.

Writing Workshop

Activity A: Formatting

Instructions: Select a paper that you have previously written and revise it using APA or ASA format and citation style. Include the following parts:

- Title page

- Abstract

- Introduction

- Body (two or more pages; use at least two heading levels)

- Conclusion

- Reference page

Activity B: Process Message

Instructions: Write your instructor a process message explaining the kinds of changes you made from your original draft as you converted it to APA or ASA style. (For all process messages, use a greeting that includes your professor's name along with a closing; sign off with your name.)

References

1   APA. (2010). *Publication manual of the American Psychological Association* (6th ed.). Washington, DC: American Psychological Association.

2   ASA. (2014). *American Sociological Association style guide* (5th ed). Washington, DC: American Sociological Association.

3   The University of Chicago. (2017). *The Chicago manual of style* (17th ed). Chicago, IL: University of Chicago Press.

Editing for Clarity

Cohesive Paragraphs and Transitions

The paragraph is the basic unit of academic writing. Once you know how to write a good paragraph, you are much closer to being able to write a good paper. All types of writing depend on well-written paragraphs: readers are confused when writers present ideas haphazardly, jumping from one idea to another without developing a line of thought. Readers also assimilate information in chunks, and reading long narratives with no breaks can become wearing. Thus, whether you are writing an e-mail or a research paper, making good paragraphing decisions is an essential part of the process.

While you cannot depend on a recipe to write a paragraph, you can rely on a few guidelines. By applying principles of *information flow*, you can develop paragraphs that are *cohesive* and *coherent*. By constructing a *topic sentence* that builds into a *topic string*, you develop a logical flow. By breaking your writing into manageable chunks, you make your ideas accessible. To further enhance the flow of your writing, use transitions to bridge ideas and highlight connections for the reader.

The principles in this chapter assist you in constructing paragraphs that are reader friendly and that present your content in a substantial style. In the process, you analyze your writing, probing deeper into the content: while shaping your writing for your reader, you gain insight into which ideas are key, which provide support, and which merit cutting. If you have not yet focused on how you create paragraph breaks, now you can.

When you have completed this chapter, you will be able to:

- Develop cohesive and coherent paragraphs.

- Build effective paragraphs by using a topic sentence and a topic string.

- Edit and revise paragraphs for effective information flow.

- Identify transitional elements and apply them to paragraphing decisions.

- Use conjunctions to bridge ideas, provide cues about key concepts, and create effective transitions.

Developing effective paragraphs is a matter of editing: when you compose, write freely. When you edit, shape your writing for your reader. Let's start by reviewing guidelines for effective paragraph length.

Paragraphing: Process and Length

While the general guideline for sentence length is 10 to 25 words, a general guideline for paragraph length is four to eight sentences.

However, neither sentence length nor paragraph length is governed by rules—these are guidelines and suggestions. While all sentences are not equal, neither are all paragraphs. For example, a paragraph could be as short as a sentence or two or longer than eight sentences. When you make paragraphing decisions, shape your writing for your reader with the intent of making ideas accessible. In part, the type of writing dictates the parameters and expectations for paragraphing:

- For *academic papers*, paragraphs tend to be longer because ideas are developed in depth.

- For *professional writing*, such as e-mail, paragraphs are best kept short. E-mail messages tend to be conversational, and short paragraphs can stress key information.

- For *fiction writing*, paragraphs can be any length and can even consist of a single word.

- For *blogs* and other types of *online writing*, short- to medium-length paragraphs catch and keep the reader's attention and convey ideas readily.

Academic writing, especially, is rife with examples of exceedingly long paragraphs. While paragraphs tend to be longer in academic papers than for other types of writing, paragraphs still need to be a reasonable length. When a paragraph seems to go on forever, readers lose their concentration and interest. Here is how to use paragraph length as a cue for editing:

- Count the *number of sentences*: keep most paragraphs between four and eight sentences. When a paragraph goes beyond eight sentences, check if you have shifted to a new topic and need to create a fresh paragraph.

- Do a *word count*: if you keep paragraphs between 100 and 200 words, they remain manageable.

- Assess your writing *at a glance*: if a paragraph goes beyond a half page, review the content to see if you have shifted topics that signal the start of a new paragraph.

- Keep paragraph length *proportional* to the length of the paper: for shorter papers, aim for shorter paragraphs.

Once you develop skill with paragraphing, you will break your writing into paragraphs naturally as you compose and then refine them when you edit and revise. Read your writing out loud or have someone read it to you. When you hear a new topic, start a new paragraph. By mixing up paragraph length, you add variety for the reader, which enhances attention and thus understanding. Short paragraphs grab the reader's attention, so use short paragraphs when you want to add emphasis. However, all paragraphs, even short ones, need to be *cohesive* and *coherent*.

Cohesive and Coherent Paragraphs

Effective paragraphs have two important qualities: they are cohesive *and* coherent.[1]

- *Cohesive* paragraphs develop only *one main idea* or *topic*, demonstrating a *connectedness* among ideas that support that topic. Adequate details support the main idea so that the reader understands the main point.

- *Coherent* paragraphs develop the main idea through a *logical flow of ideas*: one point leads to the next.

To develop a cohesive paragraph, the first step when editing is to identify its **topic sentence**. The next step is ensuring that each sentence in the paragraph develops the topic, creating a **topic string**.

- A *topic sentence* gives an overview of the paragraph; a topic sentence contains broad and general information.

- A *topic string* is a series of sentences that develop the main idea of the topic sentence. Each sentence extends the controlling idea, giving specifics that illustrate the main idea of the topic sentence.

As you compose, do not be concerned about writing a topic sentence or building a topic string. In fact, you will gain clarity about your topic as you write about it, and you may find that one of the latter sentences in your draft paragraph often becomes the topic sentence.

Here is a step-by-step process for *editing* paragraphs:

1   Identify the topic sentence: select the sentence that develops the topic in a broad and general way.

2   Bring the topic sentence to the beginning of the paragraph as the first (or second) sentence.

3   Build a topic string with sentences that explain, expand, and support the topic sentence.

4   Cut sentences that do not fit, or use them to start a new paragraph.

Read the draft paragraph on the next page in Box 7.1. As you read the paragraph, ask the following:

- What is the main topic? Which sentence expresses the main topic best?

- Which sentences seem off topic and belong in a different paragraph?

Does the paragraph seem to ramble on, in part because of the changing topic?

In Box 7.1 below, the edited version 1 focuses on how to edit but leaves out the writer's own experience. Version 2 takes the writer's point of view: notice how the voice shifts to the *I* viewpoint. Version 3 takes the third-person point of view, giving it an academic tone.

7.1 DRAFT

I believe editing is important, and I even knew an editor once. But I never knew how to edit before, and I was always confused about how to improve my writing. Before, I didn't take the time to edit, now I do because I know how to make corrections and how to revise a document. Editing is an important part of the writing process. When you edit, correct errors in grammar and punctuation and try to improve the flow of the writing. Editing also involves putting the purpose up front and then cutting what doesn't belong. When I read papers that are not edited well, I can tell because the writer jumps from one topic to another. Editing can turn a mediocre paper into a good one. Poorly written documents also seem to ramble on and on without paragraph breaks, so add paragraph breaks where they are needed. Take time to edit, and you will see an improvement in your final document.

Edited Version 1

Editing is an important part of the writing process. When you edit, correct errors in grammar and punctuation and improve the flow of the writing. Put purpose up front and then cut what doesn't belong. Also, add paragraph breaks where they are needed. If you take time to edit, you will see an improvement in your final document.

Edited Version 2

Editing is important. In the past, I didn't take the time to edit, but now I do because I know how to correct and revise a document. When I edit, I correct errors in grammar and punctuation and try to improve the flow of the writing. I also put the purpose up front and then cut what doesn't belong. When I take time to edit, I see an improvement in my final document.

Edited Version 3

Editing is an important part of the writing process. Editing involves shaping writing for the audience. For all types of writing, purpose is the most important element and should be placed at the beginning. Information that does not support the thesis should be cut, along with redundant or empty information. In addition, paragraph breaks should be added where needed. When writers edit effectively, they see an improvement in their final documents.

For a paragraph to be *coherent*, ideas must flow logically. In other words, writing should not contain disjointed ideas. However, as you compose, disjointed ideas may seem to make sense. To edit the flow, step away from your work for a while so that you can evaluate your writing objectively.

Here are some steps for revising paragraphs.

- *Print out a copy.* Writing sometimes reads differently in hard copy from the way it reads on the screen.

- *Read your writing out loud.* Writing also sounds different when the words are spoken, which is an important test of writing fluency: use your speech as a guide to revise complicated words and passages, especially for professional writing—*If you wouldn't say it that way, don't write it that way.*

- *Have a peer read it.* Ask for specific changes that you can make to upgrade the quality of your writing.

- *Keep an open mind.* Others will see things that you cannot; try new ideas, even if they feel uncomfortable at first. You can toss out ideas that don't work after you have given them a chance to expand your thinking.

While paragraph length is a judgment call, keeping paragraphs between four and eight sentences helps ensure your writing remains reader friendly. When papers are short, keep your paragraphs short. For a shorter paragraph, use three or four sentences to explain, expand, and support your topic sentence. When papers are long, give yourself a bit more leeway.

Paragraphs and Viewpoint

Viewpoint can be described as *the eyes through which writing is being portrayed* and can emanate from first, second, or third person, singular or plural. Consistent pronoun viewpoint not only ensures that writing is grammatically correct but also helps ensure that a paragraph is *coherent*. For example, when writing shifts from one viewpoint to another, readers are challenged because meaning becomes clouded.

As discussed in chapter 1, academic writing, for the most part, stresses the third-person viewpoint: *it/they* could represent the topic about which you are writing. For example, if you were writing a summary about the relationship between sociology and social work, you would write it from the third person point of view, with "sociology/sociologists" and "social work/social workers" being topics (shown in italics in the following example written by sociologist J. H. Turner).

> People outside sociology and social work often consider the two
> areas synonymous. They are not. *Social work* is a profession for

helping people. As such *it* draws upon knowledge from all the social sciences and from the individual social worker's intuition and life experiences. Of course, many *social workers* have received sociological training, for *sociology* is highly relevant to their work, but *sociologists* try to understand why certain situations (i.e., crime and poverty) exist. *Sociologists* do not usually try to intervene in the social world. Rather *they* attempt to provide knowledge for those who do intervene. [However, *sociologists* disagree] over their proper role and responsibility. Should *they* be detached, or should *they* be activists and try to change human affairs? The answers tend to vary from sociologist to sociologist.[2]

Once you establish a point of view for a particular piece of writing, remain consistent with that point of view within sentences, paragraphs, and the entire document.

Practice 7.1

Pronoun Point of View and Consistency

Instructions: Edit the following short paragraph by correcting for pronoun consistency. Apply the "we" viewpoint. (*Note*: The following paragraph was adapted from *The Thinker's Guide to Analytic Thinking* and was originally written from the "we" viewpoint.)

You begin to reason from the moment you wake up in the morning. We reason when you figure out what to eat for breakfast, what to wear, whether to make certain purchases, whether to go with this or that friend to lunch. A person reasons as they interpret the oncoming flow of traffic, when we react to the decisions of the other drivers, when you speed up or slow down. One can draw conclusions then, about everyday events or, really, about anything at all: about poems, microbes, people, numbers, historical events, social settings, psychological states, character traits, the past, the present, the future.[3]

Note: See page 415 for the key to the above exercise.

Information Flow

Principles of information flow can also assist you in understanding how to adjust your writing so that it is reader friendly. As you learned in

Chapter 2, "Process, Strategy, and Style," information flow orders ideas so that readers have an easier time connecting how one idea relates to another.

* *Old information* is familiar information that provides a context for your reader.

* *New information* is unfamiliar information that extends the reader's understanding.

* *Empty information* is irrelevant to the topic at hand.

Information flow can create smooth transitions between ideas that would otherwise sound disconnected. Below are three versions of a paragraph about *listening* (which is considered the topic and is old information). As you read each paragraph, analyze the information flow, identifying old, new, and empty information.

Example 1

Can you identify the empty, irrelevant information in the paragraph below?

> Listening is an important part of doing research. *If you take the time to listen* to them, most people will tell you about their lives. *As you listen*, ask questions, and most people will reveal more about themselves. I once had a job doing focus groups, and a big part of the job was *listening*. I didn't do well when I first started because *I wasn't a good listener. Once you become a better listener*, you will understand people, even if they think differently from the way that you think.

Example 2

Once the irrelevant, empty information is removed, the paragraph flows more effectively. *Can you see how the flow of the paragraph improves with the empty information removed?*

> Listening is an important part of doing research. *If you take the time to listen*, most people will tell you about their lives. *As you listen*, ask questions, and most people will reveal more about themselves. *Once you become a better listener*, you will understand people, even if they think differently from the way that you think.

Example 3

In the following paragraph, information flow is reversed: new information appears at the beginning of each sentence and the consistent topic *listening* appears at the end. *Does the following paragraph lose its flow and sound choppy? As a reader, do you need to work harder to find meaning?*

> An important part of doing research is *listening*. Most people will take the time to tell you about their lives *if you listen*. Ask questions, and most people will reveal more about themselves *as long as you take the time to listen*. You will understand people, even if they think differently from the way that you think, *once you become a better listener*.

As you compose, you may naturally put new information on the page first and then connect it to your topic (or old information). As you edit, revise the flow of sentences that start with new information by presenting old information first.

Here is the same paragraph one more time, but this time the topic sentence appears at the end:

> If you take the time to listen to them, most people will tell you about their lives. As you listen, ask questions, and most people will reveal more about themselves. Once you become a better listener, you will understand people, even if they think differently from the way that you do. Listening is an important part of doing research.

Can you see how the topic sentence provides the context for the paragraph? Can you see how the emphasis shifts based on the topic sentence?

Apply the principles of information flow in the practice below.

Practice 7.2

Paragraphs and Information Flow

Instructions: In the following paragraph, adjust the information flow by:

1   Identifying the old information or topic in each sentence.

2   Adjusting information flow so that sentences begin with old information and end with new information.

The search for common patterns in social relations is the key to the
sociological perspective, which distinguishes it from other disciplines.
To discover the ways that social relationships reveal order, consistency,
and predictable change, even when change involves violence and
volatility if the job of the sociologist. To all human affairs—those of the
past and present, those involving economic processes, those revolving
around power and politics, and those involving people's personalities,
there is an underlying organization. Only sociology and (at times)
anthropology seek to put the pieces together, but each social science
looks at a piece of social reality.[4]

Note: See page 415 for a suggested revision; answers may vary.

Basic Structure: The Beginning, Middle, and End

All documents, even short ones, have a beginning, a middle, and an end.
It might sound trite to discuss this topic; however, many writers think
basic structure applies only to longer documents or formal ones. In fact,
some writers pay no attention to beginnings and endings which is a serious
oversight.

- The *beginning* of any document should connect your purpose with your
  reader. With short, informal documents, the beginning sets the tone of
  the message. With formal documents, the introduction is critical and
  must be developed meticulously.

- The *middle* contains the body of evidence and examples to support
  your purpose, validating its relevance. If a bit of information does not
  support your purpose, cut it. Every time you give the reader excess or
  irrelevant information, it diminishes your purpose.

- The *ending* brings closure for the reader and indicates next steps,
  defining action for the reader and/or the writer. For formal
  documents, tie the ending back to the problem posed in the
  introduction, opening the door for further discussion or research.
  The conclusion may reveal new questions for readers to explore. For
  informal documents such as e-mail, bring closure by ending with a
  short closing.

Let's review the purpose of each part.

Introduction

- States the purpose and provides an overview.

- Explains why the purpose is relevant.

- Connects the reader to the purpose.

- At times, poses questions.

Body

- Breaks the topic into component parts.

- Covers all main points.

- Supports main points with evidence, examples, and details.

- Answers questions that may be posed in the introduction.

Conclusion

- Summarizes and draws conclusions for readers.

- Clarifies and restates main points.

- Reinforces the introduction, solidly establishing the purpose.

- At times, reveals new questions and suggests additional research.

The introduction is usually the most difficult part of any document to write. A good beginning captures the essence of the entire document, but you may be unclear about your purpose when you begin to write. Once you have composed your document, your purpose should be clear and meaningful to you.

Rather than relying on "introduction, body, and conclusion," the **PEER model** breaks down each part on the basis of purpose (see Chapter 3, "Research and Evidence-Based Writing"). Use this model during the composing or revising stage for documents of any length. If you loosely apply the PEER model as you compose, your content will be somewhat structured before you revise. The letters in *PEER* correspond to the four elements of the model:

P   What is the *purpose*? What points are you making, and why are they relevant?

E   What *evidence* demonstrates your main points? What are the facts and details?

E   What *explanation* do you need to make or what *examples* do you need to provide so that the reader understands the evidence and its significance?

R   What are your *recommendations* for your reader? How can you *resolve* your thesis? *Recap* main points and draw conclusions.

Next, let us review how transitional sentences support information flow, making broad connections between old information and new information.

Transitional Sentences

Transitional sentences provide logical connections between paragraphs. The transitional sentence glances forward and links the topic of one paragraph with the main idea of the next, for example:

> In the next section, our analysis demonstrates the strengths and weaknesses of the model that we applied in our study.

> Next, we discuss how polling projects the results of political election.

> Although production waste has economic implications, toxic waste and its dispersion also has social implications.

Transitional sentences prepare the reader to understand the content of the next paragraph by seeding its purpose and familiarizing the reader with new key ideas.

Transitional Paragraphs

In addition to transitional sentences, **transitional paragraphs** assist readers by achieving the following:

- Summarizing the key ideas of the current section.

- Indicating how the major theme of the document will be developed in the next section.

Here is a transitional paragraph that summarizes the key ideas of a current section:

In this section, we highlight the major differences between the traditional and modern food systems, with emphasis placed upon the production process. We review how industrialization has transformed agricultural production, ensuring the security of food supplies in developed countries. The evolution of the modern food system is also closely associated with industrialization as well as other changes in the nature of the labor market.[5]

Here is a transitional paragraph that glances forward to a next section:

As we have demonstrated, the intricate connections between a person's eating patterns and the state of health are a focus of human concern. Modern societies have witnessed a fundamental and far-reaching transformation in the ways in which these concerns are conceptualized. Traditional beliefs are plausible ways to explain events and experiences relating to health and illness which might otherwise be perceived as driven by arbitrary forces, which is discussed in the next section.[6]

As you have seen, old-to-new information flow helps create smooth transitions between ideas. Another way to create smooth transitions is to use conjunctions. Let us examine how to use conjunctions to make transitions.

Connectors as Transitions

Do you recall the Sesame Street song, *Conjunction Junction*: "Conjunction Junction, what's your function?" If you remember the song, you may begin to smile as the tune sets in. Here are the three types of conjunctions:

- coordinating
- subordinating
- adverbial

While conjunctions are not a core element of sentence structure, such as subjects and verbs, they play a critical role in grammar, punctuation, and writing style:

- Conjunctions show relationships and bridge ideas, adding smooth transitions to choppy writing.
- Conjunctions pull the reader's thinking along with the writer's intention.

As you use conjunctions more effectively, your writing style also improves. By pulling the reader's thinking along with yours, you help the reader connect ideas and draw conclusions. Conjunctions focus the reader on key points, making writing clearer and easier to understand. In addition, conjunctions play a key role in punctuation by signaling where to place commas and semicolons: conjunctions are *comma signals* (see Chapter 13, "Comma Rules").

Understand how conjunctions *function*, and you will be a big step closer to using them effectively in your writing. Though the terms themselves might put you off, realize that it only takes a bit of practice to use the terms *coordinating*, *subordinating*, and *adverbial* with ease.

Coordinating Conjunctions

Coordinating conjunctions connect equal grammatical parts. There are only seven of them, and they are as follows:

- and
- but
- or
- for
- nor
- so
- yet

Together they spell the acronym FANBOYS: *for, and, nor, but, or, yet, so*. The most commonly used coordinating conjunctions are *and, but,* and *or*. The *equal grammatical parts* that conjunctions connect are *sentences, words,* and *phrases*, which Chapter 13, "Comma Rules," covers in more detail.

Though using a coordinating conjunction as the first word of a sentence is acceptable, it is not preferred and should be used sparingly. But when you do start a sentence with a coordinating conjunction, you are likely to get the reader's attention. In general, the adverbial conjunction *however* is a good substitute for the coordinating conjunction *but*. Thus, if you find yourself starting a sentence with "but," change it to "however."

Subordinating Conjunctions

Subordinating conjunctions show relationships between ideas and, in the process, make one idea dependent on another; they appear as single words or short phrases. Subordinating conjunctions also play an important role in grammar: when you put a subordinating conjunction at the beginning of a complete sentence, the sentence becomes a dependent clause.

Here is a list of some common subordinating conjunctions:

after	because	since	until
although	before	so that	when
as	even though	though	whereas
as soon as	if	unless	while

In addition to subordinating conjunctions, adverbial conjunctions contribute to a reader-friendly writing style.

Adverbial Conjunctions

Adverbial conjunctions bridge ideas, and they are known as *transition* words. Adverbial conjunctions help pull the reader's thinking along with the writer's intention. Use an adverbial conjunction at the beginning of a sentence to *introduce* it, in the middle of a sentence to *interrupt* the flow of thought, or between two sentences as a *bridge*.

Here are some examples of common adverbial conjunctions:

as a result	for example	in conclusion	otherwise
finally	hence	in general	therefore
generally	however	in other words	thus

Here are examples of adverbial conjunctions and the roles they play:

Introducing: *Therefore*, I will not be able to attend the conference.

Interrupting: Social systems theory, *however*, does not apply to this problem.

Bridging: George will attend the conference in my place; *as a result*, I will be able to assist you on the new project.

Here are some adverbial conjunctions and the kinds of transitions that they make:

Compare or contrast:	however, in contrast, on the other hand, on the contrary, conversely, nevertheless, otherwise
Summarize:	in summary, in conclusion, as a result, thus, therefore, hence
Illustrate:	for example, for instance, hence, in general, thus, mostly
Add information:	in addition, additionally, also, furthermore, moreover, too
Show results:	fortunately, unfortunately, consequently, as usual, of course
Sequence or show time:	first, second, third, finally, meanwhile, in the meantime, to begin with
Conclude:	finally, in summary, in conclusion

As a reader, use these transition words and phrases to identify key points. As a writer, use these transition words in a conscious way to pull your reader's thinking along with yours.

Conjunctions as Connectors

Here is an example of how you can apply conjunctions to choppy writing to make it flow.

Original:	The construction for the ninth floor conference room was extended two more weeks. We were not informed until Friday. Our meetings for the following week needed to be reassigned to different rooms. None was available. Jane Simmons agreed to let us use her office. Several serious conflicts were avoided.
Revised:	The construction for the ninth floor conference room was extended two more weeks. *However,* we were not informed until Friday. *As a result,* our meetings for the following week needed to be reassigned to different rooms, *but* none was available. *Fortunately,* Jane Simmons agreed to let us use her office, *and* several serious conflicts were avoided.

Do you see the difference that well-placed conjunctions make in creating writing that flows well? Before you go on to the next chapter, complete the exercises at the end of this chapter.

Recap

In this chapter, you have worked on paragraphing; you have also reviewed the three types of conjunctions and how they function as connectors and transition words.

- Paragraphs break up information into manageable chunks for the reader.

- Every paragraph contains a topic sentence, which is then developed into a topic string.

- Cohesive paragraphs focus on one topic.

- Coherent paragraphs have a logical flow of ideas, which is developed through editing and revising.

- A consistent viewpoint helps ensure that a paragraph is grammatically correct as well as coherent.

- Conjunctions build bridges between ideas and provide cues about a writer's key points.

- As a review, here are the three types of conjunctions with examples:

Coordinating conjunctions:	and, but, or, for, nor, so, yet
Subordinating conjunctions:	if, since, although, because, before, after, while
Adverbial conjunctions:	however, therefore, for example, consequently

In Chapter 13, "Comma Rules," you learn about the role that conjunctions play when using commas.

Writing Workshop

Activity A. Editing Paragraphs

Instructions: Select a paper that you have written within the last year. Analyze each part to identify how you might edit and revise the paper, improving the quality based on the principles in this chapter.

1 **Review the introductory paragraph:**

    1.1 What is the thesis or purpose statement? Where in the paragraph is it placed?

    1.2 Does the introduction provide an overview?

    1.3 Does the introduction explain why the purpose is relevant?

2 **Identify the longest paragraph in your paper:**

    2.1 How many sentences does the paragraph have?

    2.2 What is the topic sentence?

    2.3 Does every sentence in the paragraph relate to the topic sentence? Has an effective topic string been developed?

    2.4 Does the paragraph have a consistent viewpoint? What is that viewpoint?

    2.5 Have transitions been used effectively?

3 **Review the evidence:**

    3.1 Does each paragraph contain evidence to support your thesis?

    3.2 What facts and details support key points?

    3.3 Can you identify empty information to cut?

4 **Review the conclusion:**

    4.1 Does the conclusion tie to the introduction, clarifying main points?

    4.2 Does the conclusion summarize and draw conclusions for readers?

    4.3 Does the conclusion reveal new questions or next steps?

Activity B. Peer Editing

Instructions: Exchange papers with a partner and analyze your partner's paper using the questions above.

If you wish, give your partner the original version of your paper that you have already edited. You can then compare your edits with your partner's edits of your paper.

References

1   Williams, J. M. (2000). *Style: Ten lessons in clarity and grace.* Longman, New York.

2   Adapted from Turner, J. H. (2006). *Sociology.* Upper Saddle River, NJ: Pearson Education, p. 26.

3   Adapted from Elder, L., & Paul, R. (2016). *The thinker's guide to analytic thinking.* Tomales, CA: Foundation for Critical Thinking Press, p. 6.

4   Adapted from Turner (2006) Op. cit., p. 26.

5   Adapted from Beardsworth, A., & and Keil, T. (1997). *Sociology on the menu.* London: Routledge, p. 45.

6   Ibid., p. 149.

Active Voice

When you find yourself struggling to understand what you are reading, check to see if passive voice is the primary voice. Passive voice complicates meaning because the passive verb does not perform action: its subject is a grammatical "place holder" and not a *real subject* that drives action.

- With **passive voice**, the verb *describes* action.

- With **active voice**, the verb *performs* action.

Active voice is clearer and more concise precisely because the verb and its subject play their designated roles: the verb performs action, and a *real subject* drives that action.

To further complicate meaning, passive writing also encourages the use of *nominalizations* or verbs that have been transformed into their noun forms. When writers revise nominalizations back into active verbs, writing comes to life and meaning becomes more easily accessible. However, in academic writing, passive voice coupled with nominalizations is common. Writers become attached to the passive voice, using it even when it is not necessary. In fact, writers can incorrectly assume that complicated, wordy writing sounds "smarter." As Abraham Lincoln once observed of a political foe, "*He can compress the most words into the smallest idea of any man I ever met.*"[1]

Though active voice is generally the voice of choice, passive voice has a legitimate and necessary place in all types of writing when used *purposely*. In fact, in scientific writing, the passive voice is used to place focus on a method or procedure, rather than the person who is carrying it out.

When you have completed this chapter, you will be able to:

- Use active voice to shape your writing style so that it is clear and direct.

- Revise sentences from passive to active voice.

- Identify nominalizations and turn them back into active verbs.

- Apply passive voice in situations that call for tact.

As you review active voice, realize that you are also developing an effective writing style in line with the American Sociological Association (ASA) and American Psychological Association (APA) writing guidelines: ASA and APA both recommend using active voice over passive voice, *when possible*.

> *Note*: To track your use of the passive voice, you can use a proofing option through Microsoft Word (and possibly other software programs). To find out how to turn on tracking for passive voice, search "passive voice tool in Word," and you will find tutorials to show you how to activate it.

Grammatical Subjects versus Real Subjects

While every sentence has a *grammatical subject*, not all sentences have a *real subject*.[2] Until now, you may not have thought about the difference between the two or even realized that a difference existed. Here is the role each type of subject plays:

- The grammatical subject precedes the verb.

- The real subject drives the action of the verb.

When the real subject (RS) precedes the verb, the real subject and grammatical subject (GS) are the same, for example:

Jane's <u>professor</u> assigned her to lead a focus group.
     GS/RS

However, in the following sentence, the real subject (professor) is not the grammatical subject (Jane).

Jane was given an assignment to lead a focus group by her professor.
GS   RS

In a passive sentence, the *grammatical subject* is not its *real subject*: real subjects drive the action of verbs; and in a passive sentence, there is no action. Since the real subject appears in the sentence, the above example is considered a **full passive**. In comparison, the following sentence has a grammatical subject, but not a real subject.

An assignment to lead a focus group was given to Jane.
GS

What is the real subject (RS)? Who gave Jane the assignment? Based on the above sentence, we do not know. When a passive sentence does not contain a real subject, it is called a **truncated passive.**

Though you briefly covered active voice in Chapter 2, "Process, Strategy, and Style," the following is a step-by-step process to turn passive sentences into active voice.

Active Voice

The active voice is the most clear, direct, and concise way to phrase a sentence because each part of the sentence fills its prescribed role. Let us start with a passive sentence and then revise it to active voice:

Passive: The papers were sent to Sue by Bob.

To change the above passive sentence to active voice, first identify the main verb, which is *sent*. Next, identify the real subject by asking who performed the action: *Who sent the papers? Bob did.* Finally, change the order in the sentence so that the real subject (Bob) is also the grammatical subject.

Active: Bob sent the papers to Sue.

Here are the steps to change a sentence from passive voice to active voice:

1. Identify the main verb.

2. Identify the real subject by asking, *who performed the action of the verb?*

3. Place the real subject (along with modifying words) at the beginning of the sentence, which is the position of the grammatical subject.

4. Follow the real subject with the verb, *adjusting for agreement.*

5. Complete the sentence.

In a shorter form, here is the process:

1.   Main verb?

2.   Real subject?

3&4.   Real subject + verb (*agreement and tense?*)

5.   S → V → O

Here is another sentence to revise from passive voice to active voice:

Passive: The polling was completed by the research group.

1.	Main verb?	completed
2.	Real subject?	the research group
3&4.	Real subject + verb	the research group completed
5.	Complete sentence:	The research group completed the polling.

Here is the structure for the **active voice:**

Who *did/does/will do* what.

Here is the structure for the **passive voice**:

What *was done/is done/will be done* by whom.

This step-by-step analysis makes revising sentences from passive voice to active voice sound simple. In fact, the process is simple, even with complex sentences. The challenges arise when you start revising your own writing because you also need to revise your thinking.

At first, it may be difficult to identify sentences that you have written in the passive voice. That is partly because writing in a complicated way feels "natural." Reading your own writing also feels comfortable because you are already familiar with the ideas. To analyze your writing with an open mind, begin to notice your reaction *as a reader* to various types of writing that others produce.

Practice 8.1

Active Voice

Instructions: Edit the following sentences by changing passive voice to active voice.

Passive: An urgent message was left by Miguel for my project manager.

Active: Miguel left an urgent message for my project manager.

1. Sean was asked by his manager to lead the diversity team.

2. Phelps was given another chance by his coach to swim in the relay.

3. The holiday event was hosted by our department last year.

4. A new policy on reimbursement for travel expenses was implemented by our president.

5. The program was cancelled by the mayor due to lack of interest.

    Note: See page 416 for the key to the above exercise.

Passive Voice, the Tactful Voice

Since the real subject does not need to be present in a passive sentence, there are times when passive voice is preferred over active voice.

*   Whenever you do not want to focus on a specific person because it would be more tactful not to sound accusatory, use passive voice, for example:

    Passive: A mistake was made on the surveys.

Who made the mistake? An active sentence needs an actor or agent performing the action of its verb; however, a passive sentence does not need an actor or agent because its verb does not create action.

- Whenever you do not know *who* performed an action, use passive voice, for example:

  Passive: The bank was robbed at gunpoint.

For these situations, the passive voice is necessary, and you will find that you use the truncated passive naturally as you speak or write. While truncated passives play a vital role in writing, full passives that are unnecessary interfere with the quality and the flow of writing.

Another element that complicates writing is *nominals*, which are often used in conjunction with the passive voice. After working on the practice below, you work on getting rid of unnecessary nominals.

Practice 8.2

Passive Voice, the Tactful Voice

Instructions: Edit the following sentences by changing passive voice to active voice. Then determine which sentences would sound more tactful written in the passive voice.

Passive:	Your check should have been mailed last week to avoid a penalty.
Active:	You should have mailed your check last week to avoid a penalty.
Active or passive?	Passive is more tactful.

1. An error in invoicing was made on your account (by Meyers).

2. If you wanted to avoid an overdraft, your check should have been deposited before 4 p.m.

3. Your receipt should have been enclosed with your return item.

4. Your order was sent to the wrong address and apologies are being made.

5. Your invoice needed to be paid before the first of the month to avoid penalties.

   Note: See page 416 for the key to the above exercise.

Nominalization

A *nominal* is a noun that originated as a verb. The term for transforming a verb into a noun is *nominalization*. For example, the verb *appreciate* becomes *appreciation* in its nominalized form. Using a nominal often makes writing more complicated.[3]

> **Nominalized:** I want to express my **appreciation** for your help.
>
> **Active:**   I **appreciate** your help.

As in the above example, the nominal may displace an action verb, replacing it with a weak verb such as make, give, or have. As a result, using nominals encourages complicated, passive writing.

Sometimes writers prefer to use nominals because they think using longer, more challenging words sounds smarter. However, as a writer, your goal is to make complex messages as simple as you can. Though there is no exact formula, most nominals are formed by adding *-tion* or *-ment* to the base of the verb. Here are a few examples:

Verb	Nominal	Verb	Nominal
transport	transportation	encourage	encouragement
develop	development	facilitate	facilitation
dedicate	dedication	accomplish	accomplishment
separate	separation	evaluate	evaluation

A few nominals form in other ways:

Verb	Nominal
analyze	analysis
criticize	criticism
believe	belief

At times, nominals are necessary; however, use them only when they improve the efficiency and quality of your writing. When nominals do not improve the writing, the reader has a more difficult time decoding the message.

Here is an example using the verb *commit* and its nominalized form *commitment:*

> **Nominalized:** A **commitment** of resources for the study on poverty
>   was made by the foundation.

Active: The foundation **committed** resources for the study on poverty.

Here is another example showing how the passive voice and nominalization are used together:

Nominalized: **Encouragement** was given to me by my coach and teammates.

Passive: I **was encouraged** by my coach and teammates.

Active: My coach and teammates **encouraged** me.

In the first sentence above, the nominalization *encouragement* is used in a passive sentence. In the second, the nominal is removed, but the sentence is still passive. In the third, *encourage* is used as an active verb in its past tense form.

Understanding these principles is much easier than actually applying them to your own writing. To achieve active writing, you need to be committed; the more committed you are, the more changes you will make in your writing. To get practice, complete the following exercise.

Practice 8.3

Nominals

Instructions: Rewrite the following sentences by changing nominalizations into active verbs.

Passive: The distribution of the product was made by Mary Lou.

Active: Mary Lou distributed the product.

1. The implementation of the policy was made official by management in August.

2. A suggestion was made by Jane that all new hires start on the first day of the month.

3. Information about that research was given to us by our professor.

4. A discussion of the new survey occurred at our last team meeting.

5. An announcement about the research grant was made by our
    department chair before the resources were awarded.

    Note: See pages 416–417 for the key to the above exercise.

APA and ASA Style, Active Voice, and Tone

Academic writing has the reputation of being passive, over-nominalized, and abstract—in other words, much academic writing is not reader friendly because it is more complicated than it needs to be. In contrast, APA and ASA guidelines recommend active, clear, concise, readable writing as the preferred style for academic papers.[4,5]

However, many academic writers still cling to passive, complicated writing. One of the biggest arguments against letting go of the passive voice is that changing a sentence from passive voice to active voice changes its meaning. However, shifting from one voice to another does not necessarily change the meaning, but it does change the tone.

When all actors are present in a sentence, changing from passive voice to active voice is an exercise in *translation*. Active voice is direct and clear. Passive voice is indirect and abstract to the point that the person performing the action is not necessarily in the sentence, for example:

Passive: The problem will be solved.

However, who *is solving the problem?*

Passive: A solution will be developed.

However, who *is developing a solution?*

For the above sentences to be active, each would need a *real subject* performing the action. Also, in sentences that do not include a real subject, no one is taking responsibility for any actions that the sentence may contain.

When sentences are long and complicated, the tone of the writing is much different from sentences that are clear and to the point. With passive voice, writers do not connect with their own words in the way that they must with active voice, for example:

Passive: A discussion of the issue ensued at length before an
acceptable compromise could be established.

Once again, *who discussed the issue?* By adding *actors* or *agents* (people) to
drive the action of the verb, the sentence becomes more reader friendly, for
example:

Active: We discussed the issue at length before we reached a
compromise.

Though passive voice sounds more formal, today's academic culture now
recognizes that clear, concise, active writing can get the job done just as well.
However, changing your style of writing is difficult: breaking out of a passive,
nominalized writing style takes courage and commitment.

Always keep in mind that when you write in the active voice, your readers
appreciate your clear, direct writing style because its simplicity saves them
time and energy. According to Ralph Waldo Emerson, "Nothing is more
simple than greatness; indeed, to be simple is to be great."[6]

The next chapter covers parallel structure, another topic that ranks high in
making your writing effective.

Recap

Using active voice improves the quality and readability of writing.

- Active voice is clear, concise, and direct.

- Passive voice is complicated and abstract but perfect for situations that
  call for tact.

- Nominalization removes the action from verbs and complicates writing.

- When feasible, turn nominals back into active verbs.

If you are now identifying passive sentences in your own writing and revising
them to active voice, savor your sense of accomplishment. Stay committed in
your quest to write actively: active voice makes writing powerful because it
brings writing to life.

Writing Workshop

Writing Practice

Instructions: Identify active voice and passive voice in your writing and in the writing of others.

1 **Take out a paper that you have written within the last year.**

　　1.1 How many passive sentences can you find?

　　1.2 How many nominalizations can you find?

　　1.3 Are you able to revise those sentences to active voice?

　　1.4 If so, does it improve the flow and clarity of your writing?

2 **Exchange a paper with a colleague and analyze it based on the above questions.**

3 **Find a newspaper or a magazine article that interests you. Assess the writer's use of active and passive voice. Can you see the difference voice makes?**

References

1　　Lederer, R. (2013, June 25). "Lincoln as Jokester." *The Saturday Evening Post.* Retrieved from http://www.saturdayeveningpost.com/2013/06/25/history/lincoln-jokes.html

2　　Young, D. J. (2008). *Business English: Writing for the global workplace.* Burr Ridge, IL: McGraw-Hill Higher Education.

3　　Williams, J. M. (1990). *Style: Toward clarity and grace.* Chicago, IL: University of Chicago Press.

4　　APA. (2010). *Publication manual of the American Psychological Association* (6th ed). Washington, DC: American Psychological Association.

5　　ASA. (2014). *American Sociological Association style guide* (5th ed). Washington, DC: American Sociological Association.

6　　Emerson, R. W. (1838). *Literary ethics.* New York: Thomas Y. Crowell & Company, p. 9.

Parallel Structure

When writing sounds choppy and disjointed, check to see if it is lacking parallel structure. Parallel structure involves expressing similar sentence elements in the same grammatical form, creating balance, rhythm, and flow. As a result, parallel structure adds clarity and enhances understanding, which readers appreciate.

Though you may not have focused on parallel structure before, building skill with it now can enhance the flow of your daily professional writing as well as your academic papers. Parallel structure is also an important element in writing clear instructions and in listing consistent bullet points on your résumé. When editing sentences, look for parallel structure with the following:

- Active and passive voice

- Verb tense

- Gerunds and infinitives

Throughout the centuries, speakers and writers have used parallelism in a variety of ways to draw attention to their point. On a micro level, parallel structure involves the syntax of individual sentences. On a macro level, parallel structure involves using repetitive phrases or sentences to draw readers in and build their expectations. For example, consider the parallel features of Dr. Martin Luther King's speech, "I Have a Dream."[1] Dr. King's repetition not only built up listeners' expectations but also added an indelible rhythm to his speech. When you listen to an especially effective speech, consider if the speaker uses parallel repetition to draw you in. On all levels, parallel structure creates rhythm and flow.

When you have completed this chapter, you will be able to:

- Write sentences that demonstrate parallel structure.

- Apply parallel structure when using correlative conjunctions.

- Achieve parallel structure with bulleted lists using gerunds, infinitives, or verbs.

- Use the imperative voice when writing instructions.

- Write job duties using active verbs in parallel structure on a résumé.

Nouns

Writers have various ways of shifting structure when using nouns, thereby losing parallel structure.

Inconsistent: You need *rest, relaxation*, and *weather that is warm.*

Parallel: You need *rest, relaxation*, and *warm weather.*

Inconsistent: During summers, I worked as *a teaching assistant, lab supervisor*, and *did tutoring.*

Parallel: During summers, I worked as *a teaching assistant, lab supervisor*, and *tutor.*

Another common way to lose parallel structure is to shift from infinitives to gerunds. Infinitives and gerunds are nominals, so they function as nouns, not as verbs.

- An infinitive is the base form of the verb plus *to*, as in *to see, to go*, and *to keep.*

- A gerund is the base form of the verb plus *ing*, as in *seeing, going*, and *keeping.*

For parallel structure, the key to using gerunds and infinitives is using one or the other, but not both.

Inconsistent: My favorite activities are *to jog, swimming*, and *to go golfing.*

Parallel: My favorite activities are *jogging, swimming*, and *golfing.*

Next, you will work with parallel structure using adjectives.

Adjectives

With lists of adjectives, writers sometimes drift from an adjective to a phrase or a clause.

Inconsistent: The research project is not very interesting and costs a lot but is relevant.

Parallel: The research project is boring and expensive but relevant.

Inconsistent: The program is *short, intense,* and *many people like it.*

Parallel: The program is *short, intense,* and *popular.*

When you see yourself shifting from an adjective to a phrase, revise your sentence so that it is parallel.

Phrases

Parallel agreement with phrases can be tricky, especially with prepositional phrases. For example, a preposition may not fit all of the phrases that follow it, necessitating the addition of a preposition that would fit:

Inconsistent: I am disappointed *about the situation* and *the people* who caused it.

Parallel: I am disappointed *about the situation* and *with the people* who caused it.

You may find a prepositional phrase followed by another type of structure:

Inconsistent: Our task force applauds them *for their dedication* and *because they are passionate about their cause.*

Parallel: Our task force applauds them *for their dedication to* and *for their passion about* their cause.

Once again, edit these kinds of inconsistencies out of your writing.

Clauses

When a sentence shifts from active voice to passive voice, or vice versa, the sentence lacks parallel structure, for example:

Inconsistent:	Bob received his brother's old car because a new car was bought by his brother. (active–passive)
Parallel:	Bob received his brother's old car because his brother bought a new car. (active–active)
Inconsistent:	We ran out of money in our budget, so that project was dropped. (active–passive)
Parallel:	We ran out of money in our budget, so we dropped that project. (active–active)

The following sentences will give you practice applying parallel structure.

Practice 9.1

Clauses

Instructions: Edit the following sentences for parallel structure.

Inconsistent:	I am going to compile the data and will be assisted by my team.
Parallel:	I am going to compile the data, and my team will assist me.

1   The control group will meet on next week, and arriving early on Friday was his suggestion.

2   My research design needs input from the committee, and suggestions will be made for them for me.

3   Though I gave input, my schedule was planned by my department chair.

4   If my schedule can be adjusted, I will take time off to complete my research.

5   The extra time was approved by my department chair, so now I must change my schedule.

   Note: See page 417 for the key to the above exercise.

Tenses

Do not shift verb tense unnecessarily. In other words, stay in present tense or past tense unless the meaning of the sentence requires that you change tense.

Inconsistent:	Tim *tells* me last week that the polling *was completed.*
Parallel:	Tim *told* me last week that the polling *was completed.*
Inconsistent:	My professor *says* that our project *was accepted.*
Parallel:	My professor *said* that our project *was accepted.*

To gain skill using verb tense consistently, complete the following exercise.

Practice 9.2

Tenses

Instructions: The following sentences shift tense unnecessarily. Change the verbs so that tenses are consistent.

Inconsistent:	The registrar says I needed to turn the form in yesterday.
Parallel:	The registrar said that I needed to turn the form in yesterday.

1   The message is not clear and needed to be changed.

2   The project assistant says that their participation was inactive for some time now.

3   The new computers arrive today, so then I had to install them.

4   Yesterday my co-worker tells me that I was supposed to attend the budget meeting.

5   First Mary says that she wants the position then she says that she didn't.

   Note: See page 417 for the key to the above exercise.

Lists and the Imperative Voice

When displaying lists, you can use various styles, but remain consistent. For example, you can display items using active voice, nouns, gerund phrases, or infinitive phrases.

However, when you write a list of instructions, the most effective style is the *imperative mood* or *voice*, which makes a command or request. The imperative voice occurs in the second person, and the subject is *you* (which is the same as using the base form of the verb). The imperative voice communicates to the reader what must be done in the most simple, direct way; for example, (you) *attend* the meeting and (you) *take* notes. (The imperative voice is also equivalent to active voice in second person.)

Below is an inconsistent list which is then displayed in the various styles: the base form of verbs, nouns, gerund phrases, and infinitive phrases.

Incorrect:

1 Paper on environmental risks

2 Selecting a location for meeting

3 Topics for meeting agenda

Corrected:

*Verbs (base form or **imperative voice**):*

1 Write paper on environmental risks

2 Select a location for meeting

3 Identify topics for meeting agenda

Nouns:

1 Paper on environmental risks

2 Location for meeting

3 Topics for meeting agenda

Gerund phrases:

1 Writing paper on environmental risks

2 Selecting a location for meeting

3 Identifying topics for meeting agenda

Infinitive phrases:

1 To write a paper on environmental risks

2 To select a location for meeting

3 To identify topics for meeting agenda

Here is a list of instructions that lacks parallel structure:

Instructions for tallying the call volume

1 A tally should be taken of the call volume.

2 You need to complete the tally by 9 a.m. for the previous day's calls.

3 The call volume is recorded in the black binder labeled *Call Volume*.

4 Then you should report the number to the project manager.

5 When you are finished, the binder must be returned.

Here is the same list using verbs (base form or imperative voice):

Call volume tally

1 Tally the previous day's sales calls by 9 a.m.

2 Record the number in the black binder labeled *Call Volume*.

3 Report the number to the project manager.

4 Return the binder.

In the exercise below, put the items in parallel structure.

The following list is displayed as *nouns*:

Here are items to discuss at our next meeting:

• Ground rules

• Holiday schedule

• Summer hours

You can represent the same list using *verbs* (the *imperative voice*):

At our next meeting, we need to do the following:

- Revise ground rules
- Review holiday schedule
- Implement summer hours

Adding *-ing* to the verbs turns them into *gerunds* (a noun form):

The following are topics for our next meeting:

- Revising ground rules
- Reviewing holiday schedule
- Implementing summer hours

You can also use complete sentences:

Here is what we expect to accomplish at our next meeting:

- We will revise the ground rules.
- We will clarify our holiday schedule.
- We will establish summer hours and a date to implement them.

Practice 9.3

Parallel lists

Instructions: Make the following list parallel by using the base form or the verb (or the imperative voice).

1   Development of questions for survey

2   Identification of effective communication skills

3   Compilation of the requirements for the study

4   Conflict resolution among the group

5   Recruitment and retention of project leaders

6   Valuing personality differences in committees

7   Climate assessment in change efforts

Note: See pages 417–418 for the key to the above exercise.

Bulleted Lists on Résumés

Apply parallel structure when listing job duties on a résumé. Start each bullet point with an active verb: for current positions, use present tense; for past positions, use past tense.

Here is a list of sample job duties for a current position:

- Develop and implement training programs
- Schedule and conduct interviews
- Tabulate daily call volume and weekly inventory
- Prepare and organize schedules
- Negotiate contracts for polling projects

Here is a list of sample job duties for a past position:

- Maintained status updates
- Supervised interns
- Planned and administered policy changes
- Secured funding for special projects
- Ensured compliance of federal standards

Correlative Conjunctions

Here are common pairs of conjunctions—notice that the second word in the pair is a coordinating conjunction:

either . . . or

neither . . . nor

both . . . and

not . . . but

not only . . . but also

whether . . . or

When using correlative conjunctions, follow the second part of the correlative with the same structure as the first part.

Inconsistent:	We will *not only* upgrade your account *but also* are providing monthly reports.
Parallel:	We *not only* will upgrade your account *but also* will provide monthly reports.
Parallel:	We will *not only* upgrade your account *but also* provide monthly reports.

Complete the following exercise for additional practice.

Practice 9.4

Correlative Conjunctions

Instructions: Edit the following sentences for parallel structure.

Incorrect:	Barbara will either go to the meeting or she will not go.
Corrected:	Barbara will either go to the meeting or not (go to the meeting).

1   My associate not only asked me to complete the report but also presenting it at the meeting was required.

2   Milly applied both for the job and got it.

3   Our team neither focused on getting funding nor to show interest in the project.

4   The solution makes not only sense but also saves time.

5   Neither my new project has been approved nor is it being considered.

Note: See page 418 for the key to the above exercise.

Recap

Parallel structure comes in all shapes and forms. Developing a keen eye for similar sentence elements takes time and commitment. As you focus attention on parallel structure, you will see connections that you did not previously see.

- Express similar sentence elements in the same grammatical form: noun for noun, verb for verb, phrase for phrase, and clause for clause.

- Start bulleted lists with gerunds, infinitives, or verbs.

- Use the imperative voice when writing instructions (which is equivalent to using the base form of the verb or active voice in second person).

- Pay special attention to parallel structure when using correlative conjunctions.

- Use parallel structure when listing job duties on your résumé.

Writing Workshop

Activity A. Writing Practice

Instructions: Use parallel structure to give instructions on how to accomplish a task.

1   Select a task that takes several steps to complete, such as writing a paper, completing a project, or following directions to a specific location. If you wish, select something fun, such as cooking a recipe.

2   Next, break the task down into steps, listing each step in the active (or imperative) voice.

Write your list of instructions so that anyone could pick up your list and accomplish your chosen task.

Activity B. Job Duties for Résumé

Instructions: Make a list of job duties that you perform for a current job as well as duties that you have performed for past positions—paid or volunteer.

1   Put your job duties in parallel structure using active verbs in present time.

2   Now put your job duties in parallel structure using active verbs in past time.

Reference

1   King, M. L., Jr. (1963, August 28). "I Have a Dream." Speech. Lincoln Memorial, Washington, DC.

Pronouns and Viewpoint

Since pronouns are a core element of everything that you write, gaining control of pronoun viewpoint is key to developing your voice—or rather, your *various voices*: academic, professional, and reflective.

For example, each type of writing has different requirements for the use of pronouns and verbs. To achieve the best results, adapt your use of pronouns to meet the needs and expectations of each audience. In Chapter 1, "Purpose, Voice, and Viewpoint," you reviewed the following:

- *Academic writing* relies on the third person. The second person "you" viewpoint is not used; and only under defined contexts is the first person "I" viewpoint used.

- *Professional writing* focuses on the "you" viewpoint. However, the first person or "I" viewpoint is also effective, depending on the context.

- *Reflective writing* emanates from the first person or "I" viewpoint. When writing reflectively, you write from your own experience.

The first section of this chapter, *Pronoun Viewpoint*, provides explanation and exercises to develop expertise with writing in each viewpoint consistently. The second section, *Pronoun Basics*, reviews how pronouns function. (*Note*: If you find the first part of the chapter challenging or confusing, work on the second part of the chapter first.)

When you have completed this chapter, you will be able to:

- Adapt pronoun use for context: academic, professional, or reflective

- Display consistent use of point of view in sentences and paragraphs

- Understand how to use pronouns to avoid gender bias

- Distinguish between subjective case and objective case pronouns

- Understand the use of *who, whom,* and *that*

- Apply singular and plural indefinite pronouns correctly

- Understand correct usage of collective nouns, such as *data* and *committee*

Learning a few basic principles will give you control in using pronouns. In case you need a refresher, a *pronoun* is a word that is used in place of a noun or another pronoun; for example, *I, you, he, she, it, we,* and *they* as well as *who, that, which, someone,* among others.

Pronoun Viewpoint

Pronoun viewpoint refers to the *point of view* from which a document is written, which can be from *first, second,* or *third person, singular* or *plural.* In this part, you start reviewing how to use pronouns consistently and then work on pronoun and antecedent agreement.

Here are the points covered in this section:

- Viewpoint and consistency

- Pronoun and antecedent agreement

- APA and ASA style and pronoun usage

- Professional writing and the *you* viewpoint

While these topics contribute to developing an academic and a professional voice, the basics for using pronouns correctly are covered in Part 2 (see pages 226–237).

Viewpoint and Consistency

Using pronouns correctly enables you to adapt your voice for your audience, and one element of using pronouns correctly is to use them consistently: *once you start writing within a viewpoint, stay within that viewpoint.*

Pronoun viewpoint can emanate from first, second, or third person, singular or plural.

	Singular	**Plural**
First Person	I	we
Second Person	you	you
Third Person	a person	people

The following examples use the various viewpoints consistently within a sentence:

> When *I* write, *I* must pay attention to *my* audience.
>
> When *you* write, *you* must pay attention to *your* audience.
>
> When a *person* writes, *he* or *she* must pay attention to *his* or *her* audience.
>
> When *we* write, *we* must pay attention to *our* audience.
>
> When *people* write, *they* must pay attention to *their* audience.
>
> When *one* writes, *one* must pay attention to *one's* audience.

Though the *one* viewpoint is not commonly used in the United States, other English-speaking countries do use the *one* viewpoint. An error many writers make, however, is to use the pronoun *one* "randomly" within a sentence when they are unsure of pronoun choice, for example:

Example 1

Incorrect: *I* think *one* should write daily because *you* improve *your* skills.

Example 2

Incorrect: If *one* arrives on time, *they* will receive prompt service.

As you read the following corrected versions of the sentences above, notice the consistency in various voices:

Example 1

Corrected: *I* should write daily because *I* will improve *my* skills.

Corrected: *You* should write daily because *you* will improve your skills.

Corrected: *One* should write daily because *one* will improve *one's* skills.

Example 2

Corrected: If *they* arrive on time, *they* will receive prompt service.

Corrected: If *you* arrive on time, *you* will receive prompt service.

Corrected: If *one* arrives on time, *one* will receive prompt service.

Do you ever write instructions? If so, use the *you* viewpoint, which is clear and direct. Here is an example of instructions written in the *you* viewpoint and active voice:

> (You) Fill out the application immediately so that your project is eligible for funding.

> (You) Answer all questions completely.

> (You) Send your application by October 15.

As you compose, write freely. However, when you edit, correct pronoun usage for consistency, and agreement: *Do not shift point of view within sentences or even paragraphs.*

- Select the point of view that meets the expectations of your audience, whether that be academic (third person), professional (first and second persons), or reflective (first person).

- When you select a point of view, use that viewpoint consistently.

Practice 10.1

Consistent Point of View

Instructions: Correct the following sentences for pronoun–antecedent agreement. You can correct each sentence in various viewpoints—the key is consistency, for example:

Incorrect:	A person who does their best will achieve the best possible outcome.
Awkward:	A person who does *his or her* best will achieve the best possible outcome.
Corrected:	*People* who do *their* best will achieve the best possible outcome.
	If *you* do *your* best, *you* will achieve the best possible outcome.

1 One sometimes thinks another situation is better until you experience it.

2 We generally follow the rules unless you are told otherwise.

3 If a student is conscientious, they will do well in their class.

4 One does not always follow instructions, but we should.

5 Everyone must make their own reservations.

6 John went to the meeting with Gary to ensure that he gave a complete report.

Note: See page 418 for the key to this activity.

Pronoun and Antecedent Agreement

Pronouns can be used in place of nouns and other pronouns, and the words that pronouns refer to are known as *antecedents*.

• Pronouns must agree in number and gender with their antecedents.

• Many antecedents are not gender specific, such as *person, doctor, engineer, lawyer, teacher,* and so on.

Because singular pronouns, such as "he" and "she," are gender specific, writers sometimes face a dilemma. For example, when writing about a "teacher," would a feminine or a masculine antecedent be best used?

Until recently, the masculine antecedent was traditionally used. When it became apparent that this approach was biased, writers chose different solutions, such as the following, *none of which is recommended*:

- Shifting between masculine and feminine antecedents: for example, in one instance, referring to "teacher" as "he" then the next time as "she."

- Combining "he" and "she" to create an alternative form, such as "s/he."

- Using "they" as an antecedent to *singular* gender-neutral nouns.

- Inventing new words such as "Ne," "Ve," "Ze," or "Xe."

As you can see, the English language has no good solution for singular antecedents that are gender neutral. However, you have the following options for writing correctly in an unbiased way:*

- When you can, use the plural form of gender-neutral nouns: *teachers . . . they*

- When you refer to a person and are unaware of the person's gender, refer to the person by name. While this may become redundant, redundancy is preferred to being offensive. (And when feasible, do some research or ask.)

- At times, a person will ask to be referred to in a specific way; when that happens, it is appropriate to respect the request. Applying a diverse usage for specific documents would be a matter for etiquette, not grammar.

    **Note*: This topic is also discussed in Chapter 18, "Word Usage."

Let us take a look at applying the plural form to gender-neutral nouns. In the following example, *managers* is the antecedent of *they* and *their*.

> All *managers* said that *they* would submit *their* quarterly reports by Friday.

Here is another example with *person* and *people* used as *antecedents*:

Incorrect: In an emergency, a *person* must do what *they* are asked.

Corrected: In an emergency, *people* must do what *they* are asked.

Here are a few more examples:

Awkward: When a *researcher* performs *his* or *her* duties, *he* or *she* must remain attentive to *his* or *her* research subjects.

Revised: When *researchers* perform *their* duties, *they* must remain
                 attentive to *their* research subjects.

Incorrect: *Every team member* should bring *their* own *laptop*.

Corrected: *All team members* should bring *their* own *laptops*.

Notice in the above example that *laptops* becomes plural along with *team members*. Within a sentence, grammatical agreement is applied to all related elements.

As another option, edit out the pronoun, for example:

Corrected: *Every team member* should bring *a laptop*.

At times, when two or more antecedents appear in a sentence, pronoun reference can be unclear. For example, in the following, to which person does the pronoun *she* refer?

Sue and *Martha* completed their report by Tuesday so that *she* could present the findings in a conference on Thursday.

When meaning is unclear, restate the antecedent:

Sue and *Martha* completed their report by Tuesday so that *Martha* could present the findings in a conference on Thursday.

Practice 10.2

Pronoun and Antecedent Agreement

Instructions: Correct the following sentences for pronoun–antecedent agreement.

Incorrect: Ask a friend for their help only when you really need it.

Awkward: Ask a friend for his or her help only when you really
                 need it.

Corrected: Ask *friends* for *their* help only when you really need it.

1   When an employee calls in sick, they should give a reason.

2   When a sociologist does not relate well to their clients, they need more training.

3   A social worker is going beyond their job description when they assist a client's guests.

4   A criminologist's job is challenging because they work under difficult conditions.

5   When a customer does not have a receipt, they may not be able to return an item.

6   Charley said that John should be on his team because he would be available during his training.

> *Note*: See page 419 for the key to this activity.

To reinforce academic requirements for using pronouns, let us next review APA and ASA guidelines.

APA and ASA Style and Pronoun Usage

APA and ASA styles encourage clear and concise writing and give directives about using pronouns effectively.[1,2] Therefore, let us look at the following three pronoun viewpoints and how they fit into your academic writing, which requires a formal tone:

*   Third-person viewpoint

*   *I* Viewpoint

*   *We* viewpoint (aka *editorial we*)

Third-Person Viewpoint

For academic writing, the third-person viewpoint is the most commonly used point of view. When you summarize the work of others or speak about a topic, choose the third-person viewpoint, for example:

Third person: *Barnes argues* that too much time spent on the Internet . . .

The *internet distracts* learners when . . .

APA and ASA styles also recommend that writing should focus on the research and not the researchers conducting it. Therefore, when you summarize a research article, start by stating the author's name but then shift your focus to the research itself, for example:

> *Barnes* (2010) *argues* that the internet can divert users from their original objective, causing them to lose time and focus. The research specifically identifies students as being at risk for getting sidetracked from academic tasks. Findings include data about distracted learners who experience more stress than value from experiences in which they lose focus.

> The *internet has* many uses, ranging from personal interests to being an academic research vehicle. Unfortunately, sites such as Facebook actually interfere with student learning and their research on the internet (Johnson 2016).

Since most of your academic writing will be in the *third-person viewpoint*, learn to speak with consistency in that viewpoint. Otherwise, you may unknowingly make errors that distract your readers and cause you to lose credibility. At times, however, the *first-person viewpoint* is not only necessary but also desirable.

I Viewpoint

When you describe research that you have conducted, use the *I* viewpoint. Also use the *I* viewpoint in academic papers when you make concluding remarks and state your recommendations. If you avoid using "I" altogether, your writing is likely to become unnecessarily complicated and awkward.

For example, the *I* viewpoint is preferred to the passive voice below:

Passive:	A recommendation is being made that further research in this area . . .
I **viewpoint:**	*I* recommend that further research in this area explore . . .

To avoid overusing the "I" viewpoint, keep the focus on the research and not yourself:

I viewpoint:	*I* found that . . .
Third person:	The results of the research indicate that . . .

When you conduct research with others, use the *we* viewpoint instead.

We Viewpoint

When you work with others on a project, use the *we* viewpoint (also known as the *editorial we*). For example, the *editorial we* is preferred to you and your colleagues referring to yourselves in the third person:

Third Person   *The authors* received a grant to cover the cost of
                    resources.

We Viewpoint   *We* received a grant to cover the cost of resources.

Since the third-person viewpoint is an essential viewpoint of academic writing, complete the exercise below to hone your skills.

Practice 10.3

Pronoun Consistency

Instructions: Edit the following paragraph, screening for pronoun consistency.

> I enjoy working on team projects because you learn so much from your teammates. A team member needs to be helpful because they never know when they will need assistance from his or her colleagues. When you are on a team, every member needs to carry their weight. That is, teammates who do not do his or her share of the work can be a burden to the team and jeopardize their project.
>
> If a team member stays motivated, you are more valuable to the team. I always strive to do my best because you never know when you will need to count on your team members.

Note: See page 419 for the key to the above exercise.

Professional Writing and the You *Viewpoint*

While academic writing is highly formal, professional writing is neither highly formal nor casual: professional writing falls in the category of medium formality.[3] Follow standard rules for grammar and capitalization, and do not use texting language. Use your professional voice when you write e-mail messages, business letters, and memos.

To create a professional tone, use the following viewpoints:

- *You* viewpoint

- *I* viewpoint and *we* viewpoint (aka *editorial we*)

When you write from your *professional voice*, your aim is to connect with readers through simple, clear, concise writing. Therefore, use first-person and second-person pronouns (such as *I*, *you*, and *we*) so that you may refer to your reader and yourself in a direct and personal way.

You Viewpoint

While the *you* viewpoint is not an option for academic writing, it is a critical element of professional writing because the *you* viewpoint speaks directly to your reader.

I **viewpoint:**	*I* am writing to let you know that *I* would like to invite you to our next meeting.
You **viewpoint:**	Would *you* be interested in attending our next meeting?

By speaking directly to your reader through the *you* viewpoint, you engage your reader and tune in to their needs. Here are more examples:

I **viewpoint:**	*I* am interested in the position in research.
	I would like to know what you think about the change.
	I would like to encourage you to apply for the position.
You **viewpoint:**	(*You*) Please tell me about the position in research.
	What do *you* think about the change?
	You should apply for the position.

At times, the subject of a sentence is implied or understood, as in the first "you" viewpoint example above. The "you understood" subject is represented as "(you)."

While it is important to limit your use of the *I* viewpoint, at times it is necessary and desirable. Otherwise your writing will become awkward, and awkward writing is never effective. For professional writing, here's a general approach:

> *If you wouldn't say it that way, don't write it that way.*

Thus, when you are writing about your own experience, use the *I* point of view.

Awkward:	When the project was started by me, a request was made . . .
I viewpoint:	When *I* started this project, *I* requested . . .

In business, writers also use the *we viewpoint*, also known as the *editorial we*, to stress that they represent their company, as in the following:

We viewpoint:	*We* at Focus Research Group value your support.

While the *you* viewpoint puts focus on the reader, the *I* viewpoint comes more naturally when composing. When you compose, let your words flow freely. When you edit, shift to the *you* viewpoint. *Compose for yourself, then edit for your reader.*

Practice 10.4

Pronoun and Antecedent Agreement

Instructions: Correct the following sentences for pronoun-antecedent agreement.

Incorrect:	When an employee calls in sick, they should give a reason.
Corrected:	When *employees* call in sick, *they* should give a reason.

1 When a pollster does not relate well to the public, they need more training.

2 A server is going beyond her job description when they prepare carry-out orders for customers.

3   A pilot has a challenging job because they work long hours under difficult conditions.

4   When a lab assistant does not turn in their work, they should expect negative feedback.

5   A writer needs to submit their work in a timely manner.

Note: See page 419 for the key to the above exercise.

Pronoun Basics

While verbs may be complicated and thus troublesome, pronouns probably give writers more problems. Most people are not aware of the mistakes that they make with pronouns. A common mistake is using a formal-sounding pronoun such as *I* in place of a less-formal sounding pronoun such as *me*. For example, it is common to hear a phrase such as "between you and *I*" when usage dictates "between you and *me*" is correct. That kind of mistake is called a *hypercorrection*, and hypercorrection is common.

Unsure speakers pick up incorrect pronoun use easily, changing their speech so that it sounds "right." If you want to use pronouns correctly, base your decisions on how they *function* in a sentence, not on how others use them; then you will have sound and principle on your side.

Here are the points covered in this section:

- Pronoun case

- Subjects versus objects

- Pronouns following *between* and *than*

- Relative pronouns: who, whom, and that

- Relative pronouns: that and which

- Indefinite pronouns

Pronoun Case

To start, pronouns are classified by *case:* the four cases of personal pronouns are *subjective*, *objective*, *possessive*, and *reflexive*. In this part, you review how pronouns function based on case; you also review other types of pronouns, *relative* and *indefinite pronouns*.

Box 10.1 presents a quick refresher of personal pronouns.

10.1 PERSONAL PRONOUNS

	Subjective	Objective	Possessive	Reflexive
Singular				
1st Person	I	me	my, mine	myself
2nd Person	you	you	your, yours	yourself
3rd Person	he	him	his	himself
	she	her	hers	herself
	it	it	its	itself
Plural				
1st Person	we	us	our, ours	ourselves
2nd Person	you	you	your, yours	yourselves
3rd Person	they	them	their, theirs	themselves

10.2 THE ROLE EACH CASE PLAYS IN A SENTENCE

- *Subjective* case pronouns function as *subjects* of verbs, and thus a subjective case pronoun is used as the subject of a sentence.

- *Objective* case pronouns function as *objects*, usually of verbs or prepositions.

- *Possessive* case pronouns *show possession* of nouns or other pronouns.

- *Reflexive* case pronouns reflect back to subjective case pronouns; reflexive case pronouns are also known as *intensive case pronouns*.

Subjects versus Objects

Your first step in gaining control of pronouns lies in using subjective case and objective case pronouns correctly. At the core of pronoun use, here is the question you need to answer:

> Does the pronoun function as a *subject* or as an *object*?

Here is why many writers make mistakes with subjective-case and objective-case pronouns:

- Subjective case pronouns sound more formal than objective case pronouns. An unsure speaker will use *I* or *he* as an object, when *me* or *him* would be correct.

- When a pronoun is part of a pair, incorrect pronoun use can sound correct.

Here are some examples:

Incorrect: Bill asked Mike and *I* to assist him.

Correct: Bill asked Mike and *me* to assist him.

Incorrect: George and *me* went to the game last Friday.

Correct: George and *I* went to the meeting last Friday.

In place of a subjective case pronoun or an objective case pronoun, some writers incorrectly substitute a reflexive case pronoun.

Incorrect: George and *myself* went to the meeting last Friday.

Incorrect: Bill asked Mike and *myself* to assist him.

Incorrect: Sue and *yourself* can work on the project.

Instead, use reflexive case pronouns only when they refer to a subjective case pronoun or a noun that is already part of the sentence. Here are some examples using reflexive case pronouns correctly:

I will do the work *myself.*

You can complete the project *yourself,* if you have the time.

Susan referred to *herself* as the person in charge of hiring.

The *dog* bit *himself* in the foot, mistaking *his* foot for a bone!

To use subjective-case and objective-case pronouns correctly, first identify whether the pronoun functions as a *subject* or as an *object*. If the pronoun stands alone, it is easier to test by sound. If the pronoun is part of a pair, use the following substitutions:

- Use *I* if you could substitute *we*:

  Sam and I went to the conference: *We* went to the conference.

- Use *me* if you could substitute *us*:

  Sally asked *Juan and me* for help: Sally asked *us* for help.

- Use *he* or *she* if you could substitute *they*:

  Martin and he finished the project: *they* finished the project.

- Use *him* or *her* if you could substitute *them*:

  Melissa encouraged *LaTika and her* to go: Melissa encouraged *them*.

Another way would be to simplify your sentence by taking out the other person and then testing for sound. Using examples from above, here is how you would test your pronoun based on sound:

Incorrect: Sam and *me* went to the conference.

Simplify: ~~Sam and~~ *me* went to the conference.

Correct: Sam and *I* went to the conference.

Incorrect: Sally asked Juan and *I* for help.

Simplify: Sally asked ~~Juan and~~ *I* for help.

Correct: Sally asked Juan and *me* for help.

Incorrect: Martin and *him* finished the project.

Simplify: ~~Martin and~~ *him* finished the project.

Correct: Martin and *he* finished the project.

Incorrect:	Bill asked Mike and *myself* to assist him.
Simplify:	Bill asked ~~Mike and~~ *myself* to assist him.
Correct:	Bill asked Mike and *me* to assist him.

Writing Tip

Rule of thumb substitution:

- If you can substitute *we* for a pair, use *I*
- If you can substitute *us*, use *me*

Practice 10.5

Subjects and Objects

Instructions: Correct the following sentences for pronoun usage.

Incorrect:	When you call the office, ask for myself or Alice.
Corrected:	When you call the office, ask for *me* or Alice.

1   If you can't reach anyone else, feel free to call myself.

2   The director told Catie and I to role play again.

3   Fred and her collected for the local food drive.

4   His manager and him have two more reports to complete.

5   That decision was made by Jim and I.

Note: See page 420 for the key to the above exercise.

Pronouns Following **Between** *and* **Than**

Using pronouns after *between* and *than* can be confusing, and often the correct version sounds more awkward than incorrect usage. For example, which of the following sounds correct to you? (Select your choice *before* you read the explanation that follows.)

Choice 1:   Between you and *I*, we have too much work.

Choice 2:   Between you and *me*, we have too much work.

The word *between* is a preposition, and an object would follow it. When *between* is followed by a pronoun, the correct choice would be an objective-case pronoun such as *me* or *him* or *her* or *them*. Therefore, the correct choice is "between you and *me*."

The conjunction *than* causes challenges for speakers and writers alike. Which of the following sounds correct to you?

Choice 1:   Paco is taller than *me*.

Choice 2:   Paco is taller than *I*.

Since the word *than* is a conjunction, a subject *and* a verb would follow it. Oftentimes the verb is implied, which makes an objective case pronoun sound correct even when it is not correct. If you selected the second choice above, you would be correct. The statement actually reads, "Paco is taller than I (am)."

Here is what you need to know:

- Use the objective case after the preposition *between*.

  Incorrect: You can split the project between *Bob* and *I*.

  Corrected: You can split the project between *Bob* and *me*.

You can split the project between *us*.

  Incorrect: That issue should remain between *yourself* and *I*.

  Corrected: That issue should remain between *you* and *me*.

- Use the subjective case after the conjunction *than* when a subject and implied verb follow it. To be correct without sounding too formal, include the implied verb in your speech and writing.

  Incorrect: Mitchell has more time than *me*.

  Corrected: Mitchell has more time than *I (have)*.

  Incorrect: Erin runs faster than *me*.

  Corrected: Erin faster than *I (run)*.

Once again, using pronouns correctly involves basing usage on principle rather than sound, especially if you are in the habit of hypercorrecting. In other words, until you can apply the principle, you cannot use the "way it sounds" as a guide.

Practice 10.6

Pronouns Following Between *and* Than

Instructions: Correct the following sentences for pronoun usage.

> **Incorrect:**   The discussion was between John and I.
>
> **Corrected:**   The discussion was between John and *me*.

1   Between you and I, who has more time?

2   Beatrice collects data better than me.

3   The decision is between Bob and yourself.

4   The other work group is more competitive than us.

5   You can split the work between Margaret and I so that it gets done on time.

> *Note*: See page 420 for the key to the above exercise.

Relative Pronouns: Who, Whom, *and* That

When writers do not know how to use *whom* correctly, they often use the pronouns *who* and *that* incorrectly.

Here is a review of how to use each pronoun correctly.

- Use w*ho* as the subject of a clause or a sentence.

  Who gave you the report?

  Who said that the program starts now?

- Use w*hom* as an object of a preposition, a verb, an infinitive, or other verb phrase.

To whom are you referring?

You are referring to whom?

- Use *that* when referring to things, not people.

The annotated bibliography is the part *that* is due.

Not: Mary is the person *that* spoke first.

- Use *who* as a subject complement of a linking verb such as *is, are, was,* or *were.*

Who do you want to be when you grow up?

You want to be *who* when you grow up?

When you are having difficulty choosing among the relative pronouns *who, whom,* and *that,* choose **who**. Here is why:

- *Whom* is falling out of use: only a small fraction of the population use *whom* correctly.

- People who use *whom* correctly reserve its use for highly formal situations.

- Using *whom* incorrectly sounds strange.

To improve your speech as well as your writing, instead focus on pronouncing your words clearly.

Local language: *Whoja* go to the keynote speech with?

Informal English: *Who* did you go to the keynote speech with?

Formal English: With *whom* did you go to the keynote speech?

Work on Practice 10.7 to gain additional practice using *who, whom,* and *that.*

Practice 10.7

Relative Pronouns: Who, Whom, and That

Instructions: In the following sentences, circle the pronoun for correct usage.

Incorrect: Michael is the person (who, that) collects the data.

Corrected: Michael is the person (**who**, that) collects the data.

1   (Who, Whom) completed the monthly report?

2   (Who, Whom) are you going to the meeting with?

3   Is Jim the person (who, whom) spoke with you?

4   The consultant (that, who, whom) saw you yesterday is not available.

5   Every person (who, that) arrives late will be turned away.

Note: See page 420 for the key to the above exercise.

Relative Pronouns: **That** *and* **Which**

Though *that* and *which* are somewhat interchangeable, here is how to choose between the two.

- Use *that* with *restrictive* information, which is information that should not be removed if the meaning is to remain clear.

- Use *which* with *nonrestrictive* information, which is information that can be set off with commas and removed.

Here are some examples with a brief explanation following each:

Example 1:   Our report that we wrote last quarter needs a new introduction.

Example 1 gives the impression that more than one report was written—it is the report that was written last quarter that needs a new introduction.

Example 2:   Our report, which we wrote last summer, needs a new introduction.

Example 2 indicates that only one report was written, and that report was written last quarter.

Example 3:   The report that came out in August reveals our position.

Example 3 indicates that more than one report came out, and the report of interest is the one that came out in August.

Example 4: The report, which came out in August, reveals our position.

Example 4 indicates that there was only one report, and that one report came out in August.

Indefinite Pronouns and Collective Nouns

Indefinite pronouns are words that replace nouns without specifying the noun they are replacing. To use an indefinite pronoun correctly, first determine whether it is singular or plural.

Singular Indefinite Pronouns:

another	everybody	each	neither	somebody
anyone	everything	either	nobody	something
anybody	much	every	one	someone
everyone	nothing	no one		

Singular indefinite pronouns always take a singular verb:

> *Every* situation *calls* for a different response.

> *Neither* of the girls *works* here.

> *Someone is* ready for a promotion.

Plural Indefinite Pronouns:

> both, few, many, others, several

Plural indefinite pronouns always take a plural verb:

> *Many* (of the participants) *were* unprepared.

> *Several* (invoices) *arrive* daily.

Indefinite Pronouns, Singular or Plural:

> all, none, any, some, more, most

Indefinite pronouns that can be singular or plural are generally followed by a prepositional phrase that contains a noun. If the noun that the indefinite pronoun refers to is singular, then the pronoun is singular. If the noun is plural, then the pronoun is plural.

Here are examples of indefinite pronouns; make special note of the noun in the prepositional phrase that follows each:

> *None* of the work *was* completed.
>
> *None* of the projects *were* done.
>
> *All* of the information *has been taken into account.*
>
> *All* of the results *are* valid.

Collective Nouns

In addition to indefinite pronouns, *collective nouns* can also be singular or plural: a collective noun is singular in form but represents a group or unit; for example:

board	corporation	group	organization
class	council	jury	public
committee	department	majority	society
company	faculty	minority	staff

A collective noun is singular when treated as a unit but plural when referring to individual items; for example:

> A *group* of sociologists are planning the symposium.
>
> The *group* is expected to agree on the plan.

The word "data" is now considered a collective noun. ("Data" is the plural of "datum," which has gone out of use.) When "data" is used as a noncount noun, which means that the items cannot be counted, use the singular form. When you are using data of multiple types or from multiple sources, consider it plural. Here are examples of using data as a singular and plural noun:

> All of the data has been tallied.
>
> None of the data that we have reviewed are compelling.
>
> The data is valid.
>
> The data from all of the studies have been carefully analyzed.

Work on Practice 10.8; also make a list of the indefinite pronouns that are troublesome for you, and practice using them until you build your skill.

Practice 10.8

Indefinite Pronouns

Instructions: Correct the following sentences for pronoun usage and agreement.

> **Incorrect:**   Throw away any of the pens that doesn't work.
>
> **Corrected:** Throw away any of the pens that *don't* work.

1   Either one of the programs work perfectly.

2   Everyone who finished the project are free to go.

3   None of the employees sends e-mail on Saturday.

4   Some of the assignments needs to be distributed before noon today.

5   Everything run much better when we are all on time.

Note: See page 420–421 for the key to the above exercise.

Recap

To make a correct choice with pronouns, focus on the way that the pronoun functions in the sentence: is the pronoun being used as a subject or as an object?

- For most academic writing, use the third-person viewpoint.

- Use the *I* viewpoint when you discuss research that you conducted; use the *editorial we* when you discuss research that you have conducted with others.

- Pronouns must agree in number and gender with their antecedents.

- One key to using pronouns and antecedents consistently is to use plural antecedents.

- *Who* refers to people; *that* refers to objects: When in doubt, choose *who*.

- When using an indefinite pronoun or collective noun, determine if it is being used as singular or plural (and then check the verb for agreement).

Writing Workshop

Activity A. Pronoun Consistency: First Person Singular

Instructions: Edit the following paragraph; using the first person singular or "I" viewpoint, correct for pronoun consistency.

> **For example:**   I enjoy going to meetings because ~~you~~ I find out about current projects.
>
> I enjoy working on team projects because you learn so much from your teammates. A team member needs to be supportive because they never know when they will need assistance from his or her colleagues. When you are on a team, every member needs to carry their weight. That is, if one would not do his or her share of the work can, they can be a burden to the team and jeopardize their project. If a team member stays motivated, you are more valuable to the team. I always strive to do my best because you never know when you will need to count on your team members.

Activity B. Pronoun Consistency: Third Person Plural

Instructions: Edit the paragraph above using the third person plural viewpoint.

> *Note*: See page 421 for the key to the above activities.

References

1   APA. (2010). *Publication manual of the American Psychological Association* (6th ed). Washington, DC: American Psychological Association.

2   American Sociological Association. (2014). *American Sociological Association style guide* (5th ed). Washington, DC: American Sociological Association.

3   Young, D. J. (2006). *Foundations of business communication*. Burr Ridge, IL: McGraw-Hill/Irwin.

Conciseness

Being concise is about knowing what you want to say and saying it clearly: readers have easy access to important points, and the writing sounds effortless. The irony, however, is that clear and concise writing takes effort to produce, and even seasoned writers struggle with their words until their thoughts become clear. As one writer said, "This would have been shorter if I had more time."

Compose freely until you understand your point. Once you understand your *purpose*, you can edit your writing so that you say what you mean in the simplest way. That's because purpose clarifies the difference between information that is important and information that is unimportant (or even irritating for the reader).

The more you explain it, the more I don't understand it.

—Mark Twain

Whether your chosen profession is in sociology or another field, you will use e-communication daily through e-mail messages or other media. The first part of this chapter covers how to structure e-mail messages and then reviews what you should aim to edit out of all types of writing. As you edit for conciseness, apply the principle *less is more*:

- Simple words convey information more effectively than complex words.

- Short messages get the job done better than long messages. (When you need to write a long message, consider following it up with a phone call.)

- Using big, four-syllable words is *not* a sign of intelligence.

When you have completed this chapter, you will be able to:

- Identify key points and put purpose first.

- Be indirect when writing "bad news" messages.

- Cut redundant modifiers and vague nouns.

- Eliminate the obvious, and avoid outdated phrases and legalese.

- Edit out background information, opinions, and beliefs.

- Use simple language.

Let us get started by examining how purpose relates to being concise.

Put Purpose First

Since purpose defines context, readers have an easier time finding meaning when they understand purpose up front. However, when you start writing, you may not be able to state your purpose clearly. As you compose, you gain additional insight; once you can state your key point clearly, follow these steps:

1 Paste your key point to the beginning of your message.

2 Identify and cut information that the reader does not need to know.

You may find yourself cutting quite a bit of irrelevant or empty information. For example, your reader does not need to know the background information that led you to your key point. As you read the following e-mail, take special note of where the writer's purpose finally becomes clear:

> Dear Ms. Holloway:
>
> My name is Donald Draper, and I recently attended a local job fair where I met an associate of yours. His name is Roger Sterling, and he was representing your company at the job fair.
>
> Mr. Sterling suggested that I write you because you are the person in charge of the intern program at your company. To give you a little background about myself, I am currently completing my degree at Best College, and I am scheduled to receive my degree in marketing next spring. My purpose in writing you is to find out if you have any openings in your intern program this coming winter. I would be pleased to send you my resume. I look forward to hearing from you.
>
> Best regards,
>
> Donald Draper

To revise the above message, follow these steps:

1   Identify the key point.

2   Bring the key point to the beginning of the message.

3   Cut irrelevant information.

Revise the above message before reviewing the revision in Box 11.1.

11.1   REVISED E-MAIL TO MS. HOLLOWAY

Dear Ms. Holloway:

Do you have any openings in your intern program this winter?

At a recent job fair, your associate Roger Sterling suggested that I write you. I will receive my degree in marketing from Best College this spring, and my résumé is attached.

I will follow up with you in a week or so; in the meantime, I look forward to hearing from you.

Best regards,

Donald Draper

Was the revised message more accessible? How did the tone change? What other changes improved the message?

While most messages take a direct approach, at times you will need to write a message that intentionally takes an indirect approach. For example, you will encounter times when you disagree with someone's point of view or need to convey a disappointing decision. For those occasions, write an indirect message.

Be Indirect for "Bad News"

At times, everyone needs to convey news the reader does not expect or would prefer not to receive. A *bad news message* is one of the few times when an indirect message achieves better results than a direct message. (However, when bad news is personal, avoid putting it in writing; instead, make a phone call or meet with the person. If you must put personal news in writing, send a letter, not an e-mail message.)

In an indirect message, include an explanation and details before stating outcomes or conclusions. By explaining the logic and background details first, you give the reader an opportunity to understand the *why* of the unwelcome decision, for example:

11.2 "BAD NEWS" MESSAGE: INDIRECT AND DIRECT

Charley,

Here's information about your request.

I checked with corporate, and they said they were already over budget for this summer's conference. However, they thought your suggestion to plan in a team-building workshop was excellent, and they will put that on the priority list for next year.

In the meantime, can you find another solution? Let me know what you think.

Best regards,

John

Compare the tone of the message above with the less tactful direct approach in the message below:

Charley,

Your request for a team-building workshop has been denied.

I checked with corporate, and they said they were already over budget for this summer's conference. However, they thought your suggestion to plan in a team-building workshop was excellent, and they will put that on the priority list for next year.

John

Indirect or *Bad News* Message

- Connect with the reader
- State general purpose
- Give supporting details
- State outcome or conclusion
- Close with cordial words (and next steps if they apply)

Next, let us take a look at empty information, which comes in various categories, starting with redundancies and outdated language.

Eliminate Redundant Pairings

Some redundant pairings have been passed on for centuries, such as *various and sundry* and *first and foremost*. Do you even know what *sundry* means? If you list something *first*, isn't it also *foremost*? For the pairings below, which word or words would you cut? To turn this into a learning activity, cover the revised list as you go through the words on the original list.

Original	Revised
and so on and so forth	and so on
any and all	any *or* all
basic and fundamental	basic
each and every	each *or* every
fair and equitable	fair
first and foremost	first
full and complete	complete
if and when	if *or* when
hopes and desires	hopes
hope and trust	trust
issues and concerns	issues
more and more	more
null and void	void
questions and problems	questions
true and accurate	accurate

Also cut unnecessary verb add ons:

Verb add ons	Revised
add up	add
add together	add
advance forward	advance
continue on	continue

combine together	combine
refer back	refer
repeat again	repeat
rise up	rise

Cut Redundant Modifiers

Some words simply do not need to be modified. For example, have you ever wondered about *free gifts*? If gifts are not free, are they still gifts? What about *personal beliefs* and *advance reservations*? Aren't all beliefs personal and all reservations made in advance?

Redundant modifiers come in all shapes and sizes. Once again, cover the revised words as you work through the redundant modifiers.

Original	Revised	Outdated	Revised
absolutely essential	essential	cold temperature	cold
combine together	combine	completely eliminate	eliminate
completely finish	finish	difficult dilemma	dilemma
end result	result	exactly the same	the same
final outcome	outcome	five different groups	five groups
foreign imports	imports	future plans	plans
general public	public	honest truth	truth
new breakthrough	breakthrough	past memories	memories
personal beliefs	beliefs	total of 12 attendees	12 attendees
true facts	facts	unexpected surprise	surprise
very unique	unique	12 noon/12 midnight	noon *or* midnight
100 percent true	true		

Work on Practice 11.1 to gain practice cutting unnecessary words.

Practice 11.1

Cut Redundant Modifiers

Instructions: Edit the following sentences to remove empty information, redundancy, and outdated expressions.

Wordy: Before you finish this step to go on to the next step in the process, please review and examine all the items in your shopping cart.

Revised: Before you go on to the next step, review the items in your shopping cart.

1   We hope and trust that you find our services helpful and worthwhile.

2   Our new breakthrough in design makes our laptop even more perfect than it was before.

3   The final outcome of this project depends on each individual participant doing his or her best.

4   We want you to be absolutely certain that you have not ordered multiple items that are exactly alike.

Note: See pages 421–422 for the key to the above exercise.

Cut Vague Nouns

Do you use vague nouns? Nouns such as *area, factor, manner, situation, topic,* and even *purpose* are often fillers during the composing phase. Remove vague nouns when you edit, for example:

Wordy: My field of study is the area of sociology.
Revised: I am studying sociology.

Wordy: I have found myself in a situation in which I am forced to make a decision.
Revised: I am forced to make a decision.

Wordy: The topic that I have chosen to write about is gender differences.
Revised: Gender differences answer common questions about miscommunication . . .

Wordy:	The purpose of my paper is to explore self-esteem in adolescents.
Revised:	The self-esteem of an adolescent is a critical factor in determining. . .

Can you think of any vague nouns that you use?

Eliminate the Obvious

Isn't *round* a shape and *red* a color? In the list below, cut the obvious.

audible to the ear	of an uncertain condition
brief in duration	period of time
bright in color	rate of speed
consensus of opinion	red in color
dull in appearance	re-elected for another term
extreme in degree	round in shape
filled to capacity	small in size
heavy in weight	soft to the touch
honest in character	visible to the eye

When you find yourself using any of the following phrases, simply delete them and get right to your point:

all things considered	in a manner of speaking
as a matter of fact	in my opinion
as far as I am concerned	my purpose for writing is
for the most part	the point I am trying to make
for the purpose of	what I am trying to say is that
I wish to take this opportunity	what I want to make clear is

Besides stating the obvious, writers often used canned and outdated phrases.

Update Outdated Phrases

Be confident about your writing and stop using outdated phrases, even if someone you respect still uses them. For example, writing experts have considered "thank you in advance" outdated for at least **30** years now.

Once again, to turn this into a learning activity, cover the right column that shows current use as you work through the outdated column.

Outdated	**Current**
attached please find	attached is
as per our discussion	as we discussed
as per your request	as you requested
at all times	always
at the present time	now, today
at your earliest convenience	give a specific date
attached please find	attached is
due to the fact that	because
during the time that	while
gave a report to the effect	reported
gave assistance to	helped
in the event that	if
in a situation in which	when
in almost every instance	usually
in the near future	soon
in receipt of	*Thank you for* . . .
in reference to	about
is of the opinion that	believes
I wish to thank you	do not wish *and* thank
may I suggest	do not ask permission
prior to	before
subsequent to	after
sufficient number of	enough
thank you in advance	thank you

thank you again	one *thank you* is sufficient
the manner in which	how
this day and age	today
with regard to	about *or* concerning

Practice 11.2

Remove Redundancy and Outdated Expressions

Instructions: Edit the following sentences.

> **Wordy:**   In the event that you hear from George, give him the news.
>
> **Revised:**   If you hear from George, give him the news.

1. Attached please find the papers that you requested.

2. You have our complete and absolute confidence, and we appreciate and value our client relationship.

3. As per our discussion, the new policy should be received and reviewed this week.

4. You can completely eliminate any questions or problems by sending your agenda early in advance of the meeting.

5. I would like to thank you in advance for your cooperation, support, and assistance.

Note: See page 422 for the key to the above exercise.

Avoid Legalese

Today even attorneys avoid using the following terms:

Legalese	Revised
as stated heretofore	as stated
aforementioned	as mentioned
concerning the matter of	concerning
enclosed herewith please find	enclosed is

enclosed herein	enclosed is
notwithstanding	without
pursuant to	regarding
the writer/the undersigned	use *I* or *me*
until such time as	until

People who use outdated phrases do so out of habit; canned language does not engage the reader:

If you wouldn't say it that way, don't write it that way.

Use Simple Language

Some people think that using complicated words makes them sound smart. However, savvy writers choose simple words. As Albert Einstein suggested, "Make the [. . .] basic elements as simple and as few as possible."[1]

Outdated	Revised	Outdated	Revised
apprise	inform	is desirous of	wants
ascertain	find out	methodology	method
cognizant of	aware of	prior to	before
contingent upon	dependent on	render assistance	assist
deem	think	referred to as	called
endeavor	try	termination	end
facilitate	help	transpire	happen
implement	start, begin	transmit	send
initiate	begin	utilization	use

For example:

Instead of saying:	**Say this:**
We *utilize* that vendor.	We *use* that vendor.
I am *cognizant of* the change.	I am *aware* of the change.
We *endeavor* to be the best.	We *try* to be the best.
Prior to working at Pew Research . . .	*Before* working at Pew Research . . .

Complete Practice 11.3 to revise sentences applying this principle.

Practice 11.3

Use Simple Language

Instructions: Simplify the following sentences.

Weak: What transpired subsequent to their involvement?

Revised: What happened after they became involved?

1. We are utilizing that product, and the field supervisor is cognizant of our choice.

2. Subsequent to the change in policy, we have endeavored to compromise as much as possible.

3. As per your request, an omission of that information is being made.

4. If the merger is contingent upon our utilization of their facilities, we should change locations.

5. If you are cognizant of their objections, endeavor to make respective changes.

   Note: See page 422 for the key to the above exercise.

Modify Sparingly

For academic and professional writing, use modifiers sparingly. Even Stephen King, the prolific fiction writer, compares adverbs to dandelions and has a *no adverb rule*.

Two types of modifiers that commonly creep into writing are **hedges** and **emphatics**. A hedge qualifies a statement; an emphatic "supposedly" places emphasis on the word it describes. Use hedges and emphatics sparingly: getting rid of hedges and emphatics will make your point stand out. Here are some common hedges to avoid:

at times	kind of	perhaps	rather
sometimes	sort of	possibly	in my opinion
rarely	may be	more or less	tend
hardly	maybe	usually	for all intents and purposes
almost always	seemingly	supposedly	to a certain extent

Here is a sampling of common emphatics; use them sparingly or they will detract from the meaning:

very	virtually	as you know	literally
most	usually	always	as you can see
many	certainly	totally	each and every time
often	inevitably	it is quite clear that	

Example using hedges and emphatics:

As you may already know, trust is best established from the beginning and, *in my opinion*, difficult to regain once breached. Assume that *each and every* communication *may* have the potential to build *some kind of* trust and also has the potential to *totally* destroy trust.

Without the hedges and emphatics, here is the short paragraph:

Trust is best established from the beginning and difficult to regain once breached. Always assume that every communication has the potential to build trust as well as destroy trust.

Practice 11.4

Modify Sparingly

Instructions: Remove unnecessary modifiers from the sentences below.

    Wordy: First and foremost, editing is the kind of skill that is important to develop.

    Revised: Editing is an important skill.

1   In my opinion, you should feel really certain what the true facts are before you sign the contract.

2   Can you confirm that it is totally true that they might possibly back out of their agreement?

3   I would kind of like for you to speak to the person who really knows a lot about this topic, literally.

    Note: See page 422 for the key to the above exercise.

Edit Out Background Thinking

Background thinking is different from explaining an issue or giving evidence to support a point. Learn to identify the difference between your own background thinking and key information that makes a point.

As you compose your message, you may go down many different lines of thought to get to your main point. All or most of the details leading up to your main point could be background thinking. As you read the following, identify information to cut.

> After we spoke, I continued to think about the situation in which we find ourselves. Not that long ago, the economy was strong and we had an abundance of contributions coming in. The tax laws were also in our favor, encouraging wealthy constituents to make hearty contributions that were tax deductible. Now, with the sudden change in the economy and the changes in tax laws, we are faced with uncertainty—many of our contributors will be tightening their belts, and our clients will suffer from a lack of services and resources. Here's my point: we can sit back and hope that things get better or we can look for new, innovative ways to raise funds. Let's seek input from our staff and major donors to see what suggestions they come up with. What do you think?

Practice 11.5

Edit Out Background Thinking

Instructions: Write your revision in the space provided below.

_____

_____

_____

    Note: See page 423 for the key to the above example.

Leave Out Opinions and Beliefs

Though you may find that writing about your opinions helps you get to your key points, opinions are usually not relevant once you find your key point. If you find yourself rambling off the point, that is an indication to start cutting.

Be cautious when using phrases such as *I believe, I think,* and *I feel.* These types of phrases make you sound less sure of yourself; so unless you use these phrases as you give advice to a colleague, they are simply *I statements* that merit deletion. Also, do not tell your reader *how* to interpret your message; these added comments may give the reader the impression that you are unsure of your message or that you lack confidence. Remove phrases or sentences that tell your readers *how you think* they will react.

As you read the following example, identify and cut opinions and beliefs.

> I'm not sure if you are going to like this idea, but I've been thinking about this for a few weeks now, tossing over the pros and cons. In fact, one of our guys in the field mentioned it to me, and I was surprised that he was thinking about it too. But if this is just another message suggesting something you are already thinking about or have decided won't work, sorry that I wasted your time.
>
> I am suggesting that we cut our annual conference by one day this year. Generally our productivity goes down by the last day, and we could save about 20 percent of our costs and probably accomplish just as much in the shorter time frame. Let me know what you think.

Practice 11.6

Leave Out Opinions and Beliefs

Instructions: Write your revision in the space provided below.

_____

_____

_____

Note: See page 423 for the key to the above example.

Recap

When making decisions about conciseness, apply Ockham's Razor: the simplest version is usually the best.

- Put purpose first, and you will have a clear idea of what to cut.

- Edit out background thinking, opinions, and beliefs

- Modify sparingly: cut hedges and emphatics.

- Be direct and say what you mean: *If you wouldn't say it that way, don't write it that way.*

As Robert Browning wrote, *less is more.*[2]

Writing Workshop

Editing Practice: Less Is More

Instructions: Select two or three pieces of your writing. Identify information that you could cut, such as the following:

- Redundant pairings (including redundant subjects and verbs)

- Vague nouns

- Hedges and emphatics

- Background thinking and opinions

- *I think, I believe, I feel* statements

If time permits, exchange papers with a colleague: is it easier to find information to cut in someone else's writing?

References

1   Einstein, A. (1934). On the method of theoretical physics. *Philosophy of Science*, 1, 163–169.

2   Browning, R. (1855) "Andrea del Sarto," also called "The Faultless Painter."

Formatting

Formatting is an element of voice that speaks to your audience *at a glance*. In academic and professional writing, formatting is an essential element that affects the credibility of a document.

Each piece of writing that you produce—whether an e-mail message or an academic paper—has formatting guidelines and protocol; when you follow those guidelines, you develop an immediate connection with your audience. In contrast, if you neglect to format a document for purpose and audience, you may be spending extraordinary efforts to craft your message while missing the obvious.

When done well, formatting also becomes a form of *visual persuasion*. For example, when you format a paper in APA or ASA style, the reader can see instantly whether you have taken the time to learn formatting basics. Documents that are not formatted correctly give the impression that the writer either did not know how to format or simply did not care. And well-formatted documents do more than present a credible, professional image: formatting gives visual cues to aid the reader in understanding the content.

As you develop expert formatting skills, formatting will become an element of your writing style. Formatting tools include the use of headings, bullets and numbering, font, color, bold, and italics. However, the most important element may be the unused portions of the page, or **w**hite space. To present an effective finished product, all elements must work together harmoniously.

When you have completed this chapter, you will be able to:

- Use elements of formatting to create visual cues for the reader.

- Understand how formatting affects the reader's expectations and understanding.

- Format business documents, such as letters and e-mail messages, professionally.

- Use special features such as font, color, bold, and italics, as appropriate.

- Structure agendas and minutes.

By developing expert formatting skills, adapting your writing for purpose and audience will become part of your editing routine.

> *Note*: The formatting guidelines presented here for APA and ASA are requirements for manuscript publication. Since your professors might have different requirements, always check with individual professors to make sure that you are adapting your formatting for your specific audience.

Special Features and White Space

To achieve rapport between your reader and your document, break your message into manageable chunks. Position your text so that it is well-balanced on the page, and display key ideas prominently. Such visual cues allow your reader to scan the document and understand its meaning before actually reading it. Here are the topics discussed in this section:

- Displaying key ideas with bullet points or numbering.

- Organizing a topic by using headings and subheadings.

- Incorporating special features such as bold and italics.

- Setting off explanations or descriptive information with parentheses.

- Selecting fonts for ease of reading or to fulfill requirements, such as APA or ASA style.

- Following official guidelines for white space.

In addition to following official formatting guidelines, another way of adding white space is to break information into readable chunks. For example, just as a sentence is more readable under 25 words, a paragraph is easier to read when it does not appear too lengthy. Though you covered paragraphing extensively in Chapter 7, "Cohesive Paragraphs and Transitions," here are informal guidelines for paragraph length to support *reader-friendly* writing:

- For papers, keep your paragraphs to about eight lines in length or less.

- For letters, consider limiting paragraph length to six lines.

- For e-mail, keep your paragraphs to four lines or fewer. With e-mail, getting right to the point is critical, so messages are often short. As a result, even individual sentences can effectively be set off as paragraphs.

As you learn official guidelines for using formatting features and white space, you will perceive documents differently: you will develop a trained eye, an expertise for formatting documents so that they look balanced and professional, adding to their credibility.

Bullet Points and Numbering

Though you would rarely, if ever, use a bulleted list in an APA or ASA document, you will use bullet points and numbered lists in other types of writing. For example, bullet points and numbering are strong visual cues, working well in e-mail messages, letters, and proposals. They not only make key points instantly visible for your reader but also organize and prioritize your key points.

- To highlight key points or list items of equal importance, use bullets.

- For instructions or lists that contain a specific order of actions or priority, use numbers.

For bullets or numbered items, you have a variety of different styles from which to choose. Stay consistent with the bullet or numbering style throughout your document, and shift from one style to another only if you have a special purpose for changing styles. For example, use a larger bullet for major points and a smaller bullet for minor points.

Display bullet points in **parallel structure**: noun for noun, verb for verb, phrase for phrase. For example, if you start with an active verb, start every item in the list with an active verb in the same tense. See Chapter 9, "Parallel Structure," for information about creating bulleted lists that are grammatically consistent.

Have you ever written an e-mail message that included three or four questions; but when you received your response, only two questions were answered? By numbering questions in an e-mail, you make it easier for your reader to respond to all of your questions. By making your key ideas instantly visible, you aid the reader in responding to your requests, which helps you get your job done.

If you present your information in complete sentences or short phrases, you can end your bulleted or numbered points with a period. Experiment with using bullets and numbering until you feel comfortable using them.

Formatting Features and Marks

Formatting features include **bold**, <u>underline</u>, and *italics*; special marks include parentheses and quotation marks. These special features are used selectively in APA and ASA styles, so do not use them for academic papers unless you have checked to make sure that your usage is correct.

You probably understand not to use all capitals (all caps) to stress words or phrases, as all capitals connote shouting. Instead, use bold or italics to stress words, as explained below:

- *Bold:* For professional writing (but not academic writing), put words or key ideas in boldface type to make them stand out. For APA style, the only time that you would use boldface font would be for heading levels 1 through 4.

- *Brackets:* For APA and ASA styles, enclose material in brackets that is inserted in a quotation by a person other than the original writer; also use brackets to enclose parenthetical material that is already within parentheses.

- *Italics:*

    o   For APA style, use italics for heading levels 4 and 5.

    o   For ASA style, use italics to stress words, but sparingly.

    o   For APA and ASA styles, italicize freestanding works such as the titles of books, periodicals, movies, radio and TV show names, and other formally published material.[1] (Articles, chapters, and shorter words are enclosed in quotation marks.)

    o   For general use, use italics to stress words and give definitions.

- o   For all writing, use italics for uncommon foreign terms. (Common Latin abbreviations, such as i.e., et al., etc., and so on do not need to be italicized.)

- *Quotation marks:* Enclose direct quotes and technical terms presented for the first time in quotation marks. For academic papers, use quotations selectively (and rarely).

- *Parentheses:* Put parentheses around information that gives a brief explanation or that does not directly relate to your topic. Also put parentheses around a paraphrase or an abbreviation that follows a definition.

- *All capital letters (all caps):* Follow traditional capitalization guidelines; do *not* use all capital letters to make words stand out.

- *Underline:* When you are using a typewriter or writing by hand, stress keywords by underlining them. When you are using a computer, use italics or bold for stress, and do not use underlining.

Within a document, be consistent in the way that you display these features and marks.

e-Etiquette

Sometimes, especially in e-messages, writers think they are making an idea stand out by using all capitals. Instead, readers may infer that the writer is shouting at them. To stress a word or phrase in any document, including e-mail, use bold *or* italics (but not all capital letters). In fact, when writing online, do not use the underline feature to make words stand out: for online writing, an underline implies a hyperlink.

Many writers also think that putting a word between quotation marks makes the idea stand out (such as, *It's a really "good" idea*). Instead, when quotation marks are used for no valid reason, readers think that the writer is implying the *opposite* of what the word actually means. Be careful: Do not use quotation marks unless you are certain about how you are using them.

Use quotation marks to:

- Enclose a direct quote of fewer than 40 words within the body of a document.

- Identify technical terms, business jargon, or coined expressions which may be unfamiliar.

- Use words humorously or ironically (if you think your reader will miss the humor).

- Show a slang expression, poor grammar, or an intentionally misspelled word.

Use italics to:

- Refer to a word as a word; for example:

The word *listen* has many shades of meaning.

- Emphasize a word, phrase, or entire sentence.

- Display uncommon foreign terms (such as *merci, grazie, dobra, domo arigato*); different institutions' styles vary on more common Latin abbreviations (such as *i.e.* and *e.g.*).

- Display book titles.

Use parentheses to:

- Include a brief explanation within a sentence.

- Insert a sentence that does not directly relate to the topic of your paragraph.

- Supply abbreviations or acronyms following a definition.

Using parentheses tells the reader that the information relates to the broader topic without going into detail of how or why. Thus, you can sometimes avoid writing a lengthy explanation by enclosing a few words in parentheses.

Font, Point, and Color

Though numerous font styles exist, they all fall into two basic types: *serif* fonts and *sans-serif* (or *non-serif*) fonts.

- **Serif fonts**, such as Times New Roman, have "fancy edges" (the edges of letters end in short lines, or serifs, creating a sharp or pointed look). For professional writing, hard-copy documents are most often printed in serif

12.1 LATIN TERMS FOR ACADEMIC WRITING

Traditionally, Latin terms have played a major role in academic writing and citation systems. In general, Latin terms are italicized because they are part of a foreign language; however, italicizing common Latin terms in academic writing is no longer required.

For your reference, here are a few commonly used Latin terms:

cf.	*confer*	compare to
e.g.	*exempli gracia*	for example, for instance
et al.	*et allii*	and others

When listing only one author for a work with multiple authors, use *et al.* to indicate other names were omitted.

etc.	*et cetera*	and the others; and other things
ibid.	*ibidem*	in the same place

In older articles, when citing the same source consecutively, *ibid.* was written directly under the citation which gave the author's name (or other identifying information).

i.e.	*id est*	that is; in other words
[sic]		so, thus, in this manner

The term *sic* is placed within brackets to indicate that the error that occurs in a text was made by the original author, not the current writer. (Brackets [ ] are also used around words or letters added to another's quotation.)

viz.	*videlicet*	namely, that is (that is to say), as follows

Avoid using Latin abbreviations in professional writing. In fact, using a term such as *among others* instead of the Latin abbreviation *etc.* gives writing a smoother, reader-friendly style.

fonts, such as Times New Roman. (Note that APA recommends documents be submitted in Times New Roman, size 12 or Courier, size 12.)[2]

- **Sans-serif fonts,** such as Arial and Calibri, have crisp edges with no serifs at the ends and work well when viewing print on a computer screen. Therefore, use sans-serif fonts for e-mail messages, blogs, or web development. (Note that ASA recommends documents be submitted in Arial, size 12.)

Similarly to academic writing, professional writing follows conservative standards. The traditional color for print and e-mail messages is black. However, for e-mail, some professionals use blue. Colors other than blue or black may be considered unprofessional; entrants into the workforce should be aware of possible critics before being too creative with font color and size. To avoid criticism, use accents of color conservatively. Also consider the following:

- Limit font types to two per document so that your work does not appear cluttered.

- For ASA citation style, use a font such as Arial, size 12, throughout your entire paper, including your title page.

- For APA citation style, use a font such as Times New Roman (or Courier), size 12, throughout your entire paper.

For some documents, if you know that your reader has visual difficulty, increase the font size; you may also use the bold feature to make the message especially clear.

White Space and Balance

The term **white space** refers to the unused areas of your document, such as top and side margins and spacing between lines. White space controls the way your document looks *at a glance*.

White space gives your readers' eyes a place to rest and delineates the various parts of your document, providing readers with a place to make notes and comments. Official guidelines in various published style guides, such as APA, ASA, and other reference manuals, dictate a range of minimum to maximum spacing to leave between parts. After you learn guidelines for spacing, some of which are reviewed in the following pages, you will develop a trained eye for document placement—*only then should you vary from guidelines.* Before you consider any document complete, ask the following:

- Does this document look balanced, appealing, and professional?

- Does the document look as if it has a *picture frame* of white space?

Manual Spacing versus Automatic Spacing

Most documents in this chapter show *manual spacing guidelines.* However, for manual guidelines to work, **paragraph controls** must be set at **0**. Otherwise, you will leave extra white space automatically each time that you hit *enter*, and your document may look unprofessional and thus unappealing.

> *Note*: The instructions listed here and on the following pages are for Microsoft Word; if you use a different software program, research how to achieve the base settings discussed here using your software.

Until you have a trained eye for vertical spacing, use manual spacing guidelines for business letters (see page 270). Set controls correctly for each document, starting with basic settings:

- For most documents, set margins for 1-inch default margins top, bottom, and sides. Go to the **Page Layout** tab: click on **Margins** and select **Normal.** (For ASA style, set margins at 1.25 inches.)

- Set paragraph spacing at **0 pt** for **Before** and **After** (see Figure 12.1, page 265).

- For business letters and APA style, use a serif font such as Times New Roman, size 12. For ASA style, use a sans-serif font, such as Arial, size 12.

- For most documents, including APA and ASA, select **Align Text Left**, leaving right margins uneven; in other words, do *not* justify right margins by selecting Align Right.

To see if you need to make any spacing adjustments on your document *before* you print it, click on **Print**; on the right side of the screen, you will see a preview of your document.

Until you have expert skills, follow these guidelines closely.

12.2   SPACING CHART

For documents that are single-spaced, manually space down twice
(↓ 2) between most parts of your document.

When you space down twice, you *double space*, which leaves one
blank line. When you space down three times, you leave two blank
lines:

Single spacing	Double spacing	↓ 2	Triple spacing ↓ 3
Single spacing	x *(one blank line)*		x
Single spacing	Double spacing		x
Single spacing	x		Triple spacing
Single spacing	Double spacing		

- Start counting at the end of a line—each time that you hit **enter**
  counts.

- Make sure that your **paragraph settings** are correct—see the next
  section.

Paragraph Settings

For spacing guidelines to be effective, *paragraph controls must be set correctly.*
For Microsoft Word, adjust paragraph controls for each document you create:

1 Go to the **Home** tab.

2 Open the **Paragraph** tab by clicking on the arrow.

3 At the **Indents and Spacing** tab, find **Spacing**.

4 Set **Before** and **After** at **0 pt**.

5 For APA and ASA formatting, set **Line spacing** at **Double.**

6 To set tab stops for the *body* of an APA or ASA paper, under **Special**,
   select **First line**; then set **By** at **0.5 inches**.

   Note: For the tab stop on the *reference page*, under **Special** select
   Hanging, 0.5 inches.

7 To make settings the default, click **Set as Default**, located left of **OK**.

8   Click **OK** so that you are back at the **Home** tab.

9   For APA style, set font at Times New Roman (or similar), 12 points, and margins at 1 inch on all sides.

10 For ASA style, set font at Arial (or similar), 12 points, and margins at 1.25 inches on all sides.

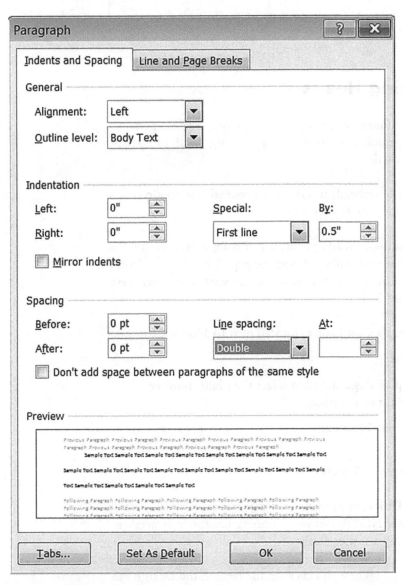

Figure 12.1 Setting Controls Step by Step

In short:

1   Home → Paragraph → Spacing → Before and After → 0 pt

2   Home → Paragraph → Line spacing → Single (*or Double for APA and ASA*) → Default → OK

3   Home → Times New Roman, Size 12

4   Page layout → Margins → Normal (for APA, 1 inch on all sides; for ASA, 1.25" on all sides)

Creating Running Heads

At times, you will use a running head, such as when you create a personal letterhead for your job-search documents or a running head for papers formatted in APA or ASA style.

To create a personalized letterhead, insert your personal information in a style of your own design into the header.

For APA and ASA formatting, creating a header is complicated because it involves multiple pages that are numbered, and the page 1 header is different from second page headers. Set up the header when you start your paper; here is one way to do it in Word 2010:

1   On the Word toolbar, click on **Insert** (located next to **Home** tab).

2   Click on **Page Number**.

3   Select the option **Top of Page** and then select the **plain number** option at the upper right of the page.

4   Check the box **Different First Page**—*this is key to setting up running heads correctly.*

5   Set **Header from Top** at **0.5 inches**.

When you check the box **Different First Page**, if the page number disappears, repeat steps **2** and **3** above. Next put in your running head, which needs to be at the left margin. Here's another method:

1   Click on your "header." (When you click on the header, the **Design** tab will open.)

2   At the **Design** tab, check the box **Different First Page**.

3   Insert the page number at the upper right margin.

4   Move your cursor to the left of the page number, and add your page 1 heading (for APA, "Running head:"; for ASA, "Running Head ="; follow with your title in all capital letters).

5   Leave your cursor after your title: to move your heading to the left margin, hit "tab" until it is at the left margin (or add spaces between your title and the page number).

6   Repeat this process on page 2, putting in the heading for second pages.

For APA style, make sure that the font for your running head and page number are both set at Times New Roman (or similar), size 12; for ASA style, Arial (or similar), size 12.

E-Mail Messages

Most professionals write e-mail messages daily. One purpose of written communication, whether with one or your professors or a colleague on the job, is to build relationships based on respect. By shaping your message effectively, you set a professional tone. Here are some points to consider.

Use a **greeting.** Greetings personalize messages and engage the reader.

- When you write to one person, use the person's name followed by a comma; if you wish, also use *Hi* or *Hello*.

- For formal messages, use the recipient's name and title. For example, if you are writing to a professor, use your professor's name: "Hi Professor Smith." (If a message is highly formal, use *Dear*.)

- When you write to several people, use a greeting such as *Hello team*, *Hi everyone*, or *Good day*.

When you expect recipients to take action based on information in your message, list their names in the *To* section, not the *Cc* section.

- Reserve Cc use for when you copy a message to someone but do not expect the recipient to take action.

- With messages that you are forwarding, add a note at the top of the message stating expected action from recipients.

Use an accurate **subject line** and update it as needed.

- As your conversation evolves, update the subject line to reflect new information.

- Include due dates in the subject line to alert the reader to needed action.

- Keep the message to about one screen in length; if your message is long and detailed, also consider phoning.

- Though e-mail may be a convenient way to communicate, consider other channels when communication becomes complicated or relationships become strained.

Use a simple **closing**. An e-mail is not as formal as a business letter, so you can use an informal closing such as the following:

Best regards,	All the best,
Enjoy your day.	Take care.

Reserve the formal closing *Sincerely* for business letters. For professional messages, include a sign-off that lists your company name, address, phone number, and other relevant contact information.

Business Letters

At times, you will need to send a formal business letter. When you do, it is critical to get the formatting correct. For most letters, use 1-inch default margins. For short or long letters, add or delete vertical space before the dateline, between the date and address, and between the closing and the signature line. In addition, apply the following standards, and your letter will be professionally formatted:

- *Letterhead.* For a company, a letterhead contains the name, address, phone number, fax number, web address, and company logo. For personal letters, including job-search documents, you could design your own letterhead with contact information.

- *Dateline.* The date appears at least three lines below the letterhead and no more than 2.5 inches from the top of the page.

- *Inside Address.* The inside address contains the name of the recipient, his or her title, the company name and address. Within the US, use two-letter state abbreviations; however, avoid using other types of abbreviations in addresses: spell out words such as "east," "street," and so on.

- *Salutation.* Use the recipient's last name *or* first name in the greeting:

  Dear Mr. Jones: (formal) or *Dear George:* (familiar).

Follow the salutation with a colon, *not* a comma (and never a semicolon). When you are unsure of the recipient's gender, use first and last names:

  Dear Pat Jones:

- *Body.* Single space; block paragraphs at the left (do not indent); leave one blank line between paragraphs; break paragraphs into *intro, body,* and *conclusion.*

- *Closing.* Use the standard closing *sincerely;* use less formal closings for e-mail.

- *Writer's Signature Block.* Type your name along with your title, when used.

- *Reference Initials.* Indicate a typist's initials, *if different from the writer.*

- *Enclosure Notation.* Use this notation to alert the recipient (and remind the writer) that something is enclosed with the letter.

- *Delivery Notation.* Use this notation to indicate that a letter was sent in a special way, such as UPS, FedEx, Express, and so on.

- *Copy Notation.* Include a *cc* notation (courtesy copy) to indicate to whom copies of the letter are being sent.

- *Postscript.* Though a postscript is considered an afterthought, presenting information in a postscript actually makes it stand out. Represent a postscript with or without periods and with or without a colon; however, use capital letters (PS, P.S., or PS:).

Blocked Letter Format

Before starting, set your paragraph controls on single spacing and 0 for "before" and "after." All lines are blocked at the left, producing a clean, uncluttered style. (Leave the right margin ragged.)

Figure 12.2 Blocked Letter Format

Sociology Network
2300 North Lake Shore Drive
Chicago, IL 60610
312-555-5555 / socwebsite.com   ↓ 3+

August 3, 2018   ↓ 4 or 5 after date

Ms. Margo Mead
Anthropology International
333 West Samoa Drive
Chicago, IL 60610   ↓ 2

Dear Ms. Mead: ↓ 2

In the introductory paragraph, state your main purpose; keep the paragraph short.

In the body, include details and examples. Use a conservative font, such as Times New Roman set at 12 points. Adjust the spacing and margins to give your letter balance. Use closed punctuation style: place a colon after the salutation and a comma after the complimentary closing.

In the last paragraph define *action needed* or next steps. Also invite the reader to contact you, if needed.   ↓ 2 before the closing

Sincerely,   ↓ 3 to 5 after closing

Bob Allison
Instructional Designer   ↓ 2 before notations

djy

Enclosure
By UPS
cc Michael Jones

PS Before you print your letter, use the *print preview function* to make sure that margins are balanced, creating a "picture frame" effect.

Agendas and Minutes

Agendas and minutes of meetings are important to sociologists for two reasons:

- Sociologists lead teams and projects and are also members of teams; when decisions are made, it is important to keep track of who did what and when.

- Sociologists do research. At times, sociologists can find valuable information—historical and current—in the minutes of groups and organizations.

Agendas and minutes are used for all types of meetings, from the most informal and casual to the most formal. An agenda is a list of topics to discuss at a meeting; minutes are a written record of what transpired. The two go together: the agenda presents the framework for the minutes.

Agendas and minutes engage participants, keeping them informed and recording progress. For example, without a written record, the same topic could be discussed, decided upon, and then readdressed at the next meeting by those who didn't agree with the decision. Keeping a record of decisions—especially controversial ones—brings closure to issues and establishes a history. In addition, an agenda keeps groups focused. An agenda can include all of the following information:

- The name of the organization (which could be a company, team, department, professional association, or a branch of the government—county, state, or federal).

- The meeting purpose and date.

- The location (if it varies from meeting to meeting).

- A list of those who are expected to attend.

- Objectives of the meeting or what the group expects to accomplish.

If you are a team leader who is creating an agenda, seek input from your group. The items to be discussed could be enumerated or listed as bullet points. If a particular item will be presented by an individual, that person's name could be listed next to the topic. Make sure participants have an agenda a day or two in advance of a meeting so that participants can add to the topics; in the meeting, they can follow along to ensure the meeting stays on track, checking off items as they are discussed. Agendas function as much as "thinking tools" as they do as time management tools.

During and after the meeting, a designated note-taker (someone other than the leader) can use the original agenda to fill in important points and the names of significant contributors. This information can be used to write up the minutes of the meeting.

For formal meetings, minutes are a *legal record* of what transpired at the meeting. Most groups assign a secretary to take the minutes. Minutes are distributed no later than the beginning of the next meeting, but preferably in advance so that members have time to read and check the minutes before the next meeting. The first item of business would be reading of the minutes (either silently or out loud) to identify corrections. Once all corrections are noted, minutes can be officially approved; some minutes become part of the public record. For example, if it were a monthly meeting of the local board of health, the minutes are available for residents to examine to see specific decisions made at the meeting. Public organizations are required by law to provide copies of minutes upon request within specific times.

Most agendas, and thus also minutes, end with *new business*. New business relates to ideas and issues brought up for the first time during the meeting. If time permits, the new business can either be discussed or tabled to become an agenda item for the next meeting.

If you are leading a formal group, you may consider adopting *Robert's Rules of Order*, which outlines parliamentary procedures for meetings and has been considered the standard for conducting meetings since it was originally published in 1876.[3]

Agendas can be formally presented or simply be an informal list of topics to discuss; individual groups define their own tone and requirements.

Think of a group you meet with regularly—does your group use an agenda? If not, would your group benefit from using one?

Figure 12.3 Sample Agenda and Sample Minutes

COMMUNITY SERVICE ASSIGNMENTS

Date: Jul 3, 2018

Place: Selma Charleston's office

Time: 3:30 p.m. to 4:30 p.m.

Coordinator: Selma

Group Leaders: Bill, Alexis, Devona, Walter, Caren, Rashid, Selma

AGENDA

1	Review minutes from last meeting and make corrections.	5 minutes
2	Introduction to Community Service Concepts.	15 minutes
3	What resources do we have to draw upon?	10 minutes
4	Establish assignment parameters.	5 minutes
5	Assign group projects.	5 minutes
6	Start developing survey, "How Do I Choose a Charity?"	10 minutes
7	New business?	5 minutes

ENVIRONMENTAL COUNCIL
BOARD OF DIRECTORS MEETING
November 22, 2018

MINUTES

The Environmental Council Board of Directors meeting was called to order by President Jack Miller at 1 p.m. at the Environmental Council offices. Present were board members President Jack Miller, Vice President Susan Vance, Secretary Jeannette Nelson, Treasurer Bob Michaels, John Maier, Michael Moor, Deborah Kerr, Elizabeth Taylor, and Robert Redford.

The July 18 minutes were presented. John Maier moved to adopt the minutes and Robert Redford seconded the motion. The March minutes were adopted as presented.

Treasurer's Report. Bob Michaels reported that nothing was out of the ordinary. Elizabeth passed out a summary of the grants. Direct mail exceeds budgeted amounts; we received $12,000 as a result of a promotion letter.

Figure 12.3 Continued

Michael Moor motioned to accept the Treasurer's Report; Jeanette Nelson seconded the motion. The motion was unanimously adopted.

Committee Reports. Deborah Kerr reported that the salary system was implemented at the end of March. We are now sending out 10 to 11 people; the base salary helps in hiring and retaining canvassers and improves job satisfaction. Their current focus is on the ground water rule; they have generated 150 letters. Susan agreed to follow up to ensure that canvassers achieve their goals.

Robert Redford moved to extend the salary structure though this year. John Maier seconded and the motion was unanimously adopted.

Development Committee Report. John and Michael reported on the spring campaign. We are purchasing new fundraising software. John will update the board on the software at the next meeting.

Robert Redford motioned to adjourn the meeting; Susan Vance seconded the motion; all were in agreement and the meeting was adjourned at 2:20 p.m.

Recap

Here are some of the points stressed in this chapter:

- Remember that formatting is a form of *visual persuasion*: by meeting formatting expectations, you create an instant rapport between you and your reader.

- Apply official guidelines for documents, leaving an appropriate amount of white space between each part.

- Structure business letters so that you include an *intro*, a *body*, and a *conclusion*, even when you write short letters.

- Adjust your computer settings so that spacing guidelines work.

- Create a header for documents that you format in APA and ASA styles; also create a header when you design your own letterhead for personal business documents.

- Use the **Print Preview** option to make sure your business letters look balanced on the page and have a picture-framed effect.

As you experiment with these tools to enhance the visual appeal of your documents, you will become more confident and use them with ease.

Writing Workshop

Formatting Practice

Instructions: Take out a paper that you have written, and format it in APA or ASA style, whichever your professor requires. If you originally formatted your paper in APA or ASA style, can you see corrections that you need to make?

12.3   APA CHECKLIST

Below is a checklist for basic formatting elements for APA style.

Have you checked your paper for the following?

Settings

- Set margins at 1 inch for all sides
- Use double spacing throughout document, including title and reference pages
- Set paragraph controls at 0 point (zero) for spacing **Before** and **After**
- Set paragraph indentation at 0.5 inches
- Use Times New Roman font, 12 point (or another serif font, such as Courier)

Running Head

- Page 1 running head: "Running head: TITLE IN 50 CHARACTERS OR LESS"

  Note: "Running head" is followed by a colon and "head" is *not* capitalized.

- Running head on following pages: title only in all capital letters at left margin
- On all pages, *including title page*, include page number in upper right corner

Note: See pages 266–267 for details about creating a running head so that page 1 is different from the second pages.

Continued . . .

cont. **Title Page**

- Center title and byline on the upper half of title page; 12 or fewer words for title

- Use Times New Roman font (or similar), size 12, *not* in boldface

- Include other information your professor may require

Abstract

- Develop a synopsis of your paper in one paragraph between 150 and 250 words

- Block first line (and all lines) at left margin; *no paragraph indentation*

- Include a keyword summary after the abstract, indenting and italicizing "Keywords" (*Keywords*: keywords follow . . .)

Body

- Present section titles differently from headings: do *not* put them in boldface type; section titles include title, abstract, reference page

- Start the introduction on page 3, using the title of your paper as the title of the introduction

- Present heading levels 1, 2, 3, and 4 in **boldface** font

- Space two times after a period

- Use "Align Left" (right margin should appear uneven)

- Indent paragraphs 0.5 inches

- Integrate short visuals (tables, graphs, or charts) within the text of your paper

- Place large visuals on separate pages at the end of your paper or in an appendix

In-Text Citations

- Use the author's last name (surname) and year of publication:

  Jones (2010) found that at-risk youth were more likely to . . .

  At-risk youth were likely to have issues with self-esteem (Jones, 2010).

  In 2010, Jones' study of at risk youth showed that . . .

- In subsequent references within the same paragraph, the date is not necessary

- When a work has *two* authors, cite both names each time they are referenced:

  Jones and Smithe (2011) found that among children who . . .

- When a work has *three*, *four*, or *five* authors, cite all of them the first time; in subsequent references, use only the surname of the first author followed by *et al.*:

Continued . . .

cont. Jones *et al.* (2011) demonstrated that more than one study . . .

- For quotations longer than 40 words, double space and indent left margin 0.5 inches; do not use quotation marks; put period before the citation

- For short quotations, place the reference inside the period:

  "Additional studies are needed to fill the gap" (Jones, 2010, p. 33).

Reference Page

- List references in alphabetical order. Do not change the order of authors within the original document cited; for example, the lead author is listed first.

- Use last name and first initial (no first names)

- For books: author's last name and initials, publication date, title of work, and publication data:

  Jones, S., & Barker, D. (2012). *Title*. City, ST: Publisher.

- Block the first line of each reference at the left margin

- Indent second lines of references 0.5 inches (hanging indentation)

- Capitalize only the first word of book titles, the first word after a colon (subtitle), and proper nouns or proper adjectives

- Type the title of a book in *sentence case*, the title of an article in *sentence case*, and the title of a journal in *title case*

- Italicize the title of a book and the title of a journal and its volume number

12.4 ASA CHECKLIST

Below is a checklist for basic formatting elements for ASA style.

Have you checked your paper for the following?

Settings

- Set margins at 1.25 inches for all sides

- Use double spacing throughout document, including title and reference pages

- Set paragraph controls at 0 point (zero) for spacing **Before** and **After**

- Set paragraph indentation at 0.5 inches

- Use a font such as Arial, 12 points

Continued . . .

cont.   **Running Head**

- Page 1 running head: "Running Head = TITLE IN 50 CHARACTERS OR LESS"

- Running head on second pages: Title only in all capital letters at left margin

- On all pages, *including title page*, include page number in upper right corner

  Note: See pages 266–267 for details about creating a header.

Title Page

- Center title and byline on upper half of title page; 12 or fewer words for title

- Use a font such as Arial, size 12, *not* in boldface

- Include other information your professor may require

Abstract

- Develop a synopsis of your paper in one paragraph no longer than 200 words

- Block first line (and all lines) at left margin; *no paragraph indentation*

- Include a keyword summary after the abstract, indenting and italicizing "Keywords" (*Keywords*: keywords follow . . .)

Body

- Start introduction on page 3; do *not* title the introduction "Introduction"

- Type first-level head in ALL CAPS; second, italicize at left margin; third, italicize and indent.

- Space one time after a period

- Use "Align Left" (right margin should appear uneven)

- Indent paragraphs 0.5 inches

- Number tables consecutively throughout the text, and include each table on a separate sheet at the end of the manuscript.

In-Text Citations

- Use the author's last name (surname) and year of publication:

  Jones (2010) found that at-risk youth were more likely to . . .

  At-risk youth were likely to have issues with self-esteem (Jones, 2010).

  In 2010, Jones' study of at risk youth showed that . . .

Continued . . .

cont.

- In subsequent references within the same paragraph, the date is not necessary

- When a work has *two* authors, cite both names each time they are referenced:

Jones and Smithe (2011) found that among children who . . .

- When a work has *three*, *four*, or *five* authors, cite all the first time; in subsequent references, use only the surname of the first author followed by *et al.*:

Jones et al. (2011) demonstrated that more than one study . . .

- For quotations longer than 40 words, double space and indent left margin 0.5 inches; do not use quotation marks; put the citation outside of the period.

- For short quotations, place the citation inside of the period:

"Additional studies are needed to fill the gap" (Jones, 2010, p. 33).

Reference Page

- List references in alphabetical order, leaving individual references in the order noted in the article or book

- Use last name and first initial (no first names)

- For books: author's last name and initials, publication date, title of work, and publication data:

Jones, S., & Barker, D. (2012). *Title*. City, ST: Publisher.

- Block the first line of each reference at the left margin

- Indent second lines of references 0.5 inches (hanging indentation)

- For books, articles, and journals, use title case (not sentence case).

- Type the title of a book in *sentence case*, the title of an article in *sentence case*, and the title of a journal in *title case*

- Italicize the title of a book and the title of a journal and its volume number

References

1   APA. (2010). *Publication manual of the American Psychological Association* (6th ed). Washington, DC: American Psychological Association.

2   ASA. (2014). *American Sociological Association style guide* (5th ed). Washington, DC: American Sociological Association, p. 32.

3   Robert, H. M. (2011). *Robert's rules of order* (11th ed). Philadelphia, PA: Da Capo Press.

Proofreading for Credibility

Comma Rules

Though you are now doing advanced academic work, are you confident with using commas? For example, what is your main reason for placing a comma in a sentence? If the word *pause* comes to mind, you are not alone. Another common response is "to take a breath." However, "pausing" is not a valid reason to use a comma, nor is "taking a breath." The only way to place commas correctly is by applying *comma rules*: the rules for using commas are based on grammar, which defines sentence structure. Punctuation is the glue that holds grammar together.

In fact, the *pause approach* turns punctuating into a guessing game, even though guessing should never be involved. As a result, commas can end up just about anywhere and sometimes everywhere; when writing is full of errors, credibility is lost. Start this chapter with a fresh way of thinking. Learn the rules; and when you use a comma, also know the rule that applies.

Go through this chapter in one or two sittings, completing all of the exercises. Once you are familiar with the comma rules, apply this strategy to your writing:

- For each comma that you use, identify the rule that applies.

- *When in doubt, leave the comma out*:

    o   When you don't know the rule that applies, do not use a comma.

    o   When uncertain, research to see if a rule applies.

    o   When all else fails, rewrite the sentence in a way that you know is correct.

As you complete the exercises in this chapter, you are asked to identify the verb and subject of each sentence. While this request may seem elementary, it may also be challenging at first. For example, your skills may be rusty, or you may never have analyzed sentences this way previously. By doing the exercises as prescribed, you are developing an understanding of structure at its core, which is key to building expert editing skills.

When you have completed this chapter, you will be able to:

- Identify the core elements of sentences.

- Understand how *coordinating*, *subordinating*, and *adverbial conjunctions* signal comma use.

- Demonstrate the correct use of the comma.

- Apply basic comma rules in composition.

- Revise fragments and run-ons into complete sentences.

Though comma rules vary slightly from source to source, the 12 comma rules presented here are consistent with other sources, including American Psychological Association (APA) and American Sociological Association (ASA) guidelines.

What is a Sentence?

Understanding sentence structure is the first step in building editing skills and enables you to correct sentence fragments and run-on sentences.

- **Define what a sentence is, or jot down any words or ideas about sentences that pop into your mind.**

- **For the answer, see Box 13.1. But first, review Rule 1, which discusses the *sentence core*.**

Rule 1: The Sentence Core

Do not separate a subject and verb with only one comma.

The core of a sentence consists of its *subject* and *verb*. In the following, the verbs are underlined twice, and the subjects once:

Incorrect: The <u>director</u> of my program, <u>stated</u> that I needed one more class.

Corrected: The <u>director</u> of my program <u>stated</u> that I needed one more class.

Incorrect: <u>Trisha</u>, my friend <u>will organize</u> the reunion.
Corrected: <u>Trisha</u>, my friend, <u>will organize</u> the reunion.
Corrected: <u>Trisha</u> my friend <u>will organize</u> the reunion.

Though this rule does not indicate where you need to place a comma, it keeps you from making serious errors: whenever you place *one comma* between a subject and its verb, either take out the comma *or* identify if you need to add a second comma.

As you identify the core of each sentence, identify the verb first and then the grammatical subject: the verb determines the subject (and the object, if there is one).

13.1   WHAT IS A SENTENCE?

Here is a definition of a sentence:

A *sentence* consists of a **subject** and a **verb** and expresses a **complete thought**.

Even if your definition does not match the above definition exactly, it can still be correct. For example:

- Some people use the word *noun* instead of *subject*.

- Some use the word *predicate* instead of *verb*.

- Some use the phrase *can stand on its own*, rather than *complete thought*.

Another term for *sentence* is **independent clause**. The word *clause* refers to *a group of words that has a subject and verb*. When a clause cannot stand on its own, it is a **dependent clause**.

When a sentence consists of an independent clause and a dependent clause, the independent clause is the **main clause**.

Rule 2: Conjunction (CONJ)

Use a comma to separate independent clauses when they are joined by a coordinating conjunction (and, but, or, for, nor, so, yet).

As you read the examples below, identify each *independent clause*. The subject of each clause is underlined once, and the verb twice, making the *sentence core* apparent at a glance:

> Bill stayed late, *and* he worked on the proposal. (CONJ)

> The book was left at the front desk, *but* George did not pick it up. (CONJ)

The two most common coordinating conjunctions are *and* and *but*. Though some writers automatically place a comma before *and*, a comma is not always needed. Be careful not to add a comma before a coordinating conjunction when only the second part of a *compound verb* follows it, for example:

> **Incorrect:** Bob worked on the proposal, *and* sent it to my supervisor.

> **Corrected:** Bob worked on the proposal *and* sent it to my supervisor.

However, place a comma before a coordinating conjunction when an independent clause precedes it and follows it, for example:

> **Incorrect:** The idea to implement the project was good *so* we plan to start next week.

> **Corrected:** The idea to implement the project was good, *so* we plan to start next week. (CONJ)

The sentence above marked *incorrect* is an example of a **run-on sentence**: *two or more sentences coming together without sufficient punctuation.*

Practice 13.1
Rule 2: Conjunction (CONJ)

Instructions: Correct the sentences below by applying the comma conjunction (CONJ) rule. For each main clause, underline the verb twice and then the subject once, for example:

> **Incorrect:** Jodie assisted with the last project so Christopher will help us with this one.

Corrected: Jodie <u>assisted</u> with the last project, so <u>Christopher</u> <u>will</u> <u>help</u> us with this one. (CONJ)

1. Mark Mallory is the new case manager and he starts on Monday.

2. Mark will be an inspiration to our staff and an excellent spokesperson for our research project.

3. You can leave him a message but he will not be able to reply until next week.

4. The facility in St. Louis also has a new probation officer and her name is Gia Rivera.

5. You can mail your information now and expect a reply within the next week.

Note: See page 423 for the key to the above exercise.

Review Point: Verbs and Subjects

Always identify the verb first and then the subject, which precedes the verb in statements. That's because the verb determines the subject and the object, if there is one. At times a sentence will have an *understood* or *implied* subject, for example:

(You) Give your information to Lucile.

(I) Thank you for your help.

Thus, when it seems difficult to identify the grammatical subject, ask yourself if the subject could be an *implied subject* such as *you understood* (You) or *I understood* (I).

Rule 3: Series (SER)

When three or more items occur in a series, separate each with a comma.

This comma rule offers an option: the comma before the *and* is optional. However, the "Oxford comma," as it is sometimes referred to, adds clarity, for example:

(You) Please complete Parts 1, 2, and 3 before you leave. (SER)

The <u>menu</u> <u>listed</u> potatoes, peas, *and* carrots for the daily special. (SER)

Mr. Jordan <u>has divided</u> his estate among Robert, Rose, Charles, *and* Sophie. (SER)

Consider the following questions:

1   In the second example, how will the peas and carrots be prepared? What if the menu had instead listed the items as "potatoes, peas and carrots"; how do you think they would have been prepared?

2   In the third example, what if Mr. Jordan's Will had omitted a comma, and it read "Divide the estate among Robert, Rose, Charles and Sophie"? Should each get an equal share, or should Charles and Sophie split one share? (When a comma is placed before *and*, there is no question.)

Also, while the comma before *and* is optional for general use, the ASA and the APA both recommend its use.

When applying this rule, make sure that you are indeed separating three items. For example, a common mistake is to place a comma before *and* when it connects only two items, particularly when the items are long phrases (shown in italics below):

Incorrect: The <u>assistant</u> <u>provided</u> *a series of examples*, and *a good recap of the meeting.*

Corrected: The <u>assistant</u> <u>provided</u> *a series of examples* and *a good recap of the meeting.*

Practice 13.2

Rule 3: Series (SER)

Instructions: Correct the sentences below by applying the comma series (SER) rule. For each main clause, underline the verb twice and then the subject once, for example:

Incorrect: Jerry asked for squash peas and carrots.

Corrected: <u>Jerry</u> <u>asked</u> for squash, peas, and carrots. (SER)

1   We were assigned Conference Rooms A and B on the first floor.

2   Make sure that you bring your laptop cell phone and client list to the meeting.

3   You should arrange the meeting call your supervisor and submit your assessment.

4   Julie John and Sally conducted the workshop on anger management.

5   They gave a workshop for Elaine Arlene Donald and Joanne on preparing a polling strategy to meet the criteria of the research.

Note: See pages 423–424 for the key to the above exercise.

Review Point: Conjunctions as Comma Signals

In Chapter 7, "Cohesive Paragraphs and Transitions," you reviewed the role conjunctions play in creating transitions and bridging ideas. Conjunctions also play a critical role in punctuation. As a refresher, here are a few examples of each:

Conjunction	Function	Examples
Coordinating	connect equal grammatical parts	and, but, or, nor, for, so, yet
Subordinating	introduce dependent clauses and phrases	if, after, while, when, as, although, because, as soon as, unless, before, since, even, even though, whereas
Adverbial	introduce or interrupt independent clauses	however, therefore, thus, for example, consequently, in general, in conclusion, as a result, fortunately, on the contrary

By memorizing a few of each type, you will have an easier time understanding certain comma rules, such as comma introductory (INTRO), which you review next.

Rule 4: Introductory (INTRO)

Place a comma after a word, phrase, or dependent clause that introduces an independent clause.

To understand this rule, you must first be familiar with subordinating conjunctions and adverbial conjunctions. Below is an explanation of "word, phrase, and dependent clause."

- *Word:* When an *adverbial conjunction* such as *therefore, however,* or *consequently* is the first word of a sentence, follow it with a comma:

  However, I <u>was</u> not able to attend the conference. (INTRO)

  Therefore, <u>we</u> <u>will convene</u> the meeting in Boston. (INTRO)

- *Phrase:* When a prepositional phrase, a gerund phrase, or an infinitive phrase begins a sentence, follow it with a comma:

  During that time, he spoke about the plan in detail. (INTRO)

  Leaving my bags at the airport, I took a taxi into the city. (INTRO)

  To arrive earlier, Michael rearranged his entire schedule. (INTRO)

- *Dependent clause:* When a *subordinating conjunction* such as *since, because, although,* or *while* creates a dependent clause at the beginning of a sentence, follow it with a comma:

  Although my <u>calendar</u> <u>is</u> full, <u>we</u> <u>can meet</u> this Friday. (INTRO)

  Before <u>you</u> <u>arrive</u> at my office, (you) <u>call</u> my assistant. (INTRO)

  Until <u>I</u> <u>am</u> available, <u>you</u> <u>can work</u> in an extra office. (INTRO)

Placing a comma after a subordinating conjunction is a common mistake, for example:

Incorrect: *Although*, the information is timely, we cannot use it.

Corrected: *Although* the information is timely, we cannot use it. (INTRO)

Pay special attention to place the comma after the dependent clause, not after the subordinating conjunction.

Practice 13.3

Rule 4: Introductory (INTRO)

Instructions: Correct the sentences below by applying the comma introductory (INTRO) rule. For each main clause, underline the verb twice and then the subject once, for example:

Incorrect: Although Mary flew to Boston she arrived a day late.

Corrected: Although <u>Mary</u> <u>flew</u> to Boston, <u>she</u> <u>arrived</u> late. (INTRO)

1   Because the proposal needed revision we were not able to respond on time.

2   However we were given an extension.

3   Although the extra time helped us we still felt pressured for time.

4   To get another extension George called their office.

5   Fortunately the director was agreeable to our request.

Note: See page 424 for the key to the above exercise.

Rule 5: Nonrestrictive (NR)

Use commas to set off explanations that are nonessential to the meaning of the sentence.

To apply this rule correctly, you must first understand the difference between *restrictive* and *nonrestrictive*.

- *Restrictive information* is *essential* and should not be set off with commas.

- *Nonrestrictive information* is *not essential* and can be set off with commas.

Whenever you set off information between two commas, you are implying that the information can be removed without disturbing the structure or meaning of the sentence. Nonrestrictive elements often come in the form of *who* or *which* clauses. The two examples below illustrate this rule (*who* clauses are italicized):

Alice <u>Walker</u>, *who is a prestigious author*, <u>will</u> <u>be</u> the keynote speaker. (NR)

The <u>woman</u> *who is a prestigious author* <u>will</u> <u>be</u> the keynote speaker.

In the first example above, you would still know who the keynote speaker would be even if the *who* clause were removed:

Alice <u>Walker</u> <u>will</u> <u>be</u> the keynote speaker.

However, in the second example, the meaning of the sentence would be unclear if the *who* clause were removed:

The <u>woman</u> <u>will</u> <u>be</u> the keynote speaker. *Which woman?*

In fact, all commas that come in sets imply that the information set off by the commas can be removed; so here is another reminder of how to use commas with *essential* and *nonessential* elements:

- *Essential information* is restrictive and should *not* be set off with commas.

- *Nonessential information* is nonrestrictive and can be set off with commas.

To reinforce your understanding, complete the following practice.

Practice 13.4

Rule 5: Nonrestrictive (NR)

Instructions: Correct the sentences below by applying the comma nonrestrictive (NR) rule. For each main clause, underline the verb twice and then the subject once (the essential and nonessential clauses are shown in italics), for example:

Incorrect: The artist, *who designed our brochure,* lives in New Orleans.

Corrected: The <u>artist</u> *who designed our brochure* <u>lives</u> in New Orleans. (no commas needed)

1   Our manager *who specializes in project grants* will assist you with this issue.

2   Tomas Phillips *who works only on weekends* will call you soon.

3   The therapist *who researched this case* is not available.

4   Nick Richards *who is in a meeting until 3 p.m.* can answer your question.

5   Your new contract *which we mailed yesterday* should arrive by Friday.

Note: See page 424 for the key to the above exercise.

Rule 6: Parenthetical (PAR)

Use commas to set off a word or expression that interrupts the flow of a sentence.

The word "parenthetical" relates to the word "parentheses": a parenthetical expression is a word, phrase, or clause that is inserted within a comment, interrupting it. This rule applies to *adverbial conjunctions* or other *short phrases* interjected into a sentence. By interrupting the flow of the sentence, a parenthetical expression places stress on the words immediately preceding it or following it. Parenthetical expressions should be set off with commas because they are nonessential and can be removed, as in the following three examples:

> Mr. Connors, *however,* arrived after the opening ceremony. (PAR)
>
> You can, *therefore,* place your order after 5 p.m. today. (PAR)
>
> The project, *in my opinion,* needs improvement. (PAR)

In the above, can you see how each adverbial conjunction (shown in italics) could be removed, leaving the sentence complete and clear in meaning? A common mistake occurs when a writer uses a semicolon in place of one of the commas, for example:

> **Incorrect:**   Ms. Philippe; in fact, approved the request last week.
>
> **Corrected:**   Ms. Philippe, in fact, approved the request last week. (PAR)

When a semicolon precedes an adverbial conjunction, generally two sentences are involved: the adverbial conjunction functions as a bridge or a transition rather than an interrupter. (See Chapter 14, "Semicolons, Colons, and Dashes.")

Another common mistake occurs when a writer uses only one comma rather than a set of commas, for example:

> **Incorrect:**   Our outreach team, therefore will assist you at your convenience.
>
> **Corrected:**   Our outreach team, therefore, will assist you at your convenience. (PAR)
>
> **Incorrect:**   Mr. Jones, however will plan this year's event.
>
> **Corrected:**   Mr. Jones, however, will plan this year's event. (PAR)

In terms of structure, adverbial conjunctions are often nonessential elements. However, these conjunctions play an important role in writing style by cueing readers and identifying key points.

Practice 13.5

Rule 6: Parenthetical (PAR)

Instructions: Correct the sentences below by applying the comma parenthetical (PAR) rule. For each main clause, underline the verb twice and then the subject once, for example:

>**Incorrect:**   Our contract however did not include fee for services.

>**Corrected:**   Our <u>contract</u>, however, <u>did</u> not <u>include</u> fee for services. (PAR)

1   Clinical Services I believe can best assist you with this issue.

2   T. J. therefore will work this weekend in my place.

3   Our invoice unfortunately was submitted incorrectly.

4   The new contract in my opinion meets specifications.

5   Social Research Corporation of course recommended us to a vendor.

>*Note*: See pages 424–425 for the key to the above exercise.

Rule 7: Direct Address (DA)

Use commas to set off the name or title of a person addressed directly.

Often the name of the person being addressed directly appears at the beginning of the sentence; however, the person's name can also appear in the middle or at the end of the sentence, as shown below:

>*Donald,* <u>you</u> <u>can</u> <u>arrange</u> the meeting in Dallas or Fort Worth. (DA)

>I <u>gave</u> the invitation to everyone in the department, *Marge.* (DA)

>Your <u>instructions</u>, *Professor,* <u>were</u> clear and to the point. (DA)

In each of the above examples, notice that the name of the person being addressed is *not* the subject of the sentence. The sentences below also contain

---

13.2 WRITING TIP: A NOTE ABOUT STYLE

Comma Parenthetical (PAR) shows you the correct way to punctuate a sentence when an adverbial conjunction occurs in the middle of a sentence, for example:

Our outreach team, *therefore*, will assist you. (PAR)

However, you can often make your sentence more reader friendly by moving the adverbial conjunction to the beginning of the sentence, for example:

Therefore, our outreach team will assist you. (INTRO)

Adverbial conjunctions play an established role in writing. However, writers often interject introductory comments such as "I believe" or "I think," for example:

I think the answer will become clear as we move forward.

Remove these types of unnecessary expressions, for example:

The answer will become clear as we move forward.

Can you see how these changes make a sentence flow more effectively?

---

a direct address, but the subject of each sentence is implied. As you read each sentence, ask yourself *who* is performing the action of the verb.

<u>Thank</u> you, *Astrid*, for speaking on my behalf. (DA)

<u>Feel</u> free to call my office at your convenience, *David*. (DA)

Traci, please <u>assist</u> me with the spring conference. (DA)

In the first sentence above, the implied subject is *I understood*; in the second and third, the implied subject is *you understood*:

[*I*] <u>thank</u> you, Astrid, for speaking on my behalf.

[*You*] <u>feel</u> free to call my office at your convenience, David.

Traci, [*you*] please <u>assist</u> me with the spring conference.

In sentences that contain a direct address, the subject is often implied.

Practice 13.6

Rule 7: Direct Address (DA)

Instructions: Correct the sentences below by applying the direct address (DA) rule. For each main clause, underline the verb twice and then the subject once, for example:

> **Incorrect:** Johnny you should study that problem in more depth.
>
> **Corrected:** Johnny, <u>you</u> <u>should</u> <u>study</u> that problem in more depth. (DA)

1   Give your report to the auditor by Friday Marcel.

2   Jason do you have tickets for the game?

3   Doctor I would like to know the results of my tests.

4   Would you like to attend the banquet Alice?

5   Thank you for inviting me George.

> *Note*: See page 425 for the key to the above exercise.

Rule 8: Appositive (AP)

Use commas to set off the restatement of a noun or pronoun.

An appositive is a restatement. When a brief explanation follows a noun or pronoun, it is considered a restatement; this restatement is usually a nonessential appositive. Here are some examples:

> Dr. Jones, my professor, will plan the conference in Seattle.
>
> Melissa Jackson, the team leader, is responsible for the policy change.
>
> (You) Please speak to Colin, my assistant, if I am not available.

Some appositives are essential (restrictive), which means that they should not be set off with commas. An **essential appositive** occurs when more than one person fits the category and the meaning would not be clear if the appositive were removed:

Diana's brother Chuck is a great golfer. (Diana has more than one brother.)

This is an essential appositive because Diana has more than one brother. If Chuck were Diana's only brother, his name would be set off with commas because the meaning would be clear *with* or *without* her brother's name:

Diana's brother, Chuck, is a great golfer. (Diana has only one brother.)

Practice 13.7

Rule 8: Appositive (AP)

Instructions: Correct the sentences below by applying the comma appositive (AP) rule. For each main clause, underline the verb twice and then the subject once, for example:

Incorrect: Elaine my cousin taught introduction to sociology.

Corrected: <u>Elaine</u>, my cousin, <u>taught</u> introduction to sociology. (AP)

1   Jacob Seinfeld our associate director decided to hire Williams.

2   My lab partner Carol Glasco applied for a job here.

3   Jim Martinez the registrar approved your request.

4   The department chair Dr. George Schmidt did not receive your transcript.

5   The director asked Clair my sister to join us for dinner.

Note: See page 425 for the key to the above exercise.

Rule 9: Addresses and Dates (AD)

Use commas to set off the parts of addresses and dates.

The term *set off* means that commas are placed on both sides of the part of the address or date to show separation. For example, notice how commas surround *Massachusetts* and *California* as well as *August 15*:

<u>Boston</u>, Massachusetts, <u>is</u> the best city to host the conference. (AD)

<u>Sally</u> <u>has</u> <u>worked</u> in Long Beach, California, for the past five years. (AD)

On Wednesday, August 15, my <u>friends</u> <u>celebrated</u> the *Ferragosto*. (AD)

Does it surprise you to learn that a comma is required *after* the state name when a city and state are written together? If so, you are not alone; the following mistake is common:

Incorrect: Dallas, <u>Texas</u> <u>is</u> a great city to start a new business.

Corrected: <u>Dallas</u>, Texas, <u>is</u> a great city to start a new business. (AD)

The same is true for dates; the second comma in the set is often left off incorrectly, as follows:

Incorrect: Jerome listed August 15, 2014 as his start date.

Corrected: Jerome listed August 15, 2014, as his start date. (AD)

Another type of error occurs when a writer puts a comma between the month and the day, for example:

Incorrect: September, 4, 2017 was the date on the application.

Corrected: September 4, 2017, was the date on the application. (AD)

Never place a comma between the month and the day, as shown in the *incorrect* example above!

Practice 13.8

Rule 9: Addresses and Dates (AD)

Instructions: Correct the sentences below by applying the comma addresses and dates (AD) rule. For each main clause, underline the verb twice and then the subject once, for example:

Incorrect: The conference is planned for August 19 2020 in Denver Colorado.

Corrected: The <u>conference</u> <u>is</u> <u>planned</u> for August 19, 2020, in Denver, Colorado. (AD)

1 Send your application by Friday December 15 to my assistant.

2 San Antonio Texas has a River Walk and Conference Center.

3 Would you prefer to meet in Myrtle Minnesota or Des Moines Iowa?

4 Springfield Massachusetts continues to be my selection.

5 We arrived in Chicago Illinois on May 22 2019 to prepare for the event.

   Note: See page 425 for the key to the above exercise.

Rule 10: Word Omitted (WO)

Use a comma in place of a word or words that play a structural role in a sentence.

This type of comma occurs infrequently. Most of the time, the word that has been omitted is either *that* or *and*.

The problem is *that* the current situation is quite grim.

The problem is, the current situation is quite grim.

Mr. Adams presented the long *and* boring report to the board.

Mr. Adams presented the long, boring report to the board.

Practice 13.9

Rule 10: Word Omitted (WO)

Instructions: Correct the sentences below by applying the comma words omitted (WO) rule. For each main clause, underline the verb twice and then the subject once, for example:

Incorrect: My suggestion is you should contain the situation now.

Corrected: My suggestion is, you should contain the situation now. (WO)

Corrected: My suggestion is *that* you should contain the situation now. (WO)

1   The president shared two intriguing confidential reports.

2   The photo shoot is on Tuesday at 5 p.m. on Wednesday at 6 p.m.

3   The problem is some of the results are not yet known.

4   Leave the materials with Alicia at the Westin with Marcia at the Hilton.

5   Silvia presented a short exciting PowerPoint on Italy.

Note: See page 426 for the key to the above exercise.

Rule 11: Direct Quotation (DQ)

Use commas to set off a direct quotation within a sentence.

A direct quotation is a person's exact words. In comparison, an indirect quotation does not give a speaker's exact words and would *not* be set off with commas.

Direct quotation:	Gabrielle said, "I have a 9 o'clock appointment," and then left abruptly.
Indirect quotation:	Gabrielle said that she had a 9 o'clock appointment and then left abruptly.
Direct quotation:	Dr. Gorman asked, "Is the environment experiencing global warming at a faster rate than previously predicted?"
Indirect quotation:	Dr. Gorman asked whether the environment is experiencing global warming at a faster rate than previously predicted.

An exception to this rule relates to short quotations: a short quotation built into the flow of a sentence does not need to be set off with commas.

Short quotations:	Marian shouted "Help!" as she slid on the ice.
	My boss told me "Do not sweat the small stuff" before he let me go.
	The advice "Give the project your best this time" sounded patronizing rather than encouraging.

With direct quotations, whether set off with commas or blending with the flow of the sentence, capitalize the first word of the quotation. For writing in the United States, apply the following *closed punctuation* guidelines.

Punctuation placement with quotation marks:

- Place commas and periods on the *inside* of quotation marks.

- Place semicolons and colons on the *outside* of quotation marks.

- Place exclamation marks and question marks based on meaning: these marks can go on the *inside* or *outside* of quotation marks.

For example:

> Mr. Jones said, "Your performance exceeds requirements," and I could not be happier.

> Refer to the item in your inbox marked, "September Meeting Cancelled."

> I had not read Chapter 5, "Social Context"; therefore, I could not respond correctly.

> Did Mark say, "Arrive promptly at 10 a.m."?

> Mark said, "Arrive promptly at 10 a.m.!"

Regardless of where the punctuation mark is placed, never double punctuate at the end of a sentence. You cover more details about punctuating with quotation marks in Chapter 15, "Quotation and Citation."

Practice 13.10

Rule 11: Direct Quotation (DQ)

Instructions: Correct the sentences below by applying the direct quotation (DQ) rule. For each main clause, underline the verb twice and then the subject once, for example:

| **Incorrect:** | Jeffery insisted go back to the beginning before you decide to give up! |
| **Corrected:** | <u>Jeffery</u> <u>insisted</u>, "Go back to the beginning before you decide to give up!" (DQ) |

1　Patrick shouted get back before we had a chance to see the falling debris.

2　According to Tyler all children can learn if they find an interest in what is taught.

3　My father warned me when you choose an insurance company, find one with good customer service.

4　Sharon encouraged me by yelling go for the gold as I was starting the race.

5　Lenny said to me good luck on your exam before I left this morning.

Note: See page 426 for the key to the above exercise.

Rule 12: Contrasting Expression or Afterthought (CEA)

Use a comma to separate a contrasting expression or afterthought from the main clause.

A contrasting expression or afterthought adds an interesting twist to writing style. The expression following a CEA comma grabs the reader's attention, for example:

> Go ahead and put the property on the market, if you can. (CEA)
>
> I asked for the information so that I could help Bill, not take the sale from him. (CEA)
>
> My associate Buddy, not Chuck, assisted me with the conference. (CEA)

In fact, omitting the CEA comma is not a serious error; however, using the CEA comma makes your comments stand out and gives your writing a conversational flow.

Practice 13.11

Rule 12: Contrasting Expression or Afterthought (CEA)

Instructions: Correct the sentences below by applying the comma contrasting expression or afterthought (CEA) rule. For each main clause, underline the verb twice and then the subject once, for example:

Incorrect: Elaine attended Southern State University not Northern State.

Corrected: <u>Elaine</u> <u>attended</u> Southern State University, not Northern State. (CEA)

1   You will find the manuscript in John's office not in Bob's.

2   Marcus secured the contract but only after negotiating for hours.

3   Chair the budget committee if you prefer.

4   Lester rather than Dan received the award.

5   Work to achieve your dreams not to run away from your fears.

Note: See page 426 for the key to the above exercise.

Recap

Have you stopped placing commas on the basis of pauses? If so, your writing decisions will become easier as the quality of your writing improves.

Analyzing comma use may seem challenging in the beginning. However, this approach ensures that you will learn how to use commas effectively, which is a benefit throughout your writing career.

When you find yourself writing a sentence too complicated to punctuate, simplify it by breaking down the information into more than one sentence. *Simplicity is key to reader-friendly writing*, which the effective use of commas helps you achieve.

Writing Workshop

Skill Building

Instructions: Make sure that you have completed every practice in this chapter according to the instructions. Do your work in pencil so that you can go back and repeat the exercises as needed. The keys are at the back of this text so that you can fill this learning gap on your own, as your sociology professor may not cover the rules in class.

13.3   COMMA RULES

Rule 1: The sentence core rules (SCR)

Do not separate a subject and verb with only one comma.

Rule 2: Conjunction (CONJ)

Use a comma to separate two independent clauses when they are joined by a coordinating conjunction (and, but, or, nor, for, so, yet).

Rule 3: Series (SER)

Use a comma to separate three or more items in a series.

Rule 4: Introductory (INTRO)

Place a comma after a word, phrase, or dependent clause that introduces an independent clause.

Rule 5: Nonrestrictive (NR)

Use commas to set off nonessential (nonrestrictive) words and phrases.

Rule 6: Parenthetical (PAR)

Use commas to set off a word or expression that interrupts the flow of a sentence.

Rule 7: Direct address (DA)

Use commas to set off the name or title of a person addressed directly.

Rule 8: Appositive (AP)

Use commas to set off the restatement of a noun or pronoun.

Rule 9: Addresses and dates (AD)

Use commas to set off the parts of addresses and dates.

Rule 10: Word omitted (WO)

Use a comma for the omission of a word or words that play a structural role in a sentence.

Rule 11: Direct quotation (DQ)

Use commas to set off direct quotations within a sentence.

Rule 12: Contrasting expression or afterthought (CEA)

Use a comma to separate a contrasting expression or afterthought.

Semicolons, Colons, and Dashes

Semicolons, colons, and dashes enhance writing because they add variety and energy. However, many writers avoid these marks because they are unsure of how to use them. As you become skilled in using these marks, you may find that punctuation speaks to your reader in subtle, yet powerful ways, for example:

- The semicolon signals readers to slight shades of meaning, drawing connections and showing relationships.

- The colon alerts the reader that the information that follows illustrates the information that precedes it.

- The dash highlights information, making it stand out.

The more practice you gain using these less-common marks, the more you will enjoy using them. These marks give you choices and options; but more importantly, they give your voice a fingerprint and add momentum to your message.

When you have completed this chapter, you will be able to:

- Demonstrate the correct use of semicolons, colons, and dashes.

- Apply diverse punctuation rules in composition.

- Understand the roles of coordinating, subordinating, and adverbial conjunctions in the use of semicolons.

- Revise fragments and run-ons into complete sentences.

Practice using the semicolon, colon, and dash until you feel comfortable using them. Then use them correctly and confidently.

The Semicolon

One of the most common errors in writing is to use a comma where a semicolon (or period) is needed. When a comma is used where a semicolon belongs, the result is a run-on sentence and is a serious grammatical error.

In this part, you learn three semicolon rules:

- Semicolon no conjunction (NC)

- Semicolon bridge (BR)

- Semicolon because of commas (BC)

As you learn the semicolon rules, stretch your skills and experiment with using semicolons in your own writing.

- The semicolon communicates to readers that ideas are close in meaning.

- Semicolons add variety and keep writing from getting choppy when sentences are short.

After you know how to use them correctly, you may actually like semicolons. As with commas, conjunctions play a key role in the use of the semicolon.

14.1	**REVIEW POINT: CONJUNCTIONS AS SIGNALS**

Conjunctions play a role in creating a reader-friendly writing style because they bridge ideas and cue the reader to subtle shades of meaning (see Chapter 7, "Cohesive Paragraphs and Transitions").

Coordinating conjunctions: and, but, or, for, nor, so, yet

Subordinating conjunctions: if, after, while, when, as, although, because, as soon as

Adverbial conjunctions: however, therefore, thus, for example, in conclusion

In this chapter, you learn that conjunctions also play a role with the use of the semicolon.

Rule 1: Semicolon No Conjunction (NC)

Use a semicolon to separate two independent clauses that are joined without a conjunction.

This semicolon is sometimes referred to as *semicolon in place of a period*. In fact, you can tell that you are using a semicolon correctly if you can substitute a period for it. A semicolon is not as strong as a period, which is a terminal mark of punctuation. Usually a semicolon is used when one or both statements are short and related in meaning; the semicolon helps the reader infer the connection between the ideas, for example:

Comma conjunction:	A<u>l</u> <u>went</u> to the store, *but* <u>he</u> <u>forgot</u> to buy bread. (CONJ)
Semicolon no conjunction:	A<u>l</u> <u>went</u> to the store; <u>he</u> <u>forgot</u> to buy bread. (NC)
Period:	<u>I</u> <u>went</u> to the store. <u>He</u> <u>forgot</u> to buy bread.

Notice how each sentence has a slightly different effect based on how it is punctuated. Do you see how choppy the writing sounds in the example above that uses a period, thereby breaking up the sentences? To avoid writing short, choppy sentences, use a semicolon instead of a period. The semicolon no conjunction (NC) rule is best applied when two sentences are closely related, especially when one or both sentences are short.

Practice 14.1

Rule 1: Semicolon No Conjunction (NC)

Instructions: Correct the sentences below by applying the semicolon no conjunction (NC) rule. Note that some sentences may need a comma conjunction (CONJ) instead. For each main clause, underline the verb twice and the subject once, for example:

Incorrect: Addison arrived at 8 o'clock, she forgot the agenda.

Corrected: <u>Addison</u> <u>arrived</u> at 8 o'clock; <u>she</u> <u>forgot</u> the agenda. (NC)

1   Keri will not approve our final report she needs more documentation.

2   Ask Bryan for the report he said that he completed it yesterday.

3   Arrive on time to tomorrow's meeting bring both of your reports.

4   A laptop was left in the conference room Johnny claimed it as his.

5   Recognize your mistakes and offer apologies as needed.

Note: See page 427 for the key to the above exercise.

Rule 2: Semicolon Bridge (BR)

Use a semicolon before and a comma after an adverbial conjunction when it acts as a bridge or transition between two independent clauses.

This rule applies when adverbial conjunctions provide transitions between independent clauses. Once again, the semicolon implies that the clauses are related in meaning.

Semicolon TRANS:　　Bob will determine the fees; *however,* he is
　　　　　　　　　　　　open to suggestions.

When writers avoid semicolons, they sometimes use commas incorrectly; for example:

Incorrect:　　Bob will determine the fees, *however,* he is open to
　　　　　　　　suggestions.

In the above example, by placing a comma where a semicolon (or a period) would belong, the result is a *run-on sentence*. Whenever an adverbial conjunction appears in the middle of a sentence, identify each independent clause; read through the sentence at least twice to ensure that your punctuation is correct.

Here are more examples of the semicolon bridge (BR) rule with adverbial conjunctions shown in italics:

Lidia wrote the grant; *therefore,* she should be on the committee. (BR)

The grant was accepted; *as a result,* we will receive funding. (BR)

You should call their office; *however,* (you) do not leave a message.
(BR)

Have you sometimes used a comma when a semicolon would have been the correct choice?

Practice 14.2

Rule 2: Semicolon Bridge (BR)

Instructions: Correct the sentences below by applying the semicolon transition (BR) rule. In each main clause, underline the verb twice and the subject once, for example:

Incorrect:	Feranda left, however, she forgot her case notes.
Corrected:	<u>Feranda</u> <u>left</u>; however, <u>she</u> <u>forgot</u> her case notes. (BR)

1 Carol suggested the topic fortunately Carlos agreed.

2 The case management team offered assistance however their time was limited.

3 Ken compiled the data therefore Mary crunched it.

4 The numbers turned out well as a result our new budget was accepted.

5 Roger ran in the marathon unfortunately he was unable to finish.

Note: See page 427 for the key to the above exercise.

Rule 3: Semicolon Because of Comma (BC)

When a clause needs major and minor separations, use semicolons for major breaks and commas for minor breaks.

Major and minor breaks don't occur very often when the writer keeps sentences simple, clear, and concise. Most often this rule applies when several cities and states or names and titles are listed:

Semicolon BC:	Joni will travel to Dallas, Texas; Buffalo, New York; and Boston, Massachusetts.
Semicolon BC:	The committee members are Jeremy Smith, director of research; Marjorie Lou Kirk, team leader; Carson Michaels, accountant; and Malory Willowbrook, research analyst.

A more complicated example would include major and minor clauses within a sentence:

Semicolon BC:	Millicent asked for a raise; and since she was a new employee, I deferred to Jackson's opinion.
Semicolon BC:	Professor Jones suggested that the project continue; but I was unable to participate, so he asked Dr. Ferretti for assistance.

Practice 14.3

Rule 3: Semicolon Because of Commas (BC)

Instructions: Correct the sentences below by applying the semicolon because of commas (BC) rule. In each main clause, underline the verb twice and the subject once, for example:

Incorrect:	Gladys has lived in Boise, Idaho, Biloxi, Mississippi, and Tallahassee, Florida.
Corrected:	<u>Gladys</u> <u>has</u> <u>lived</u> in Boise, Idaho; Biloxi, Mississippi; and Tallahassee, Florida. (BC)

1   Please include Rupert Adams social researcher Madeline Stacy community development coordinator and Mark Coleman career counselor.

2   By next week I will have traveled to St. Louis Missouri Chicago Illinois and Burlington Iowa.

3   Mike applied for jobs in Honolulu Hawaii Sacramento California and Santa Fe New Mexico.

4   Your application was received yesterday but when I reviewed it information was missing.

5   You can resubmit your application today and since my office will review it you can call me tomorrow for the results.

    Note: See pages 427–428 for the key to the above exercise.

The Colon

In general, the colon alerts readers that information will be illustrated, making the colon a strong mark of punctuation that commands attention. Use the colon for the following purposes:

- After salutations of business letters and formal e-mail messages.

- At the end of one sentence when the following sentence illustrates it.

- At the end of a sentence to alert the reader that a list follows.

- After words such as *Note* or *Caution.*

Each of the above categories is explained below.

Colons after Salutations

The most common use of a colon is after the salutation in a business letter, which is the most formal type of written communication. Only when you write a letter to a personal friend should you use a comma instead of a colon. Here are some examples of salutations using a colon:

Dear Mr. Jones: Dear Dr. Wilson: Dear Professor:

Dear Jorge: Dear Mia: Robert:

Notice that even when you use the recipient's first name, the colon is appropriate. You could also use the above salutations in an e-mail if the message were formal, such as an inquiry for a job. However, for the most part, business professionals use a comma after the greeting of an e-mail as in the following:

Dear Julia,   Mike,   Hi Sophie,

The one mark of punctuation that you would *never* use for a salutation is the semicolon; however, some writers mistakenly use it, for example:

Incorrect: Dear Charles;

Corrected: Dear Charles:

Corrected: Dear Charles,

Colons after Sentences

You have probably noticed that a colon is used to introduce lists, but have you noticed that a colon sometimes occurs at the end of one sentence when the following sentence illustrates it?

Using a colon to illustrate a complete sentence is probably the colon's least common use, but possibly its most powerful use. This type of colon use adds a nice dimension to writing style, conveying the message in a slightly more emphatic way.

Here are some examples of one sentence introducing another:

> The colon is a strong mark of punctuation: it draws the reader's attention.

> Johnson Ecology accepted our proposal: we start on Monday.

For general usage, the first word of the independent clause following a colon should be in lower case. However, capitalize the first word if you are placing special emphasis on the second clause or the second clause is a formal rule, as shown below.

Here is the principle that applies: A colon can be used in place of a period when the sentence that follows illustrates the one that precedes it.

> Update your report by Friday: The accrediting commission's site visit is next week.

> *Note*: In contrast to general usage, APA guidelines recommend *always* capitalizing the first word after the colon when a full sentence follows it.

When you use a colon to illustrate a sentence, use it sparingly. While no rule applies, limit yourself to using no more than one or two colons per page to illustrate sentences this way.

Colons Introducing Lists

Using the colon to illustrate or introduce a list of words or phrases generally requires using words such as *these, here, the following,* or *as follows* within a complete sentence. Here are some examples:

> These are the materials to bring to the meeting: your annual report and current data.

> Bring the following identification: driver's license, social security card, and current utility bill.

> Here are writing samples that you can use: Myers, Jones, and Riley.

However, do not use a colon after an incomplete sentence, for example:

Incorrect:	The items you need to bring are: a tent, a sleeping bag, and a light.
Corrected:	The items you need to bring are a tent, a sleeping bag, and a light.
Incorrect:	This package includes: a stapler and 3-hole paper punch.
Corrected:	This package includes a stapler and 3-hole paper punch.

Also notice that the colon can be used after the adverbial conjunction *for example* to alert the reader that an example follows, as shown below (and throughout this text).

Colons after Note or Caution

Use a colon after a word of caution or instruction, for example:

Note: All meetings are cancelled on Friday.

Caution: Do not use the staircase.

If a complete sentence follows *Note* or *Caution*, capitalize the first word, as shown above. Space one or two times after the colon, but be consistent in the style you choose.

Practice 14.4

The Colon

Instructions: Insert colons where needed in the following sentences.

| Incorrect: | The materials we need are: blankets, water, and cell phones. |
| Corrected: | The materials we need are blankets, water, and cell phones. |

1   I have some exciting news for you, Jeremy proposed on Friday.

2   Note, the office is closed on Monday for the 4th of July holiday.

3   The supplies we need are as follows; markers, copy paper, and staplers.

4   Giorgio said that we need: cereal, coconut milk, and bananas.

5   Here is what you should do, complete the inventory list and then work
     on the schedule.

Note: See page 428 for the key to the above exercise.

The Dash

The dash is the most versatile of all punctuation marks and can be used
on both formal and informal documents. It can substitute for a comma,
semicolon, period, or colon. There are two types of dash, the *em* **dash** and
the *en* **dash**, and each is illustrated below.

Em Dash

For general writing, the *em* dash is the traditional choice. Use two hyphens
without a space before, between, or after them. When you key in a dash as
two hyphens without a space before, between, or after them, your computer
software is likely to display the *em* dash as one solid line (about the width of
a capital "m"), for example:

> Bob called on Friday—he said he'd arrive by noon today.

> Thanks—your package arrived right before our meeting.

> Feranda Wilson—our new executive VP—will host the event.

The *em* dash adds energy, placing emphasis on the information that
follows one dash or falls between two dashes. However, when overused, the
dash gives the impression that the writer is speaking in a choppy and haphazard
fashion.

En Dash

The *en* dash is used when giving scores, directions, page numbers, or other
information involving numbers. To create an *en* dash, type one hyphen with
a space before and after it: word – word. When you hit the space bar, Word
will turn the hyphen into an *en* dash, as follows:

The London – Paris train arrives at 2 o'clock this afternoon.

Chicago defeated Green Bay, 13 – 6.

Once again, do not overuse dashes: overusing dashes is similar to overusing exclamation points. Writers enjoy using them, but readers tire of them easily. Thus, use them sparingly by limiting yourself to no more than one or two dashes per page or e-mail message. (Writing experts recommend that exclamation points never be used in academic writing and only rarely in professional writing.)

Practice 14.5

The Dash

Instructions: Place dashes where needed in the following sentences; make any other corrections, as needed.

| **Incorrect:** | Mark scheduled the meeting, how could I refuse to go? |
| **Corrected:** | Mark scheduled the meeting—how could I refuse to go? |

1   Margie called on Friday George is home!

2   Mike's parents are visiting he invited me to have dinner with them.

3   Helen Jones the new CEO asked me to join her team.

4   Call if u need anything Im always here to support you.

5   Give as much as you can to that charity it's a good cause.

Note: See page 428 for the key to the above exercise.

Writing Style: Punctuation and Flow

Using punctuation *correctly* is one element of writing. Another element is applying punctuation *effectively*: punctuation packages your words, developing a rhythm that affects the style and tone of your writing.

Writing generally does not flow well when it consists of short, choppy sentences. However, at times short, choppy sentences create a desired dramatic effect, as in the following:

> Conan arrived late today. He resigned.

When you want to reduce the choppy effect that short sentences can create, semicolons can often add flow to your writing, but not always. Consider the following example:

> Jay priced the condo lower; he needs to relocate.

In the previous example, connecting the independent clauses with a semicolon does not necessarily reduce the choppy effect. The reader needs a transitional word to build a bridge between the cause and the effect. Here are some ways to solve the problem through the use of conjunctions:

> Jay priced the condo lower *since* he needs to relocate.
>
> Jay priced the condo lower *because* he needs to relocate.
>
> Jay priced the condo lower; *unfortunately,* he needs to relocate.

In each example above, the conjunction smoothed the flow of the writing. By giving the reader a transitional word, the reader can more readily draw a connection between the meaning of the two clauses.

Recap

Punctuation is one more tool to help you connect with your reader and get your message across. Work with punctuation until you feel confident using the various marks correctly: experiment with punctuation and conjunctions until you gain a sense of how to use them effectively to express your voice.

Writing Workshop

Activity A. Writing Practice

Instructions: Take out a paper that you have written within the past two years.

1   Edit the paper for correct use of punctuation.

2   Revise three sentences using the semicolon, colon, and dash.

How many errors in punctuation did you find?

Activity B. Skill Building

Instructions: Make sure that you have completed every practice in this chapter according to the instructions. Do your work in pencil so that you can go back and repeat the exercises as needed. The keys are at the back of this text so that you can fill this learning gap on your own, just in case your sociology professor does not cover this chapter in class.

SEMICOLON RULES

Rule 1: Semicolon no conjunction (NC)

Use a semicolon to separate two independent clauses that are joined without a conjunction.

Rule 2: Semicolon bridge (BR)

Use a semicolon before and a comma after an adverbial conjunction when it acts as a bridge or transition between two independent clauses.

Rule 3: Semicolon because of comma (BC)

When a clause needs major and minor separations, use a semicolon for major breaks and a comma for minor breaks.

CHAPTER 15

Quotation and Citation

Citing sources is a critical element of evidence-based writing. By using evidence to support your claims, you add depth to your writing and enhance its credibility. By citing your sources, you also give your readers the opportunity to probe more deeply and read original research on your topic first-hand—further enhancing the effect of your work.

A major issue involving citation is *plagiarism*. One reason for plagiarism may be that developing writers lack an understanding of what plagiarism is or are uncertain about how to cite sources correctly. Another reason is that many college students plagiarize on purpose. An informal poll conducted in 2007 revealed that 60.8 percent of college students who responded admitted to cheating.[1]

Of course, intentional plagiarism is most disturbing. In fact, of those polled, 16.5 percent of those who plagiarized felt no guilt for doing so. Plagiarists justify their actions, in part, because higher grades lead to more "success." Before taking plagiarism lightly, consider the following:

> Psychologists at the University of British Columbia found that students who cheated in high school and college were likely to meet the criteria for psychopathic personality . . . . The researchers found that academic cheaters also scored high in two other personality traits: narcissism (people who suffer from grandiosity, self-centeredness and an outsized sense of entitlement) and Machiavellianism (cynical, amoral types who make it a habit to manipulate others). But of the three disordered personalities . . . psychopathy was the only trait significantly associated with student cheating.[2]

If you would like to learn more about the causes of and cures for plagiarism, excellent sites offer resources, such as **Plagiarism.org**. While citation can be intimidating at first, building skills is an effective way to overcome anxiety and build confidence about citing correctly. Only by doing the work yourself will you see *results that matter*.

- The first section, *Quotation Marks, Ellipses, and Parentheses*, reviews how to use quotation marks and other minor marks of punctuation, including brackets.

- The second section, *Citation*, reviews a few key points for in-text citation using American Psychological Association (APA) and American Sociological Association (ASA) citation styles.

When you have completed this chapter, you will be able to:

- Apply closed punctuation style with quotation marks.

- Use proper spacing with ellipsis marks, parentheses, and brackets.

- Understand the basics of in-text citation for APA and ASA citation styles.

- Know how to format a reference page.

When you use a direct quotation or a paraphrase, you need to cite it. However, for academic writing, use quotations rarely and paraphrase sparingly. Papers that are full of quotations are not well-received, especially when quotations are long.

Quotation Marks, Ellipses, and Parentheses

This section includes information on using marks of punctuation that are often associated with quotation and citation. As you review the information, also learn the correct way to type these marks. For example, for quotation marks, do you type the marks inside or outside a period? For ellipses, how many periods are used and how are they spaced?

However, before you review this section, note that for academic writing you should *use quotations sparingly*: do not hide behind quotations thinking that the results will be good. Professors are not impressed by papers full of quotations, even if they are cited correctly. Write from your own voice; if that's a challenge for you now, write every day, summarizing new information. Becoming proficient with writing is a matter of practice; becoming proficient with editing is a matter of applying principles until you know them well.

Quotation Marks

The primary reasons for using quotation marks are as follows:

- Inserting a direct quote of three or fewer lines within the body of a document.

- Identifying technical terms or coined expressions that may be unfamiliar.

- Using words humorously or ironically.

- Showing a slang expression or an intentionally misused word.

However, do not use quotation marks to make a word stand out, for example:

> **That is a really "good" idea.**

In the above example, your reader will assume that you really do not mean the idea is *good* because the reader may assume you were being sarcastic. To avoid overuse of quotation marks, follow this advice: *When in doubt, leave quotations out.*

There are two basic ways to display quotation marks: the *closed style* and the *open style*. The closed style is the correct one to use with APA and ASA styles. Here is the major difference between the two:

- **Closed style:** Place quotation marks outside commas and periods; for example: "Thank you."

- **Open style:** Place quotation marks inside commas and periods; for example: "Thank you".

While the open style is used in the UK, the closed style is used in the United States. Thus, this book, the APA, and the ASA all apply the *closed style.*

Quotation Marks and Punctuation

When using quotation marks, make sure to display them correctly in conjunction with other punctuation marks, such as *commas*, *periods*, *semicolons*, and *colons*.

When applying closed punctuation style, here are rules to remember:

- *Commas* and *periods* (including ellipses marks) are placed inside quotation marks.

  When I read the case file, "Brown et al.," I called my supervisor. In her message back to me, she stated, "Call me immediately."

- *Semicolons* and *colons* are placed outside quotation marks.

  The judge instructed, "Leave the courtroom immediately"; we all responded accordingly.

- Footnotes are placed directly outside quotation marks (no space added).

  According to the Infectious Disease Clinics (2008), the virus can spread quickly: "Insects, birds and some species of animal are carriers . . . across the continent."[2]

- The placement of *question marks* depends on the meaning. That is, does the quotation itself pose a question, or is the quotation within a sentence that poses the question. (The same pattern is followed for *exclamation points*.)

  Did Browning really say, "Less is more"?

  Was it Elizabeth who said, "What are our options?"

Finally, never double punctuate at the end of a sentence:

Incorrect: She said, "That's a great idea!".

Corrected: She said, "That's a great idea!"

Short Quotations

Incorporate direct quotes *less than 40 words long* into your narrative and set them off by using quotation marks.

Example 1: "Understanding the context of practice is an essential component of social work practice as is providing service that respects diversity" (Green, Gregory, & Mason 2009, p. 413).

Example 2: According to Nixon and Murr (2006), "the development of professional practice is based on practice learning, yet there is no consensus about its definition" (p. 798).

Long Quotations

Display quotations of *40 or more words* in block-quote format. Display the quotation separately from the text by doing the following:

- Indent the quote 0.5 inches from the left margin. (Do not use quotation marks; the indentation signals the reader to the quote.)

- In APA style, double space the quotation along with the body of your paper; in ASA, the quotation may be single spaced.

- Place the period at the end of the quote, not at the end of the citation.

    Although beginning practitioners often think that methods, approaches, or skills are the critical factors in achieving good client outcomes, clients surveyed in many research studies reported that the relationship qualities of warmth, respect, genuineness, empathy, and acceptance were most important. (Chang et al. 2009, p. 72)

Quotations within Quotations

For short quotes (less than 40 words of quoted material within text):

- Display the main quote between double quotation marks.

- Display the internal quote with single quotation marks.

    Example 1: According to Kegan (1983), "Carl Rogers's 'client-centered' or 'nondirective' therapy has had an enormous influence on the training and practice of three generations of counselors and therapists" (p. 302).

    Example 2: According to Cummins, Byers, and Pedrick (2011), "[l]ong-time policy practitioners realize that 'it is really all about relationship'" (p. 19).

Indirect Quotes or Paraphrasing

When you paraphrase, you express an author's ideas in your own words and should not use quotation marks. However, you must credit the source by using the author's last name and date. By citing the resources that informed your statement, you assure the reader that you understand the information and how it relates to your topic. Here is a paraphrase of the quote in a previous example by Chang et al.:

> According to Chang, Scott, and Decker (2009) and several other authors, clients thought the most helpful part of social services was the warm, accepting, respectful, genuine, and empathetic relationship with the practitioner.

Changing Words in Quotations

At times, you must change or add a word or two to quoted material so that the reader can make sense of the quote in its new context.

- When you add a word or two of your own, put them between brackets: [ ]

  Jones (2012) asked what "knowledge, skills, and values [were] necessary for culturally competent service provision" (p. 3).

  Note: On most keyboards, brackets are located to the right of the "p" key.

Omitting Words in Quotations

Use ellipses to show omission of a word or words. An ellipsis mark consists of three spaced periods. If the omission comes at the end of a sentence of quoted material, add one more period to indicate the end of the sentence.

> Karger and Stoesz (2010) indicated that,

> Poverty is a fluid . . . process for most Americans. The University of Michigan's Panel Study of Income Dynamics . . . followed 5,000 families for almost 10 years (1969 – 1978) and found that 2 percent of families were persistently poor throughout the entire period. (p. 112)

Since ellipses are used for more than omitting words in quotations, they are discussed in more detail below.

Ellipses

Ellipses is the plural form of *ellipsis* marks. Ellipses inform the reader that you are leaving out information. Since ellipses indicate that information is missing, their use removes an otherwise awkward gap.

In formal documents, ellipses allow writers to adapt quotations by leaving out less relevant information, making the main idea stand out. In informal documents, ellipses allow writers to jump from one idea to another without entirely completing their thoughts. Ellipses also allow the writer to convey a sense of uncertainty without coming right out and stating it.

- Ellipsis marks consist of three periods with a space before, between, and after each one, for example:

  This doesn't make sense to me . . . let me know what you think.

- The only time a fourth period would be used is when the missing information is at the end of the sentence in a formal quotation, for example:

  According to Goleman (1995), "[T]he topics taught include self-awareness, in the sense of recognizing feelings and building a vocabulary for them, and seeing the links between thoughts, feelings, and reactions . . . ." (p. 268)

- However, some software programs create ellipses when you space once, type three periods in a row, and then space once again, as follows:

  Vic was not pleased ... he will call back later.

For most academic and legal documents, unspaced ellipses are *not* acceptable. Thus, before using the unspaced ellipsis illustrated above, check to make sure that it is acceptable practice within the domain in which you are submitting your work. Use ellipsis marks sparingly, but correctly, even for informal use.

Parentheses

Parentheses are used for various reasons, citation being only one of them. Here are other reasons for using parentheses:

- Give a brief explanation within a sentence.
- Insert a sentence that does not directly relate to the topic of your paragraph.
- Supply abbreviations.
- Display phone numbers.

Using parentheses de-emphasizes information. Parentheses also help to break up information flow in a positive way: parentheses tell the reader that the information is related to the broader topic without the writer needing to give an explanation of how or why. By enclosing a few words in parentheses, you can sometimes avoid writing a lengthy explanation.

When you use parentheses, type them correctly by including a space before the first parenthesis and after the last one; for example:

Incorrect: My number is (312)555-5555.

Corrected: My number is (312) 555-5555.

Incorrect: Jones(2010) reported that . . .

Corrected: Jones (2010) reported that . . .

Incorrect: The study helped reveal the causes of homelessness (Jones, 2010).

Corrected: The study helped reveal the causes of homelessness (Jones, 2010).

Practice 15.1

Quotation Marks

Instructions: Place quotation marks where needed in the following sentences using *closed punctuation style*.

Incorrect:	Beth's exact words were, "I'll be in Boston next week".
Corrected:	Beth's exact words were, "I'll be in Boston next week."

1   My answer to your request is an enthusiastic "yes".

2   If you think that's a "good idea", then so do I!.

3   The code was "307A", not "370A".

4   All he wrote was, "Our dog can hunt".

5   If you call that "good timing", I don't know how to respond.

Note: See page 428 for the key to this exercise.

Citation

When you quote or paraphrase information, you need to cite it. However, for academic writing, use quotations rarely and paraphrase sparingly. Remember, "paraphrase" that is the same as the original with only a few changes in wording is not paraphrase. When writers "hide behind" quotations and paraphrase, it may be that they have not yet found their own voice or are not confident in it.

In-Text Citation

APA and ASA styles both use in-text citation. In-text citation refers to *parenthetical author-date references* in the body of the text.

In-text citation is markedly different from the use of footnotes and endnotes for citation. Writers accustomed to citation styles that employ footnotes, such as the Modern Library Association (MLA) and The Chicago Manual of Style (CMOS) may find using an in-text citation system challenging at first. However, note that MLA and CMOS both have "second styles" for in-text citation. The field that you are writing in determines the style that you must use; *individual professors may also have specific requirements*. In sociology, both APA and ASA styles are used; check with your professor (or publisher) before you submit a paper to make sure that you are using the correct citation style.

To adapt to in-text citation, you must also adapt your writing style. One way to coach yourself would be to use *sentence prompts* to structure your ideas. As discussed in Chapter 3, "Research and Evidence-Based Writing," the University of Manchester's Academic Phrasebank provides a multitude of examples that can help ease you into building your academic vocabulary, such as the following:[3]

Jones (2011)	found	distinct significant	differences
	observed	considerable major	between X and Y.
		only slight	

In-Text or Parenthetical Citations

Only the basics about in-text citations are included here. When you find yourself stuck with a challenging reference, refer to the *Publication Manual for APA*, 6th edition, or the *American Sociological Association Style Guide*. In addition, several online citation generators are available.

If you use a citation generator, do not simply copy and paste it to your reference page: remove the formatting and reformat the citation so that it is displayed in hanging indent style with the correct font style and size.

Here are a few basics:

- If the author's name is in the text, follow it with the publication year in parentheses:

  Jones (2010) found that at-risk youth were more likely to . . .

- If the author's name is not in the text, enclose the last name and year of publication in parentheses:

  At-risk youth were likely to have issues with self-esteem (Jones, 2010).

- If you refer to the author and publication year as part of the narrative, that is sufficient:

  In 2010, Jones' study of at-risk youth showed that . . .

- In subsequent references within the same paragraph, the date is not necessary.

- When a work has *two* authors, cite both names each time they are referenced:

  Jones and Smithe (2011) found that among children who . . .

- When a work has *three*, *four*, or *five* authors, cite all the first time; in subsequent references, use only the surname of the first author followed by *et al.*:

  Jones et al. (2011) demonstrated that additional research was warranted.

- For parenthetical citations for six or more authors, include only the last name of the first author followed by "et al." and publication year in all parenthetical citations.

- For quotations longer than 40 words, indent the left margin 0.5 inches; do not use quotation marks; put the period before the citation.

- For short quotations, place the reference inside of the period:

  "Additional studies are needed to fill the gap" (Jones, 2010, p. 33).

Reference Page

When you find yourself stuck with a challenging reference, refer to the most recent edition of the APA or ASA style guide.[4,5] Once again, if you use a citation generator, remove the formatting and reformat the citation so that it is displayed in hanging indent style with the correct font style and size.

For APA and ASA, title the reference page "References" (not "Resources" or "Works Cited"). Center the title at the top of the page and do *not* use boldface font.

- List the references in alphabetical order (However, for each title, do not change the order of authors given in the original document: the lead author should be listed first.)

- Block the first line of each reference at the left margin.

- Indent second lines of references 0.5 inches (hanging indentation).

- Italicize the title of a book and the title of a journal and its volume number.

For APA style:

- Use last name and first initial (no first names).

- For books, use authors' last names and initials, publication date, title of work, and publication data: Jones, S., & Barker, D. (2012). *Title*. City, ST: Publisher.

- Type the title of a book in *sentence case*, the title of an article in *sentence case*, and the title of a journal in *title case*.

- For sentence case, capitalize only the first word of book titles, the first word after a colon (subtitle), and proper nouns or proper adjectives.

Recap

By reviewing the basic information in this chapter, you have sufficient understanding of in-text reference systems to write a first draft. For your final draft, retrieve any additional details you need from the APA or ASA style guide.

Writing Workshop

Writing Practice: APA/ASA Formatting

Instructions: Select a paper that you have previously written and revise it using APA or ASA format and citation style; use at least two heading levels. Include the following parts:

- Title page

- Abstract

- Introduction

- Body (at least two pages)

- Conclusion

- Reference page

To refresh your knowledge of APA and ASA formatting, see Chapter 6, "APA and ASA Citation Styles," as well as Chapter 12, "Formatting." You will also find information about writing an abstract in Chapter 4, "Literature Review."

References

1   Open Education Database, https://oedb.org/ilibrarian/8-astonishing-stats-on-academic-cheating/, accessed May 20, 2018.

2   Song, S. (2010). "Profiling student cheaters: Are they psychopaths?," http://healthland.time.com/2010/09/20/profiling-student-cheaters-are-they-psychopaths/, accessed May 21, 2018

3   The University of Manchester's Academic Phrasebank, http://www.phrasebank.manchester.ac.uk/

4   APA. (2010). *Publication manual of the American Psychological Association* (6th ed). Washington, DC: American Psychological Association.

5   ASA. (2014). *American Sociological Association style guide* (5th ed). Washington, DC: American Sociological Association.

Capitalization and Number Usage

Capitalization is a writing trap. When writers are unsure of the rules, they have a tendency to capitalize too many words. And sometimes when they are "sure of the rules," they also capitalize too many words. For e-communication, unsure writers sometimes put everything in lower case . . . or everything in all capital letters, both of which garner negative responses in professional environments. In this chapter, you learn basic guidelines so that you can make correct decisions about capitalization, and some of those rules may surprise you.

When you use numbers in a document, should they be written as words or numerals? Since writing in sociology often involves numbers, you will be at an advantage to know the rules. For example, you will be including quantitative research as evidence in papers that you write; and qualitative research often contains numbers as well. When you learn the rules for numbers, you will be able to make clear, consistent decisions so that your documents are correct and credible.

However, capitalization and number rules are not "set in stone" the way that grammar and punctuation rules are—instead, some capitalization and number rules vary from one citation style to the next. As you learn basic guidelines, notice that specific requirements of American Psychological Association (APA) and American Sociological Association (ASA) are also discussed throughout the chapter.

When you have completed this chapter, you will be able to:

- Apply capitalization rules in academic and professional writing.

- Understand the difference between common nouns and proper nouns.

- Distinguish between when to spell out numbers and when to use numerals.

- Know when to use the word *percentage* as compared to *percent*.

This chapter gives you the information that you need to make most decisions on using capitalization and numbers; let's get started with capitalization. (And by the way, the personal pronoun *I* is *always* capitalized.)

Capitalization

When writers feel unsure about capitalization, they sometimes capitalize words in a seemingly random manner. Do not base your decisions on someone else's writing, as you may simply be picking up their errors and making them your own.

By learning a few basic rules, many of your questions about capitalization will be answered. Start by applying the general rule, "When in doubt, do not capitalize." Then, when you are unsure, do a bit of research to find out what the rules support. Whether you are writing a formal paper or a casual e-mail message, applying standard rules of capitalization gives your writing credibility.

Proper Nouns versus Common Nouns

Before you work on individual rules of capitalization, the most basic place to start is identifying the difference between common nouns and proper nouns.[1]

- A *proper noun* is the official name of a particular person, place, or thing.

- A *common noun* is a general term that refers to a class of things.

Proper nouns are always capitalized; common nouns are not capitalized.

Proper Noun	Common Noun
John Wilson	name, person, friend, business associate
Wilson Corporation	company, corporation, business
Water Tower Place	shopping mall
Diet Pepsi	soda, pop, soda pop
New York	state, city

Italy	country
Atlantic Ocean	ocean
American Sociological Association	sociologist
Bachelor of Arts in Sociology	bachelor's degree in sociology

Names are proper nouns, and that includes the names of people as well as the names of places and things, such as the following:

Titles of literary and artistic works	*Chicago Tribune*, the Bible
Periods of time and historical events	Great Depression, Information Age
Imaginative names and nicknames	Big Apple, Windy City
Brand and trade names	IBM, 3M, Xerox copier
Points of the compass	the North, the South, the Southwest (*referring to specific geographic regions*)
Place names	Coliseum, Eiffel Tower
Organization names	International Sociological Association
Words derived from proper nouns	English, South American
Days of the week, months, and holidays	Thanksgiving, Christmas, Chanukah
Racial and ethnic groups	Hispanic, Asian, African American, Appalachian, European

While the names of racial and ethnic groups that represent geographical locations or linguistic populations (such as those listed above) are capitalized, do not capitalize *black* and *white* when designating racial groups.

Words derived from proper nouns become *proper adjectives* and are capitalized:

Proper noun	**Derivative or proper adjective**
England	English language
Spain	Spanish olive oil
Italy	Italian cookware
French	French class

Articles, Conjunctions, and Prepositions in Titles

In titles of organizations as well as literary and artistic works, the following words would be capitalized *only* as the first word of a title or subtitle:

Articles (*the*, *a*, *an*)
Conjunctions (*and*, *but*, *or*, *nor*)
Prepositions of three or fewer letters (*to*, *at*, *in*, *for*)

- **APA style** requires that prepositions of *four or more letters* be *capitalized*.[2]

- **ASA style** requires that prepositions be in lower case, even those that have four or more letters, such as *with*, *from*, and *among*.

Here are some examples:

> The University of Chicago*
>
> *Pride and Prejudice*
>
> *Tuesdays With Morrie* (APA style)
>
> *Tuesdays with Morrie* (ASA style)

> **Note*: For ASA style, in running text do not capitalize the word *the* for institution titles such as *the University of Chicago*, *the University of Illinois System*, *the University of Wisconsin-Whitewater*, and so on.[3]

First Words

Another category of importance when it comes to capitalization is *first words*. Capitalize the first word of each of the following:

- Sentences
- Poems
- Direct quotations that are complete sentences
- Independent questions within a sentence
- Items displayed in a list or an outline
- Salutations/greetings and complimentary closings

Note: Also capitalize the first word of a complete sentence that follows a word of instruction or caution, such as *Note* or *Caution* (as illustrated here).

Professional Titles

Some writers capitalize all titles, thinking that a title is an official category or proper noun. However, a title is *not* a proper noun; here's the general rule:

* Capitalize titles when they precede a name, but not when they are part of an appositive.

* Do not capitalize titles when they follow a name.

Here are some examples:

Incorrect: John Smith, Marketing Director, will meet with us today.

Corrected: John Smith, marketing director, will meet with us today.

Corrected: Marketing Director John Smith will meet with us today.

Here are a few more examples:

Dee Sims, director of admissions, will assist you.

You can speak with Professor Ferretti at 3 p.m.

They sent the letter to A. S. Ferretti, professor, at his Rome address.

Mr. Shaun O'Brien, marketing director, will arrive shortly.

Once again, do not capitalize a title that follows the name of a person. Also, do not capitalize a title that is used as a substitute for a specific personal name. For example:

Please send this to George Martinez, president of Martinez and Associates.

The president will visit our office later; please greet President Martinez when he arrives.

However, here's an exception to this rule: Capitalize the titles of high-ranking government officials, foreign dignitaries, or international figures even when the title follows the name or stands alone.

The President met with the reporters at the White House.

The Vice President asked the president of our company to lead his campaign.

Titles versus Occupations

Though titles are capitalized when they precede a name, occupations such as lawyer, accountant, financial analyst, marketing director, human resources director, and so on, are not capitalized.

My lawyer Bert Hernandez will take care of the matter.

Your accountant Virginia Christopher can handle this.

The report was made by financial analyst Ronald DuPreis.

The term *doctor* can be either a title or an occupation; the same is true for professor. Thus, capitalize *doctor* and *professor* in a direct address.

Thank you, Professor, for responding.

I asked my doctor and my professor for advice about nutrition.

Would you, Doctor, give the information to my assistant?

When requested, Professor Jones agreed to chair the committee.

Organizational Terms

Capitalize common organizational terms in your own company, such as *marketing department, research division, human resources department,* and *board of directors.* Do not capitalize these terms when they refer to departments at another organization unless you want to show special importance.

The Board of Directors meets on the first Friday of each month.

Our Human Resource Department has not completed this year's budget.

We cannot proceed until their marketing department submits the information.

Our Marketing Department will celebrate the announcement.

In each of the above examples, using lower case for each organizational term would also have been acceptable.

Abbreviations, Acronyms, and Initialisms

An *acronym* is a form of abbreviation formed from the initial letters of other words and pronounced as one word, such as the following:

NATO   North Atlantic Treaty Organization

AIDS   Auto-Immune Deficiency Syndrome

An *initialism* is an abbreviation formed from a string of initials and generally pronounced as individual letters, such as the following:

BBC   British Broadcasting Corporation

ASA   American Sociological Association

While acronyms and initialisms are written in all-capital letters, abbreviations are generally not capitalized. For example, "a.m." and "p.m." are abbreviations for "before noon" (*ante meridian*) and "after noon" (*post meridian*). However, if the abbreviation is *uncommon* and derived from a foreign word, it is placed in italics.

Hyphenated Words

At times, you will need to determine how to capitalize hyphenated words for titles and works.

- For **ASA style**, capitalize only the first element of a hyphenated word, unless the second element is a proper noun or adjective or a spelled-out number or fraction, for example:[4]

  The Dynamic of Self-concept: A Social Psychological Perspective

  Post-Vietnam War Reconstruction: Challenges for South-East Asia

  The Transition to Adulthood in the Twenty-First Century

- For general writing, capitalize each word of a hyphenated term used in a title (except short prepositions and conjunctions, as previously noted), for example:

Up-to-Date Reports   Mid-July Conference

E-Mail Guidelines   Long-Term Outlook

APA Style: Title Case and Sentence Case

For presenting titles, APA style employs two different types of capitalization styles, *title case* and *sentence case*.

- For *title case*, type titles in upper- and lower-case letters, following the basic guidelines for capitalization presented in this chapter. For example, capitalize all words in the title except for articles, conjunctions, and prepositions of three letters or fewer. Use title case for the following:

  o   The title of your paper on the title page.

  o   The title of a book, article, or chapter *within the text of your paper*.

- For *sentence case*, capitalize the first word of the title and the first word following a colon (the subtitle) as well as proper nouns and proper adjectives; all other words are typed in lower case. Use sentence case as follows:

  o   The titles of books, articles, or websites (but not the title of the publisher or a journal) *with references listed on the reference page*.

In text: *Tuesdays With Morrie: An Old Man, a Young Man, and Life's Greatest Lesson*

Reference: *Tuesdays with Morrie: An old man, a young man, and life's greatest lesson*

Two Common Capitalization Errors

You will have made important progress with capitalization if you stop capitalizing common nouns and follow the rules discussed above. However, the following two common types of error fit into a special class of their own.

Leaving the personal pronoun *I* in lower case

The personal pronoun *I* should always be represented in upper case. Partly due to text messaging, the problem of leaving the personal pronoun *I* in lower case has escalated, for example:

Incorrect: A friend asked me if i could help, so i said that i would.

Corrected: A friend asked if I could help, so I said that I would.

Whenever you use the pronoun *I*, capitalize it; and that includes its use in e-mail messages.

Using all UPPER CASE or all lower case

When writers type messages in all upper case or all lower case, it is generally because they are unsure about writing decisions. While neither version is correct, using all upper case has earned the reputation that the writer is shouting, which often is not the intention: writing in all caps may seem like an "easy way out" of making capitalization decisions.

When writers use all lower case, it sometimes reflects a tradition within certain professional niches. For example, some computer professionals communicate primarily with other technical professionals, and they write to each other almost exclusively in lower case. When communicating with professionals outside of their inner circle, even technical professionals would enhance communication by adapting to the broader audience and applying standard rules of capitalization.

Practice 16.1

Capitalization

Instructions: In the following paragraph, correct errors in capitalization.

Next Year the President of my Company will provide a financial incentive for all employees, and I plan to participate in it. jack Edwards, Vice President of Finance, will administer the plan. Everyone in my department is looking forward to having the opportunity to save more. A pamphlet entitled, "financial incentives for long-term savings," will describe the plan and be distributed next week. If the pamphlet has not arrived by friday, I will check with the vice President's Office to find out the details.

Note: See page 429 for the key to the above exercise.

Using Numbers

In this section, you learn general guidelines about how to display numbers, with a focus on their use in **APA style** and **ASA style**. In fact, there is not one definite set of number rules that are followed universally.

When in doubt about using numbers, check the APA and ASA style guides. (Since ASA is derived from Chicago Style, you can also check *The Chicago Manual of Style, 17th Edition*, for more details.)

Number Usage in APA and ASA Style

Here are some points about basic number usage in APA and ASA style.[5,6]

Point 1: Spelling out Numbers in Words

Spell out numbers in words for the following:

- Numbers one through nine within written text
- Ordinal numbers one through nine, such as "first," "second," and so on
- The first word of a sentence, such as "Fifty participants were . . . ."
- Centuries, such as "nineteenth century" or "twentieth century"
- Common fractions, such as "one half"

Point 2: Using Figures for Numbers

Use numerals for the following:

- Numbers 10 and above within written text
- Ordinal numbers 10 and above, such as "10th," "15th," and so on
- All numbers in an abstract
- References to tables, such as "Table 5" and "Figure 3"
- Precise units of measurement, such as "2 mm" or "2 inches"
- Statistical or mathematical functions, proportions, and ratios; for example:

- o   6 divided by 2

- o   5 times as many graduates

- o   3 of the 4 applicants (proportion)

- o   a ratio of 3:1

- A sample size or specific number of participants, such as "7 participants"

- Percentages

  - o   For **APA style**, use the percent symbol after a numeral: 10%

  - o   For **ASA style**, use the word *percent* in text: 10 percent

  - o   Use the word "percent" after any number expressed as a word, such as a number that begins a sentence, title or text heading: "Five percent of the returns . . . ."

  - o   Use the word "percentage," not "percent" when no number appears with it: "a high percentage of respondents . . . ."

- Ages, for example:

  - o   The sample included 9- to 12-year-olds.

  - o   The participants of the study were 21 years old.

- Exact sums of money, such as "$15.92"

- Numbered series, parts of books, tables, such as "pages 53 – 64"

Point 3: Large Numbers

Combine numerals and words for the following:

- Numbers in the millions or higher can be written as a combination of figures and words if the number can be expressed as a whole number or as a whole number plus a simple fraction or a decimal amount, for example:

  - o   Our company extended their $1.5 million loan until April.

Point 4: Dates and Times

- Spell out the names of months; use figures for days:

  o   September 12, 2018

  o   November 2011 (no comma needed)

- Use figures for time and use the abbreviations *a.m.* and *p.m.* or the word *o'clock*, but not both.

  o   4 p.m.

  o   4 o'clock in the afternoon

- For time on the hour, you may omit the :00 (unless you want to emphasize time on the hour).

- Use the ordinal ending for dates only when the day *precedes* the month.

  o   21st of February

  Note: Use a combination of numerals and words to express back-to-back modifiers.

  The Beck Depression scale has four 10-point subscales.

  Note: Write indefinite numbers, such as *thousands* or *hundreds*, in words.

  We were pleased with the hundreds of positive responses.

Addresses and Phone Numbers

The APA and ASA styles are used for academic citation, so they do not provide guidelines for typing addresses or phone numbers. However, when you write in professional arenas, you will need to format addresses and phone numbers. One example would be your résumé. Here are some basic guidelines to apply to professional documents.

In general, do not abbreviate parts of addresses unless space is tight or you are following a specific system of addressing. However, do not abbreviate simply for convenience. Here are some rules for displaying addresses:

- Spell out parts of addresses: Do not abbreviate points of the compass such as *North* or *South* or words such as *avenue, street,* or *apartment*.

- Spell out street names *One* through *Ten*.

- Use figures for all house numbers except the number *One*.

- Add ordinal endings only when points of the compass (North, South, East, and West) are not included, for example: 1400 59th Street.

- Use two-letter state abbreviations; leave one or two spaces between the two-letter state abbreviation and the zip code.

- Do not place a period after a two-letter state abbreviation.

Here are some examples:

Mr. Alistair Cromby	Dr. Michael Jules
One West Washington Avenue	1214 79th Place, Suite 290
St. Clair, MN 56080	Chesterton, IN 46383
Mrs. Lionel Hershey	Ms. Lorel Lindsey
141 Meadow Lane South	Associate Director
Seattle, WA 92026	The Fine Arts Studio
	500 North State Street, Suite 311
	Chicago, IL 60611-6043

For foreign addresses, type the name of the country on the last line in all capital letters, as shown below:

Mr. Lucas M. Matthews	Pierluigi e Sylvia D'Amici
72 O'Manda Road	Via Davide Bello No. 1
Lake Olivia, VIC 3709	00151 ROMA
AUSTRALIA	ITALIA

Display phone numbers by using parentheses around the area code or by using a hyphen or period between parts. Displaying phone numbers in these styles makes them easier to read.

Please call (212) 555-1212 at your earliest convenience.

You can reach me at 312-555-1212.

I left the message at 502.555.1212.

Practice 16.2

Numbers

Instructions: Make corrections to the way numbers are displayed in the following sentences.

Incorrect:	Reggie sent ten copies of the report, but I received only 5.
Corrected:	Reggie sent 10 copies of the report, but I received only five.

1   We r meeting on Jan. 5 at 10 AM at our offices on Lake St.

2   Call me on Mon. at 4075551212.

3   Alex lists his address as 407 S. Maple St., Hobart, Ind. 46368.

4   We received 100s of calls about the job opening but only five résumés.

5   Purchase 12 laptops but only 7 new printers for our department.

Note: See page 429 for the key to the above exercise.

Recap

Rules create standards so that everyone can understand the meaning of the message, reducing confusion and misunderstanding. By following the rules, you are adapting your writing to your audience, which not only improves the quality of your writing but also improves your credibility as a writer.

• Capitalize proper nouns, but not common nouns.

• Always capitalize the personal pronoun *I*.

• Capitalize a business title when it precedes a person's name, but not when it follows the name.

• Spell out numbers one through nine; use figures for numbers 10 and above.

By writing correctly, you show respect for your readers, enhancing relationships as well as your ability to communicate across borders and continents.

16.1 TWO-LETTER STATE ABBREVIATIONS

Alabama	AL	Montana	MT
Alaska	AK	Nebraska	NE
Arizona	AZ	Nevada	NV
Arkansas	AR	New Hampshire	NH
California	CA	New Jersey	NJ
Colorado	CO	New Mexico	NM
Connecticut	CT	New York	NY
Delaware	DE	North Carolina	NC
District of Columbia	DC	North Dakota	ND
Florida	FL	Ohio	OH
Georgia	GA	Oklahoma	OK
Guam	GU	Oregon	OR
Hawaii	HI	Pennsylvania	PA
Idaho	ID	Puerto Rico	PR
Illinois	IL	Rhode Island	RI
Indiana	IN	South Carolina	SC
Iowa	IA	South Dakota	SD
Kansas	KS	Tennessee	TN
Kentucky	KY	Texas	TX
Louisiana	LA	Utah	UT
Maine	ME	Vermont	VT
Maryland	MD	Virgin Islands	VI
Massachusetts	MA	Virginia	VA
Michigan	MI	Washington	WA
Minnesota	MN	West Virginia	WV
Mississippi	MS	Wisconsin	WI
Missouri	MO	Wyoming	WY

Note: Do *not* put a period after a two-letter state abbreviation.

Writing Workshop

Instructions: Select two journal articles about sociological topics of interest, one article quantitative and the other qualitative.

1   Identify five examples of how numbers are represented in the text of each article. Are the numbers written in words or figures? Can you identify which rules apply?

2   Identify five examples of words that are capitalized in the text: can you identify which rules apply?

References

1   Young, D. (2008). *Business English: Writing for the global workplace.* Burr Ridge, IL: McGraw-Hill Higher Education.

2   APA. (2010). *Publication manual of the American Psychological Association* (6th ed). Washington, DC: American Psychological Association.

3   ASA. (2014). *American Sociological Association style guide* (5th ed). Washington, DC: American Sociological Association, p. 31.

4   Ibid.

5   Ibid., pp. 32–34.

6   APA (2010), Op. cit.

17 Apostrophes and Hyphens

When writers omit apostrophes and hyphens where they are needed, it may be due to uncertainty, such as about where to place an apostrophe to show possession. Possessives are difficult enough when the noun is regular and singular, but what happens if the noun is irregular and plural or ends in an *s*? And since the hyphen is used infrequently, it too is often omitted when needed, such as for compound modifiers and even phone numbers.

Then there is the use of the apostrophe with contractions: some writers omit using apostrophes with contractions, possibly a habit developed as a result of texting. This approach not only results in writing that is incorrect, it sends a message that the writer lacks professional skills. To connect with all types of audiences, adhere to the rules of language.

- The first section, *The Apostrophe*, covers singular and plural possessives along with other writing traps, such as contractions and hyphenated words. To work on possessives, you start with contractions and then review singular and plural possessives, regular and irregular.

- The second section, *The Hyphen*, covers the use of hyphens with word division, group modifiers and numbers as well as with prefixes and suffixes.

When you have completed this chapter, you will be able to:

- Punctuate regular and irregular possessives, singular and plural, correctly.

- Identify abstract nouns that are possessive.

- Punctuate group nouns, nouns in series, and abbreviations.

- Identify possessives standing alone.

- Use apostrophes to form contractions.

- Use hyphens with compound modifiers, compound numbers, and certain prefixes.

The Apostrophe

The apostrophe has two basic uses: to form contractions and to show possession. This chapter starts with the simpler application, contractions, and then moves to the more complicated, forming possessives. When apostrophes are missing from contractions and possessives, readers can be distracted. For the most part, using an apostrophe correctly is an easy problem to solve.

Contractions

Apostrophes are used to construct contractions, which make writing sound more conversational. While contractions are acceptable for use in e-mail and other informal types of writing, avoid using contractions for formal or academic writing. For example, *APA does not accept contractions.*

The most common contractions are verbs, which can be shortened by omitting a few letters and using the apostrophe in their place. When writers misspell contractions by leaving out the apostrophe, they are making spelling errors.

Verb	Contraction	Error
will not	won't	wont
cannot	can't	cant
do not	don't	dont

The above errors in spelling are possibly the result of using texting keyboards. Here is a sample of contractions that are formed with pronouns and verbs and that are also often misspelled:

Original	Contraction	Similar word
You are	You're	Your
They are	They're	Their or There
It is, it has	It's	Its
We are	We're	Were

The types of contractions listed above create different types of spelling problems for writers because they are often confused with words that sound alike but have different meanings. You will find more information on these similar words in Chapter 18, "Word Usage: Unbiased Language and *More*."

Practice 17.1

Apostrophes: Possessives and Contractions

Instructions: Make corrections where needed in the following sentences.

Incorrect: Its all in a days work.

Corrected: It's all in a day's work.

1   My supervisors report wont be ready until next week.

2   The weather report says its going to rain later, but I dont believe it.

3   Though its Junes responsibility, its in Jacks best interest to complete the task.

4   Dr. Jones office isnt located down the hall; its next to Dr. Raines.

5   If you tell me its Tess project, i'll adjust my expectations.

Note: See page 429 for the key to the above exercise.

Possessives

The most common use of the apostrophe is with possessives, which come in a variety of forms, most of which are discussed here. To start, whenever you see a noun ending in an *s*, ask yourself, *Is this noun plural or possessive or both?*

Incorrect:	Bobs arrival	a few weeks projects	todays discussion
Correct:	Bob's arrival	a few weeks' projects	today's discussion

Only nouns and pronouns can show possession or ownership of other nouns. At times, it can be tricky to identify a possessive because some nouns, such as *value* or *belief* or *hope*, are not concrete objects, but are abstract.

Concrete nouns are easier to identify because you can experience them through your five senses. However, *abstract nouns*—nouns other than persons, places, or things—are not as obvious to identify. Abstract nouns can be a quality, a state, or an action, such as *humor, thought*, or *arrival*. The easiest way to identify if a word is a noun is to place the word *the* in front of it. If the phrase sounds complete, the word was probably a noun, for example: "the idea," "the thought," "the color," and "the glare."

Singular Possessives

When a singular noun shows possession, add an apostrophe and *s* (*'s*). This category is the easiest because you are taking a noun and adding to it in a logical way. Here are some examples:

Singular Noun	**Singular Possessive**
book	book's cover
project	project's due date
week	week's assignments
day	day's activities
Mary	Mary's suggestion

Sometimes it is difficult to determine if a noun is showing possession; this is especially true with inanimate objects such as *wind* or *paper*. When in doubt, ask yourself if you can change the sentence around using the word *of*. That is, *the paper of yesterday* becomes *yesterday's paper*. Here are more examples:

the end of the semester	the semester's end
force of the wind	the wind's force
the work of one day	a day's work

the results of the poll   the poll's results

the success of our team   our team's success

At times, possessives can sound awkward, especially when a group of words string together to show possession, as in the following:

Awkward: an associate of mine's idea

my sister's accountant's advice

my manager's supervisor's request

When awkward constructions occur, show the possession by changing the word order, as shown below:

Preferred: an idea of an associate of mine (or an associate's idea)

the advice of my sister's accountant

the request of my manager's supervisor

Often when "mine" is written as "mines" or "mine's," it is a form of local language and would be incorrect according to standard usage, for example:

Incorrect: Mines are on the table.

Corrected: Mine are on the table.

Practice 17.2

Possessives: The Basics

Instructions: Change the following to the possessive form.

Example: the permission of the owner   the owner's permission

1   the price of the book

2   the cover of the report

3   the influence of the team leader

4   the advice of my professor

5   the reports of the agency

Note: See page 430 for the key to the above exercise.

Singular Nouns Ending in S

To form the possessive of a singular noun that ends in *s*, add an apostrophe alone or add an apostrophe plus an *s* (*'s*). Follow these guidelines:

- If a new syllable is formed in the pronunciation of the possessive, add an apostrophe plus *s*, as in the following:

    the witness's answer

    Dallas's downtown area

    the hostess's guest list

    the actress's role

- If the addition of an extra syllable would make the word challenging to pronounce, add only the apostrophe, as in the following:

    Mr. Jones' (*or* Mr. Jones's) office

    Mark Phillips' briefcase

    for goodness' sake

Regular Plural Possessives

To form the possessive of a regular plural noun which would end in *s* or *es*, add an apostrophe after the *s* (*s'*). In other words, make the singular form of the noun plural before you make the noun possessive.

Singular Possessive	Plural Possessive
the owner's address	a few owners' addresses
our manager's decision	all of the mangers' decisions
my shirt's collar	my shirts' collars
my friend's books	my friends' books

When the singular form of a noun already ends in s, make the noun plural by adding es to the singular. Then form the possessive by adding an apostrophe, for example:

Singular	Plural	Singular Possessive	Plural Possessive
business	businesses	business's owner	businesses' owners
virus	viruses	virus's origination	viruses' originations

Notice in the above examples that when the possessive noun is plural, the object it modifies is also plural. That's because the objects being possessed are *count nouns*, nouns that can become plural.

In contrast, some nouns come in mass and are considered *noncount nouns*; examples include *paint* or *cake* or *food*. Other examples of noncount nouns are *honor*, *integrity*, and *humor*.

Singular Possessive	Plural Possessive
a boy scout's honor	several boy scouts' honor
a person's integrity	many persons' integrity
a friend's help	our friends' help

For last names (surnames) that end in *s*, *x*, *ch*, *sh*, or *z*, add *es* to form the plural. Then form the plural by adding an apostrophe, as in the following:

Singular	Plural	Singular Possessive	Plural Possessive
Fox	the Foxes	Mr. Fox's car	the Foxes' family reunion
Banks	the Bankses	Mary Banks' schedule	the Bankses' get-together

Irregular Plural Possessives

To form the possessive of an irregular plural noun, change the singular form of the noun to the plural form and then add an apostrophe and *s* (children's).

Singular Possessive	Plural Possessive
the child's toy	the children's toys
one woman's comment	many women's comments
one man's idea	many men's ideas

a lady's suggestion   several ladies' suggestions

a woman's right   women's rights

Practice 17.3

Singular and Plural Possessives

Instructions: Turn the following nouns into singular possessives and then plural possessives.

Example:	contractor	contractor's schedule		contractors' schedules	
		Singular possessive		**Plural possessive**	
1	boss	my	office	both	offices
2	waitress	this	table	these	tables
3	year	this	schedule	both	schedules
4	secretary	my	laptop	our	laptops
5	client	the	needs	all	needs

Note: See page 430 for the key to the above exercise.

Academic Degrees

Use an apostrophe to show possession when referring to academic degrees in general terms:

bachelor's degree   master's degree   doctor's degree

However, academic degrees that are specific would not show possession:

master of science   bachelor of arts   doctorate

Note: Capitalize only the formal names of degrees, such as "Bachelor of Arts in Sociology."

Group Words

With group words or compound nouns, the apostrophe and the *s* are added to the last term. For example:

the queen of England's duties

the attorney general's job

her mother-in-law's address

Though an awkward construction, plural group words occasionally occur. To make a compound noun plural, add the *s* to the base word:

Awkward: their mothers-in-law's addresses

                 the attorney generals' statements

Preferred: the addresses of their mothers-in-law

                 the statements of the attorney generals

Nouns in Series

When two nouns joined by *and* share joint possession, add the apostrophe only to the last noun. When there is individual possession, add the apostrophe to both nouns. For example:

Joint Ownership	Individual Ownership
Mitch and Sophie's mother	Mitch's and Sophie's cars
Margaret and Bill's project	Margaret's and Bill's projects

Abbreviations

To make an abbreviation plural, simply add an *s*; for example:

three DVDs	blue, green, and yellow M&Ms
five VCRs	10 CDs

To make an abbreviation possessive, add an apostrophe and *s*, just as you would with regular possessive nouns. For example:

ASA's conference	the ADA's guidelines for dental hygiene
CNN's reporters	the NBA's new season

Possessives Standing Alone

At times, a writer or speaker will leave off the item of possession after the second noun. Be careful in these constructions as the second noun also shows possession.

> Barb's remark was similar to George's (remark).
>
> We will meet in Alex's office, not Miko's (office).
>
> Michele is working on her master's (degree).

Practice 17.4

More Possessives

Instructions: Look for possessives and make corrections where necessary. There may also be errors in spelling and grammar, for example:

> **Incorrect:**   My papers topic was not approved.
>
> **Corrected:**   My paper's topic was not approved.

1   Ambras and Lucias instructor refuse to let them work together.

2   Either Alexi or Basma's proposal will win the bid.

3   Milton suggested that we go to Ditkas for the holiday celebration.

4   My brother-in-laws attorneys opened their office last week.

5   Chandras and her roommate apartment need to be remodeled.

> *Note*: See page 430 for the key to the above exercise.

The Hyphen

Here are some of the primary uses of hyphens:

- To divide words.

- To form group modifiers.

- To display fractions and numbers above 21.

- To form certain prefixes and suffixes.

Each of these uses is reviewed below.

Word Division

When dividing words, divide only between syllables. Because computers have eliminated the need to divide words at the end of lines, most other principles for word division apply only to print material that must be justified. If you are unsure of how a word is broken into syllables, look it up: *When in doubt, check it out.* However, avoid dividing words whenever possible.

Note, however, that many rules for "dividing content" are still relevant. For example, when you write a paper, keep at least two lines of content on the same page as the heading. For example, do not put a heading at the bottom of one page with the narrative starting on the next page. The general rule is that at least two lines of a paragraph appear on the same page as the heading. (In fact, at least two lines of a paragraph should appear at the bottom of one page and two lines on the next page as well; otherwise, move the three-line paragraph to the top of the next page.)

Compound Modifiers

Using hyphens for compound modifiers is becoming a lost skill and merits attention. Compound modifiers are formed when two adjectives modify a noun jointly, for example:

long-term project	two-word modifiers
first-quarter report	short-term earnings
second-class service	first-class accommodations

When the modifier follows the noun, do not use a hyphen. In fact, that is one way to check usage, for example:

meetings that are high powered	high-powered meetings
information that is up to date	up-to-date information
homes that have two parents	two-parent homes

Another way to test if you need a hyphen is to check one word at a time to see if the combination makes sense; for example, the *long-term report* is neither a *long report* nor a *term report*. Both words together form *one unit of meaning*, which adding the hyphen accomplishes.

When two or more compound modifiers occur in sequence, use a *suspension hyphen* at the end of the first modifier and follow it with a space, as illustrated below:

> The short- and long-term prognoses are both excellent.

> The 30- and 60-day rates are available.

Compound Numbers

Here are a few points about hyphenating compound numbers.

- Hyphenate compound numbers from twenty-one to ninety-nine, for example:

  thirty-three   forty-nine   seventy-three

- Hyphenate fractions that are used as adjectives:

  one-half complete   two-thirds gone   one-quarter Irish

- Do not hyphenate fractions that are treated as nouns:

  George spent one half of the budget renovating his office.

- Use hyphens (or parentheses or periods) to break up phone numbers:

  202-555-1212   (202) 555-1212   202.555.1212

Prefixes

Here are a few points about common uses of hyphens with prefixes:

- Use a hyphen after the prefix *self* and the prefix *ex*, for example:

  self-confidence   self-esteem   self-employed

  ex-husband   ex-officio   ex-ante

- Use a hyphen if the prefix ends in a vowel and the root word starts with one:

  semi-annual   ultra-active   re-engage

- Use a hyphen after the prefix *re* when the same spelling could be confused with another word of the same spelling but with a different meaning:

  I re-sent the papers.   I resent your comment.

  He will re-sign the contract.   I will resign immediately.

  Sue will re-lease her car.   Sue will release the paperwork.

In the above examples, the spelling would generally not be considered incorrect if the hyphen were missing.

- Use a hyphen after a prefix that is attached to a proper noun, as follows:

  ex-President Carter   trans-Atlantic flight

  pro-American policy   pre-Roman period

Practice 17.5

Hyphens

Instructions: Make corrections as needed in the following sentences to show correct use of hyphens.

Incorrect: The short term progress is good.

Corrected: The short-term progress is good.

1   Your first class treatment has impressed all of us.

2   Our budget is one half spent.

3   The short and long term outlooks are quite different.

4   Twenty five people attended the conference.

5   Do you have funding for your 30 and 60 day payment schedules?

   Note: See page 430 for the key to the above exercise.

Recap

Below is a summary of how to use quotation marks, apostrophes, and hyphens.

Use the apostrophe to show possession:

- With singular nouns, use an apostrophe plus *s*: *cat's meow*.

- With plural nouns, use an apostrophe after the *s*: *dogs' toys*.

- With inanimate objects, use an apostrophe, as in the *wind's force*.

- For joint ownership, place the apostrophe after the second noun: *Reggie and Grey's report*.

- To show individual ownership, place the apostrophe after each noun: *Mary Lou's and Jake's cars*.

Use hyphens as follows:

- In group modifiers, such as *first-quarter report*.

- With compound numbers *twenty-one* through *ninety-nine*.

- For certain prefixes, such as *self-confident*.

- For words that could otherwise be confused, such as *re-sent*.

Writing Workshop

Apostrophe Practice

Instructions: Complete Activity 1, Apostrophe Usage A. If you need extra practice, review the principles in the chapter again before completing Activity 2, Apostrophe Usage B. You will find keys for these assessments on page 431.

Activity 1. Apostrophe Usage A

Instructions: Correct errors for apostrophe usage in the following; also correct errors in capitalization.

1   The womens' comments were not taken as they were meant.

2   Paul's and Mary's file was in the wrong cabinet.

3   Our Agencys' mission is to assist young people.

4   I have taken several classes' in Sociology this year.

5   Her Assistants response was that he could not do the work.

6   The men and women responses were recorded by the assistant.

7   The speakers remark sparked the audience laughter.

8   Its all in a days work!

Activity 2. Apostrophe Usage B

Instructions: Correct errors for apostrophe usage in the following; also correct errors in capitalization.

1   Amanda Wittfield, Director of marketing, will lead this weeks meeting.

2   Amanda will complete her Bachelor of Arts in Sociology this fall.

3   The childrens' toys were scattered around the play room.

4   He recommended reading the book *How To Find A Job In 30 Day's*.

5   When you receive your Masters Degree in Social Work, you can put MSW after your name.

6   Mary received her bachelors degree last year and is now working on her masters.

7   Every time that i tried to assist Barbs client, she refused my help.

8   This weeks activities were challenging.

The Effective Use of Words: Unbiased Language and *More*

Since language helps define the way that we perceive the world around us, the effective use of words is a critical element of sociological writing. In fact, sociology takes a strong and decisive position about using words "to promote inclusivity and diversity in all areas":

> [The] *ASA Style Guide* strongly urges the avoidance of language reflecting bias or stereotyping on the basis of gender, race, ethnicity, disabilities, sexual orientation, family status, religion, or other personal characteristics.[1]

Writers must not only be sensitive to using words effectively, they also need to use them correctly. To assist you in producing writing that is correct and sets an effective tone, this chapter contains three main sections that review word usage from the following perspectives:

- The first section, *Unbiased and Gender-Neutral Language*, assists you in updating your vocabulary to terms that are inclusive and that promote diversity. The discussion includes terminology for discussing race and ethnicity as well as disability and aging.

- The second section, *Similar Words and Tricky Combos*, covers common words that sound alike but are spelled differently and have different meanings, such as *its* and *it's* or *affect* and *effect*. You may find that you are regularly using some of these similar words incorrectly.

- The final section, *Spelling Tips*, covers various ways to build your vocabulary as well as providing some Greek and Latin roots.

When you have completed this chapter, you will be able to:

- Use unbiased and gender-neutral language in writing and speech.

- Apply effective language when referring to racial and ethnic groups, elderly people, and people with challenges and disabilities.

- Improve your use of similar words, such as *your/you're* and *definite/ defiant*, among others.

- Build vocabulary by understanding Greek and Latin roots, prefixes, and suffixes.

This chapter will support you in presenting your ideas and research in an unbiased and "value-free" style. In fact, using language effectively is important in every profession, not only sociology.

Unbiased and Gender-Neutral Language

Word choices create a picture, setting a tone. For the sake of accuracy and diversity, choose words that eliminate bias from your writing and your speech. The American Sociological Association (ASA) and the American Psychological Association (APA) give specific language guidelines, which are discussed in this section along with other sources.[2,3] For example, the National Association of Social Workers (NASW) publishes a pamphlet, *Press Guidelines for Describing People*; here is a summary of some key points:[4]

- Seek and use the preference of the people you are writing about.

- Be specific about age, race, and culture.

- Describe people positively by stating what they are instead of what they are not.

- Avoid using terms that label people; for example, refer to people as *people*, not as objects, using a phrase such as *people with disabilities* rather than *the disabled*.

- Do not specify sex unless it is a variable or it is essential to the discussion.

These points and others are discussed below. However, language is an ever-changing tool. For additional information, do an internet search on "language guidelines for describing people." For example, another excellent source is the National Center on Disability and Journalism, which also offers a style guide.[5] Thus, do not be limited by the few examples discussed here.

Gender-Neutral Language

The ASA Style Guide recommends the following:[6]

> Unless gendered terms are specific to analysis of data or demographics, use nongendered terms such as *person, people, individual*, or *humankind* rather than *man, men,* or *mankind*.

Gender neutrality was also discussed in Chapter 10, "Pronouns and Viewpoint," in which it was pointed out that, while there is no absolute answer, writers have a variety of ways around the issue of being gender specific. Here are some ways to avoid using gender in writing.

- Avoid slashed gender terms (*he/she*), repetition of the conjunction *or* (*he or she*), and switching gender order (*he or she* and then *she or he*, and so on). If possible, use the plural form of the noun or pronoun, for example:

Gender specific:	When *a person* gives a speech, *he or she* needs to stay on topic.
Gender neutral:	When *people* give speeches, *they* need to stay on topic.

- Replace the pronoun with a nonspecific noun, for example:

Gender specific:	The report referred to a *boy or girl* from the community.
Gender neutral:	The report referred to a *child* from the community.

- Use an article, such as "the" rather than "his" or "her," for example:

  Gender specific: During *his* interview, the reporter gave
                        complicated answers.

  Gender neutral: During *the* interview, the reporter gave
                        complicated answers.

- Delete the pronoun, for example:

  Gender specific: The director required *her* staff to arrive on time.

  Gender neutral: The director required staff to arrive on time.

Here are a few examples of some sexist terms and their gender-neutral equivalents:

Sexist	Gender Neutral
policeman	police officer
waiter/waitress	food server
stewardess	flight attendant
mailman	postal worker
salesman	sales representative
TV anchorman	news anchor
mankind	humanity
manmade	artificial, synthetic
manpower	workforce
housewife	home maker
man a project	staff a project
chairman or chairwoman	chair or chairperson
businessman or businesswoman	business executive or business person
congressman or congresswoman	congressional representative

Can you think of others?

Race and Ethnicity

To avoid stereotyping of racial and ethnic groups, writers should be as specific as possible when using racial and ethnic terms. Here are terms for some racial and ethnic groups:

African American (no hyphen)

black (not capitalized)

white (not capitalized)

American Indian, Native American (no hyphen)

Asian or Asian American (no hyphen)

However, do not use *Afro-American*, *Negro*, or *Oriental*.

Note that "Hispanic" and "Latino/Latina" are not interchangeable:

- *Spanish* is a language and also refers to people born in Spain.

- *Hispanic* is a broad term that refers to persons of Spanish-speaking origin or ancestry who share a connection to Spain.

- *Latino/Latina* refers to persons of Latin American heritage or origin who share a history of colonization from Spain.

- *Mexican* refers to Mexican citizens.

- *Chicano* refers to US citizens of Mexican descent.

Once again, in your writing, use specific language when possible:

Nonspecific	Specific
Hispanic	Cuban Americans, Mexican Americans, Puerto Ricans
Latino, Latina	People of Latin American heritage, such as Brazilians
Asian	Japanese, Chinese, Korean, Vietnamese, and so on
Middle Eastern or Arab	Egyptian, Iraqi, Jordanian, and so on

Unbiased Language and Labels

Avoid using terms that label people. For example, when people are referred to as "the disabled," they are being objectified (or referred to as objects); instead, use a phrase such as *people with disabilities*.

Biased language	Revised or alternative
schizophrenics	people who have schizophrenia
challenged	people who have challenges—state the specific challenge
wheelchair-bound	wheelchair-user

AIDS victims	people with AIDS
high-risk groups	high-risk behavior
nonwhite	*state what the population prefers to be called*
minority	*state what the population prefers to be called*
blacks	black Americans, African Americans
senior citizen or oldster	a person over 65, elderly person

Labels	**Revised or alternative**
the elderly or the aged	elderly people
the disabled or the handicapped	people with disabilities
the lower class	people who are poor
the upper class	people with high incomes
the blind	people who are blind
the hearing impaired	people who are hard of hearing or deaf

What other outdated language, biased language, or labels have you encountered?

Similar Words and Tricky Combos

Even confident writers make mistakes with the common words in this section, which are technically called "homophones": words that sound alike but have different meanings. Unfortunately, errors with these types of words detract from the quality of even the most sophisticated writing. Thus, identify the words that you find troublesome and practice them until you know them.

Note: Before reviewing this section, complete Activity 1, Similar Word Pretest, page 379–380.

Tricky Combos

Are you ready for some surprises? In all likelihood, you have been using some words incorrectly without any clue they were wrong.

alright/all right:

- The word "alright" is not considered a Standard English spelling.

- Use *all right*. Think of *all right* as being the opposite of *all wrong*.

   Are you feeling *all right* about the change?

definite/defiant:

- *Definite* is an adjective meaning *certain*, *confident*, or *convinced*.
- *Defiant* is an adjective that means *disobedient*, *insolent*, or *insubordinate*.

  Marcel has *definite* ideas about how to handle the situation.

  His colleague was *defiant* about going to the meeting.

idea/ideal:

- An *idea* is a thought; an opinion, conviction, principle.
- *Ideal* refers to a standard of perfection.

  I had a good *idea* the other day. What is your *idea*?

  The *ideal* solution does not exist.

  Titus lives by his *ideals*, which is why he always does his best.

loan/lend: Most people confuse these words and don't even realize it, even people in high-level banking positions. Here is what you need to know:

- *Loan* is a *noun*, not an action.
- *Lend* is a *verb*; its past tense form is "lent."

  The bank will *lend* you the funds you need by giving you a *loan*.

Though you cannot "loan" someone your book, you can *lend* it. Practice these words a few times, and their meanings will make more sense each time you use them correctly.

may be/maybe:

- *May be* is a verb form that suggests possibility.
- *Maybe* is an adverb that means "perhaps."

  I *may be* presenting at this week's meeting; *maybe* you can assist.

principal/principle: At one point, you may have learned that the *principal* of your school was your "pal." That's true; however, *principal* has a broader meaning:

- *Principal* is a noun meaning "the person with the highest authority," but it is also an adjective meaning "primary, predominant, or main." Are you surprised to learn that in paying back a loan, you must pay your "*principal* and interest."

- *Principle* means "theory or rule of conduct."

  What is the *principal* on your loan?

  We all try to live by our *principles*.

  I would rather pay off my *principal* than continue to pay interest!

weather/whether:

- *Weather* is usually a noun, referring to the temperature and atmospheric conditions.

- *Weather* can be a verb that figuratively means "to live through."

- *Whether* is a conjunction that introduces possibilities or alternatives:

  The *weather* is beautiful today: it's sunny and cool.

  Would you let me know *whether* or not you can attend the meeting?

  Though we had challenges, we weathered

were/where:

- *Were* is a verb (a past time form of the verb *to be*)

- *Where* is an adverb:

  Were you in the meeting? If not, *where were* you?

  Where were you when the lights went out?

Tricky Verbs

If you have challenges with contractions, stop using them and spell out words completely. However, when you use contractions, use an apostrophe: writers lose credibility when they make those kinds of misspellings; for example, for *do not*, the contraction is "don't" not "dont."

affect/effect: Though each of these words can be a noun and a verb, here's their primary use:

- *Affect* is a verb meaning "to influence."
- *Effect* is a noun meaning "result."

As a noun, *affect* refers to emotions and is used primarily within the field of mental health; as a verb, *effect* means "to cause to happen" or "to bring about."

> My sister was diagnosed with an *affective* (emotional) disorder.
>
> The new policy will *effect* (bring about) change within our agency.

assure/ensure/insure: These three verbs are somewhat similar in sound and meaning, but they have distinct uses:

- *Assure* means "to give *someone* confidence."
- *Ensure* means "to make certain" that *something* will happen.
- *Insure* means "to protect against loss."

When you use *assure*, make sure that a person is the object:

> I *assure* you that we will do everything we can.

When you use *ensure*, make sure that a "thing" is the object:

> I *ensure* that the grant proposal will arrive on time.

When you use *insure*, make sure that it refers to "insurance."

> You can *insure* against losses with our company.

don't/doesn't:

- *Don't* and *doesn't* are both contractions of *do not*.
- At times speakers use *don't* for third person singular when they should be using *doesn't* for correct Edited American English usage.

- APA does not accept contractions; however, you can use contractions in less formal writing, such as e-mail messages.

- Spelling a contraction without an apostrophe (such as "dont" for "don't") is a serious spelling error that can cause a writer to lose credibility.

  Alice *does not* like math, and she *doesn't* like history either.

has/have: Developing writers sometimes use *have* for third person singular when they should be using *has*.

- *Has* and *have* are both present tense forms of *to have.*

- Use *has* for third person singular (he *has*, she *has*, and it *has*) and *have* for all other persons: I *have*, you *have*, we *have* and they *have*.

  Rob *has* an exam on Friday.

  We *have* an exam every Friday.

infer/imply: These two verbs are opposite in meaning.

- *Infer* means to *deduce, conclude,* or *assume.*
- *Imply* means to *express* or *state indirectly.*

  The client *implied* that she needed money.

  I *inferred* that she was telling the truth.

Tricky Pronouns

For the words that give you challenges, write a few sentences using them correctly. You can even start by writing a sentence using the word incorrectly and then revise it using the correct spelling, following the same pattern as the examples below.

its/it's:

- *Its* is a possessive pronoun
- *It's* is a contraction of *it is* or *it has.*

It's a beautiful day for a walk.

The project lost *its* appeal after the chairperson resigned.

their/there/they're:

- *Their* is the possessive form of *they* and will always be followed by a noun.

- *There* is an adverb meaning "in or at *that* place" or a pronoun which functions as an anticipating subject.

- *They're* is the contracted form of *they are.*

   Their car would not start.

   Put the file over *there.*

   There are many issues to discuss.

   They're running late today.

who's/whose:

- The contraction *who's* stands for *who is* or *who has.*

- *Whose* is the possessive pronoun of *who.*

   Who's (who is) submitting the proposal?

   Whose turn is it to chair the meeting?

you're/your:

- *You're* is a contraction for *you are.*

- *Your* is a possessive pronoun for *you.*

   You're the best person for the job.

   Your opinion matters.

Tricky Prepositions

A preposition often precedes a noun or pronoun and indicates a relation of one word to another.

among/between:

- *Among* is a preposition meaning *together with* or *along with* and is used when three or more people or objects are involved.

- *Between* is a preposition that means basically the same thing as *among*, but *between* is used when two people or objects are discussed.

  Between you and me, we should be able to get the job done.

  Among all of the applicants, Jose did the best.

through/threw/thorough/thru:

- *Through* is a preposition meaning *by means of, from beginning to end*, or *because of*.

- *Threw* is a verb and the past participle of *throw*.

- *Thorough* is an adjective meaning *carried through to completion*.

  Note: Thru is a "word" that does not exist in Standard English—use it only as a part of the term "drive-thru."

  When you go *through* the door, be careful.

  Billy *threw* the ball to Alice.

  Do a *thorough* job on the report.

  If you need a quick meal, go *through* a drive-*thru*.

to/too: The preposition *to* is often used when the adverb *too* is appropriate.

- Use the adverb *too* when you are describing something that relates to quantity. Also use *too* when you could substitute the word *also*.

  I have *too* much work to do and *too* little time in which to do it.

  Would you like to go to the meeting *too*?

  If he has *too* many concerns, we should cancel the project.

  Do you feel that way *too*?

  Going to the conference after working all day was *too* much.

More Similar Words

Which of the following give you challenges?

advice/advise:

- *Advice* is a noun and means *recommendation*.

- *Advise* is a verb and it means *to give advice or to make a recommendation*.

  I *advise* you to listen to your supervisor's *advice*.

appraise/apprise:

- *Appraise* is a verb meaning *to assess* or *evaluate*.

- *Apprise* is a verb meaning *to inform*.

  After you *appraise* the situation, *apprise* us of your results.

customer/costumer:

- A *customer* is a *client, patron*.

- A *costumer* is a person who makes costumes for theater and films.

  Your *customer* appreciates your good service and fast response.
  The *costumer* will adjust your costume for the play.

everyday/every day:

- Use *everyday* as a modifier meaning "ordinary" or "daily."

- Use *every day* if you can insert the word "single" between *every* and *day*.

  Answering messages is an *everyday* activity on the job.
  You will hear from me *every (single) day* this week.

farther/further:

- *Farther* refers to actual distance that can be measured.

- *Further* indicates progress that is intangible and not measurable, such as "to a greater or lesser degree or extent."

  I live *farther* from work than you do by at least 5 miles.

  We are *further* along on the project than we realize.

sight/site/cite:

- *Sight* is a noun referring to vision or mental perception.

- *Site* is also a noun that refers to a location, as in website.

- *Cite* is a verb meaning *to quote* or *to name.*

  Sue's favorite saying is, "Out of *sight*, out of mind."

  Our agency does all of its training on *site*.

  Cite your references correctly according to APA style.

supposed to/used to: Because speakers do not always pronounce words clearly, the past time ending is sometimes erroneously left off when these words are written.

- *Supposed to* and *used to* are regular verbs in past tense and require the –ed ending.

  I am *supposed to* take Friday as a vacation day.

  Tanya *used to* work in my agency.

than/then:

- *Than* is a conjunction used in comparisons.

- *Then* is an adverb referring to time, as in "after that." To help remember, use *then* when it has to do with a "*when*."

  I would rather go to the meeting *than* work on the report.

  I will go to the meeting and *then* work on the report.

try to/"try and": The verb *try* is followed by an infinitive, such *to be, to see, to go*, and so on. In other words, do *not* use the construction "try and."

  Try to be on time. Also, *try to* relax when you give your presentation.

The similar words listed here are only a handful of similar words that you will come across. For a more complete list, go to the internet and search "homophones": *words that are pronounced the same but differ in meaning.*

Note: Now that you have completed this section, complete Activity 3, Similar Word Posttest, page 381.

Spelling Tips

One of the reasons spelling is difficult is that only about 40 percent of English words are spelled according to phonetics, which is how they sound. In other words, about 60 percent of English words are written with silent letters or other non-phonetic qualities, thereby requiring them to be memorized. Use the following suggestions to improve your spelling and vocabulary usage.

- *Read the glossaries of your textbooks.* Most of your sociology textbooks, especially introductory texts, have well developed glossaries that provide a thorough list of sociological terms and their definitions. Set a goal of learning two or three new words a day (or a week). By familiarizing yourself up front with significant terms, you will improve your reading fluency and comprehension.

- *Make a running list of words that you find challenging.* The way that you use language is unique. Your reading, writing, and spelling skills have different strengths and weaknesses from everyone else. To build your skills, work on the specific words that challenge you. As you read, circle the words that you do not understand, and look them up.

- *Subscribe to online vocabulary-building newsletters.* For example, Merriam-Webster (www.merriam-webster.com) has a *word of the day* as does Wordsmith (www.wordsmith.org).

- *Use new words in context: write two or three sentences with each new word.* To learn a new word, practice it in context. By writing two or three sentences, you are applying the new word in a way that will make it easier to remember and use correctly.

- *As you learn a new word, check the correct pronunciation.* Break up the new word into syllables and use the dictionary guidelines for pronunciation. Ask a friend to pronounce the word for you; say the word out loud several times until you feel comfortable.

- *Use spelling rules that are easy to remember.* Use spelling rules that you find helpful. For example, the rule "use *i* before *e* except after *c* or when the sound is like *a* as in *neighbor*" is easy to remember and helpful. However, learning complex spelling rules that have a lot of exceptions may not be as helpful. Go to the internet and search *spelling rules*. Glean what you need, and then move on.

- *Learn Latin and Greek roots as well as prefixes and suffixes.* Learning *word roots*, *prefixes*, and *suffixes* will help you figure out new words and gain a deeper understanding of the words you already know. A few are listed below; for a complete list do an internet search on "Greek and Latin roots, stems, and prefixes."

A Sampling of Roots, Prefixes, and Suffixes

Root	Meaning	Origin
anthro	man	Greek
biblio	book	Greek
cent	one hundred	Latin
equ	equal, fair	Latin
geo	earth	Greek
hydro	water	Greek
ortho	straight	Greek
poli	city	Greek
psych	mind, soul, spirit	Greek
soci	group	Latin
sci	to know	Latin
supra	above, over	Latin
techn	art, skill	Greek
viv, vit	life	Latin

Prefix	Meaning	Example
a- or *an-*	not, without	amoral, apolitical
ab-	away from	abduction
ambi-	both	ambidextrous
anti-	against	antisocial
bene-	good	beneficial
bi-	two	biannual
contra	against	contradict
de-	not	derail
dis-	not	disengage

ex-	out from	exhale
hyper-	over	hypertension, hyperactive
il-, im-, in-	not	illegal, impossible, indivisible
inter-	between	interstate
ir-	not	irreversible
macro-	large	macrocosm
micro-	small	microcosm
mis-	not	misconduct, misplace
mono-	one	monologue
post-	after	postpone
pre-	before	pretest
pseudo-	false	pseudonym
re-	again	repeat
semi-	half	semiannual
sub-	under	subversive
trans-	across	transport
un-	not	unable

Suffix	**Meaning**	**Example**
-able	able to	durable
-age	result of action	courage
-er	doer of	teacher
	more	greater
-ectomy	cutting	appendectomy
-ful	full of	peaceful
-ic, -tic, -ical	having to do with	dramatic, Biblical
-ism	the belief in	mysticism
-logy	the study of	psychology, biology
-ly or -y	like	friendly
-ment	state of	judgment
-ness	quality	kindness
-phobia	fear	claustrophobia
-ship	condition, status	ownership
-ous	full of	ridiculous

Recap

Improving your vocabulary improves your reading and critical thinking skills as well as your writing skills. Practice new words in context: write two or three sentences with each new word so that you can use it with confidence.

Writing Workshop

The writing workshop contains the following:

- Activity 1, Similar Word Pretest

- Activity 2, Gender-Neutral and Unbiased Language

- Activity 3, Similar Word Posttest

Instructions: Before you start this chapter, complete Activity 1, Similar Word Pretest. Then when you have completed the chapter, take Activity 3, Similar Word Posttest, on page 381. So that you can compare your results, you will find keys for these assessments and Activity 2 on pages 431–433.

Activity 1. Similar Word Pretest

Instructions: In the sentences below, cross out any words that are used incorrectly, and write in the correct word above it or to the right of the sentence. (See pages 431–432 for the key to this activity.)

1 Will that decision effect you in a positive way?

2 The principle on my loan is due on the 1st of the month.

3 My advise is for you to get a job before you buy that new car.

4 Please ensure my manager that I will return in one-half hour.

5 Its been a challenging day, but things are getting better.

6 Their are a few issues that we need to discuss.

7 The agency gave are report a new title.

8 Pat lives further from work than I do.

9 You can have a meeting everyday, if you prefer.

10 Whose going to the ballgame?

11 I enjoy movies more then I enjoy plays.

12 Megan assured that the project would be successful

13 It's alright for you to contact the manager directly.

14 I didn't mean to infer that you were late on purpose.

15 Try and be on time for the next meeting.

Activity 2. Gender-Neutral and Unbiased Language

Instructions: For the outdated and biased words and phrases below, provide a revised or alternative term. (See pages 432–433 for the key to this exercise.)

Outdated

1 Policeman

2 Waiter/waitress

3 Fireman

4 Mailman

5 Salesman

6 TV anchorman

7 Mankind

8 Chairman

9 Oriental

10 Afro-American

11 Man a project

12 challenged

13 wheelchair-bound

14 AIDS victims

15 high-risk groups

16 nonwhite

17 minority

18 the disabled or the handicapped

19 the lower class

20 the blind

Activity 3. Similar Word Posttest

Instructions: In the sentences below, cross out any words that are used incorrectly, and write in the correct word above it or to the right of the sentence.

1 The affect of that decision is not yet known.

2 When you know principle on your loan, let me know.

3 Her advise was that you take the other part-time job.

4 Can you assure the quality of your work?

5 The dog chased it's tail, amusing several children.

6 They are a few issues that we need to discuss.

7 Is that are new computer?

8 You are farther along on the project than I am.

9 We meet everyday at 3 p.m.

10 Who's book is that?

11 Sue was taller then Mary last year.

12 Melanie ensured me that we would be finished by Friday

13 Its alright for you to contact the manager directly.

14 I'm not trying to infer that you were late on purpose.

   Note: See page 433 for the key to the above exercise.

References

1   ASA. (2014). *American Sociological Association style guide* (5th ed). Washington, DC: American Sociological Association.

2   Ibid.

3   APA. *Guidelines for nonhandicapping language in APA journals.* American Psychological Association. Retrieved from: http://www.apastyle.org/manual/related/nonhandicapping-language.aspx

4   NASW. *NASW press guidelines for describing people.* National Association for
        Social Workers. Retrieved from: http://www.pcar.org/sites/default/files/
        resource-pdfs/press-guidelines-describing-people-nasw.pdf

5   NCDJ. *Disability language style guide.* National Center on Disability and
        Journalism. Retrieved from: http://ncdj.org/style-guide/

6   ASA (2014) Op. cit., p. 4.

Quick Guides

Getting a Job

The universe is change; our life is what our thoughts make it. – Marcus Aurelius[1]

Sociologists understand change on a deeper level than most: sociologists study human behavior across a broad spectrum of social environments, becoming experts in trends and other types of social change. Though there are few positions with the title "sociologist," having a sociological mindset is valuable in a wide range of professions, from being a social worker to a criminologist, a human resource manager, or a teacher.

Though you may expect this chapter to be about using the internet to find a job, it is not: this chapter helps you define your unique career profile, defining the skills that you developed through your studies in sociology. You can then use your career portfolio in networking activities, rather than activities that might end up being fruitless, such as "surfing the net." As research shows, networking is still the best way to find a job, with "some [estimating] that upwards of 85 percent of open positions are filled through networking."[2]

Regardless of your accomplishments, looking for a job can make you question everything that you have ever achieved. That is because as you search for a job, you are not just using your talents to solve a problem: you have become the *central theme* of the project. Finding a job is a full-time job. Whether you like it or not, *you* are the focal point, and the job itself is secondary.

Right now, you may feel more confident using your skills than talking about them; but with a bit of preparation, you can do both. Verbalizing your job survival skills equates to marketing yourself; to do that, you first need to identify your unique qualities so that you can prepare your résumé and ready yourself for interviewing.

When you have completed this chapter, you will be able to:

- Identify your unique career profile, specifying your transferable skills and experience.

- Develop a career portfolio that includes a hard-copy résumé, e-résumé, and business card.

- Compose a cover letter and a thank-you message.

- Develop a strategy to engage in networking opportunities, online and on site.

- Develop an elevator pitch and a keyword summary for your job search.

By comprehensively assessing your skills, you will have flexibility using online sites such as Indeed.com, CareerBuilder.com, and LinkedIn. As you create your career portfolio, you may also feel motivated to network in local or national organizations, on site and online.

Networking

Networking is the best way to secure a job. According to Matt Youngquist, president of Career Horizons,

> At least 70 percent, if not 80 percent, of jobs are not published, [and] yet most people – they are spending 70 or 80 percent of their time surfing the net versus getting out there, talking to employers, taking some chances [and] realizing that the vast [majority] of hiring is friends and acquaintances hiring other trusted friends and acquaintances.[3]

For many job postings, if not most, the first line of screening is through computer software that detects keywords for the job being recruited for. According to Trisha Svehla, president of Managing the Mosaic, "To ensure that your resume gets to the correct people, if you have a contact within that company, use it. If you fail the screen, you may still get in to see a hiring manager.[4]

In addition, according to Ilana Gershon of *Harvard Business Review*, what hiring managers "value most is a strong recommendation from someone who actually knows the applicant as a worker and can assure them that the person will be a good hire."[5] Gershon goes on to say that people who were the most useful were those "who could talk knowledgeably and convincingly about what the applicant was like as a worker and colleague." So personal friends are not your best network allies but rather people who have had direct contact with your work on the job, such as past managers, clients, coworkers, and so on.

Start to build your network now. Professional networking groups give you a steady stream of new contacts. By doing an online search of groups that target your interests, you will find opportunities to use your social skills to build your reputation and credibility.

- *Connect with people who have similar goals and values.* Stay active and involved on site and online.

- *Build your network before you need it.* Start now and network on an ongoing basis so that you make contacts, remain visible, and get the support you need.

- *View networking as a communication exchange, not a one-sided dialog.* Before you call on someone to network, articulate why the meeting would be *mutually* beneficial. Look for common interests, experiences, or shared acquaintances.

- *Reciprocate favors: when you ask people for help, also ask what you can do for them in return.* You may find that an opportunity that did not work out for you is perfect for someone else.

- *View organizations within your field as career opportunities.* Through professional organizations, you will meet new people and have experiences that enhance your leadership skills.

- *Continue to network within your organization.* This will help you build relationships as you promote your visibility and flexibility.

Volunteer to serve on committees, participate in focus groups, and attend activities related to your interests. Find new friends by attending fundraising events for not-for-profit organizations. Treat everyone with respect, including support staff such as mailroom and cleaning personnel.

Career Portfolio

All job seekers need to be organized and ready to present their credentials so that employers recognize their skills at a glance: the first screening of an applicant lasts only seconds, and employers seek to eliminate applicants at the beginning of the process. Something that sounds small, such as using an incorrect salutation in your cover letter, can be reason enough for some to toss out your letter and résumé.

Your first position is only the first step in your career: you may find that you need to continue to reinvent yourself throughout your career. If you keep your mindset geared toward change, you will succeed. Here are some suggestions about what to include in your portfolio:

- *Purpose statement.* To gain clarity and make effective career choices, write a purpose statement that reflects your life's mission.

- *Résumé.* Prepare your traditional and electronic résumés, tailoring your résumé for each job. Keep your résumé to two pages at *most*. For international corporations, prepare a curriculum vitae (CV).

- *Work samples.* Select a few exhibits of your best work from previous jobs or classes: a letter, a report, a paper, and so on.

- *Reference letters.* If you ask for letters up front, before you need them, you can use the salutation "Dear Hiring Manager" or the basic "To Whom It May Concern." However, for specific positions, ask your reference to use the name of the person requesting the letter.

- *Networking contacts.* Become an expert at networking on site and online. Networking is still the best way to find a job, including e-networking on websites such as LinkedIn.

- *Business card.* Design your own job-search card with your name, e-mail address, phone number, and vital points about your skills.

Start with a three-ring binder; use tabs to organize the various parts. Keep an electronic file of everything you collect so that you can transform your hard copy into an *e-portfolio.*

- If you have a Facebook page, now is the time to edit it: prospective employers routinely screen applicants' social networking activity and photos.

- If you do not have a professional-sounding e-mail address, create one now. Use some form of your name, if possible, such as "myname@ e-mail.com."

- If you use other types of social media or post online at blogs, know that your electronic footprint follows you for a long, long time and may *never* go away.

The most important part of your job search is being able to verbalize your skills, qualities, and experience, so keep that in mind as you work through the remainder of this chapter.

Skills, Not Titles or Degrees

Has anyone ever asked you, *what do you want to be when you . . .* ? Most of us fumble with this question until we can answer it with a job title such as teacher, nurse, lawyer, engineer, and so on. However, among titles, "sociologist" is rarely used—being a sociologist refers more to a skillset and a mindset rather than a job title. Thus, while a job title of "sociologist" would limit your opportunities, the skills you learn as a sociology major (or minor) will make you valuable in a wide range of careers. Identify your skills and how they transfer to *any* business environment, and you gain a broader understanding of what you can offer.

Transferable Skills

Defining marketable skills is a challenge, especially when you think you don't have any. By defining what you have achieved, you are able to see the unique qualities that you bring to an employer. Every exercise you do in this chapter helps ready you for your interview.

Some of your skills have come from interests or hobbies, and you may not even be aware of what you have learned. Start to develop your job-search profile by exploring these basic areas:

- Working with people

- Identifying knowledge you can apply

- Identifying personal qualities

Working with people. *How do you work with people?* Consider formal and informal experiences at school, at your place of worship, with volunteer groups, on part- and full-time jobs, in sports activities, and in associations. Here are some terms to open up your thinking; as you go through the list, notice your impressions as well as specific experiences that come to mind.

Counseling	Giving feedback	Receiving feedback
Working in teams	Supervising	Working independently
Marketing	Expressing humor	Listening actively
Leading	Organizing projects	Organizing events
Delegating	Care giving	Selling
Advising	Negotiating	Mediating
Entertaining	Serving	Phoning or canvassing
Training	Being compassionate	Managing stress
Cleaning and organizing	Evaluating	Facilitating

Identifying knowledge you can apply. *What are your areas of expertise?* In addition to formal learning, consider hobbies and interests. Read through the list below and circle three or more of the items that reflect your abilities:

Writing (composing, editing, revising) / Languages (speaking, writing, translating, interpreting) / Social science research / Public policy / Political analysis / Group practice / Global communication / Diversity / Public relations / Journalism / Business management / Social work / Counseling / Statistics / Conflict management / Crisis management / Budgeting / Child care / Early child development / Education: elementary or secondary / Film making / Archeology / Anthropology / Law: criminal or civil / Police science / Political science / History / Sports / Organizational development / Human resource development / Fundraising / Graphic arts or design / Web development

What other subjects or major areas can you identify? Take out your college catalog and list specific classes and assignments that were particularly meaningful.

Working on tasks. *What kinds of tasks can you perform well? Which do you enjoy?* Consider all of the classes that you have taken as well as job experience, paid or volunteer. Also consider your hobbies and interests; these activities are important to employers. Use the random list of nouns and verbs below to generate a list of tasks that you do well:

> Administer surveys and questionnaires / Counsel / E-mail / PowerPoint / Microsoft Excel / Microsoft Word / Case notes / Web design / Code data / Facilitate focus groups and group discussions / Perform two-way correlations / Create charts and graphs / Perform descriptive statistical tests / Mediate disagreements / Identify signs of conflict / Assess demographic trends / Project outcomes / Manage / Work with children / Analyze data / Trouble shoot / Conduct interviews / Gather information / Write research proposals / Identify patterns and trends / Analyze work roles / Interpret issues from diverse viewpoints / Develop public policy recommendations / Care for children and elderly / Design / Gather information / Organize and file / Spreadsheets / Tables / Graphs / Letters / Behavior management plans / Agendas / Minutes / Reports / Proposals / Set goals / Meet quotas / Edit / Coach / Supervise / Anger management / Greet and receive / Construct research models / Compose reports / Harvard Graphics / Calendar Creator Plus / Communicate with diverse populations / Observe and record

Identifying personal qualities. You are unique whether you realize it or not. *What personal qualities shape you into who you are? Which of the following qualities describe you?*

reliable	dependable	motivated	self-starter
persistent	optimistic	self-reliant	strong
independent	capable	fast learner	supportive
eager	focused	purposeful	task-oriented
disciplined	friendly	persuasive	artistic
committed	easy-going	encouraging	flexible
balanced	open minded	accepting	prompt
courteous	patient	dedicated	supportive
loyal	adaptable	credible	ethical
competent	kind	helpful	determined
confident	decisive	creative	enthusiastic
honest	responsible	self-learner	passionate

Work experience. Make a list of all paid or volunteer jobs you have had; for each, specify how long you had the job. Instead of giving start and end dates, you can just list the months and years and then quantify the time. For example:

Supportive	January to March, 2016	7 weeks
care, part-time	July to August, 2017	6 weeks
caregiver	December, 2017	3 weeks
	Total	about 4 months

Though you are concerned with dates, you also want to have an idea of the amount of time on the job. Quantify your experiences in terms of years and months or even weeks. After you tally the specifics, you can list your experience as follows:

| Supportive Care, part-time | January to December, 2015 | 4 months |
| caregiver | | |

When you attend an interview, be prepared with an example to demonstrate an achievement. Perhaps you are the first person in your family to graduate from college or maybe you recently won an award. These types of notable experiences give prospective employers insight into your personality and interests as well as how you apply your skills.

Of course, use discretion in choosing which achievements to cite. A prospective employer does not want to hear about personal milestones such as engagements or weddings; and no matter how cute your children are, save those stories for your friends and relatives.

Business Cards

Especially if you are new to the job market, create a business card. Select a few accomplishments and list them as bullet points on your card.

Charles Wright Mills   **312.555.1212**

                                          cwrightmills@email.com

BA, University of Texas

- Political analyst and pollster

- Compassionate, creative, focused, and motivated

- Excellent GPA and references

Your new business card is a useful tool for networking, providing your contact information and reminding associates of your skills.

COACHING TIP: Voicemail Messages

Have you ever received a rambling voicemail message? Have you ever left one? To get the best results, plan your message before you call.

Here are guidelines for leaving voice mail messages:

1 Mind map the message before you call.

2 Start your message by *slowly* stating your name and phone number.

3 State the purpose of your call: give the most important details first.

4 Include a time frame: when do you need the information you are requesting?

5 Make sure you include the best times you can be reached.

6 Repeat your phone number *slowly* at the end of the message.

Job-Search Letters

Letters are important tools for initiating, developing, and following up with contacts and job prospects. Even though e-communication is prevalent, a hard-copy letter still makes a strong impression. Here are two types of letters to include in your job-search process:

- Cover letter
- Thank-you letter

Tailor every letter you write to the specific position you are going after and the organization to which you are sending it. In addition, some prospective employers prefer that all application letters and résumés be submitted online; others prefer to receive hard copies. Check each organization's preference as you customize each letter for each job.

Cover Letters

Send a cover letter with your résumé (or a *cover message*, if you send your résumé online). State why you would be the best person for the job and highlight your accomplishments. While your letter—or message—may not get you the job, a poorly written one will keep you from getting in the door to apply. Here are some guidelines that relate to job-search letters.

- *Know the name and title of the person to whom you are writing.* Do *not* address a letter to *Dear Sir* or *Dear Madam*. Go to the company website or call to find out the addressee's name and its correct spelling.

- *Find out whether the preference for receiving résumés is online or through the mail.* If you submit an application letter and résumé online, e-mail it to yourself first and print out your file to make sure it looks professional.

- *Stress what you can offer the organization.* Rather than focus on what you are looking for in a position, instead stress how your skills can benefit the organization.

- *Develop a plan for follow-up.* Take charge: do not expect others to contact you after they receive your information.

- *Aim for perfection: your written communication creates a strong first impression.* A letter of application presents high stakes. Write in active voice, use *you viewpoint*, and be concise.

A strong cover letter has an opening to capture the reader's attention and identifies the job for which you are applying.

> The opportunity listed with CareerBuilder for a home health care social worker is a great fit with my background and qualifications; my résumé is enclosed.

> Our mutual colleague Jennifer Lopez suggested that I have the talent and qualifications that you are looking for in a bilingual pollster. My enclosed résumé highlights some of that experience.

In the next paragraph, explain your special skills by listing some of your major accomplishments or qualifications that are relevant to the position you are seeking.

> As a recent college graduate, I have experience in youth and family services. My degree in sociology includes a minor in social work and a three-month internship. As an intern, I supported three case managers who trusted me with clients and managing their paperwork.

In the final part of your cover letter, request an interview. State that you will call within a specific time frame to find a mutually agreeable time to meet.

> Would you have time to meet with me to discuss how my background can benefit your agency? I will contact you the week of June 12 to see if we can meet.

Thus, the first paragraph identifies the job, the second paragraph explains your special skills, and the third paragraph is the call to action. Be sure to follow up with your commitment to call. If the person is not available, ask if there is another time that would be convenient for you to call back. Leave your name and number, but do not feel slighted if you do not get a callback: the responsibility for communication is on your shoulders.

Follow-Up Letters and Thank-You Notes

Two of the most powerful tools in your job search toolkit are a follow-up e-mail and a handwritten thank-you note. Get a business card from each of your contacts so that sending a note or an e-mail takes less effort. Surprisingly, no matter how good the results are when thank-you notes are received, few people actually send them.

Your note will make a new networking associate or potential employer feel good for meeting with you or for making a call or two on your behalf. By writing a formal thank-you letter, you have an opportunity to highlight strengths of the company and show appreciation to your "host."

Elaine:

Thank you for sharing your valuable time and advice for my job search.

I have contacted Joe, as you suggested and will keep you informed on my progress. If I can assist you in any way, do not hesitate to contact me. I would be pleased to put my strong research skills to use on your behalf.

Good luck with assisting your clients at the new community center.

All the best,

Sophie

Write a letter that is simple, friendly, and genuine. Do not use a boiler-plate, *one-size-fits-all* message. Customize each letter, e-mail message, and handwritten note by specifically referring to something you discussed. And remember, *less is more.*

Keep your cover letter short, and a prospective employer is more likely to read it. Write your letter so the reader can pick up key information from a glance.

Rosalie D. Lindsey
1212 Arquilla Lane
Winter Haven, FL 35319
(813) 555-5555 – rdl@e-mail.com

January 6, 2019

Ms. Jane Fleming
Director of Marketing
Market Research, Inc.
8007 Nashville Boulevard
Tallahassee, FL 35316

Dear Ms. Fleming:

Thank you for the time that you spent with me at the Sociology Network conference discussing opportunities at your company.

I will receive my BA from Best College this spring; my résumé is enclosed. As you can see, I have had a few part-time jobs that would contribute to my success as a market research analyst. In addition, during my volunteer work at our community youth program, my research identified activities that doubled participation in the program during the summer months.

I will follow up with you soon to find out if there is a convenient time for us to meet.

Sincerely,

Robert L. Harris
Enclosure: Résumé

COACHING TIP: Social Media Alert

Potential employers are not impressed by the same things that your friends are impressed by, so "clean up" your social media sites *before* you start searching for your dream job.

Also, be very selective about what you tweet or post online, or it may follow you throughout your career. Many hearts have been broken by a moment of indiscretion.

Finally, if you don't have a professional-sounding e-mail address for your résumé and other job-search documents, *get one now*.

The Résumé

Human resource executives and hiring managers receive hundreds of résumés for every job opening. Customize your résumé for each potential position, but be cautious about trying to make your résumé stand out:

- Brevity is critical: highlight your experience effectively on one page; at any rate, do not exceed two pages.

- Do not use flamboyant fonts or fancy paper: use conservative fonts such as Times New Roman and Arial; use one style of font for the body and another for your letterhead and headings.

- Use crisp, white, heavy-weight bond paper.

Chronological Formatting

The *chronological format* lists your education, work experience, and accomplishments in order, starting with the most recent and working backward. This format is the more traditional, so readers find it easy to see a history of steady promotions or increased responsibility. Here are some tips:

- Use *career focus* or *summary* rather than *objective*.

- Make sure that prospective employers can tell at a glance the job or job category for which you are applying; tailor your résumé for each job you seek.

- Be specific about accomplishments; quantify your achievements when possible.

- Apply parallel structure (represent words in a consistent form).

- Keep your résumé to one page if you can, two pages if you cannot.

Write your résumé to answer questions *before* they arise. On your cover letter, fill in gaps of unemployment that might appear on your résumé.

ROSALINE D. LINDSEY

1212 Arquilla Lane
Winter Haven, FL 35319
(813) 555-1212 (H) • (813) 555-1212 (C)
rdl@email.com

CAREER FOCUS

Research and teaching: sociology of education, social research methods, sociology of organizations, criminal behavior and social control; proven ability to develop and implement strategies for effective teaching.

TEACHING EXPERIENCE

Teaching Assistant, State University   June 2016 to Present

Sociology and Graduate School of Education

- Assisting with the development of course materials.

- Reviewing lectures in small groups and tutoring students with special needs.

- Keeping records, tracking attendance, and grading.

- Providing support in large lecture classes.

EDUCATION

BA, Sociology, Best University, 2016

MA, Sociology, State University, degree in progress

SKILLS

Highly developed qualitative research skills and strong analytical skills.

Expert skills with Word, Excel, PowerPoint, and Statistical Package for Social Scientists.

Employers assume you are telling the truth until they find out otherwise. When employers check specific details, they usually do so only after they have already decided to hire you.

Rather than use a template, develop your own résumé design. To enhance the design, use a serif font for the body and a non-serif font for the headings.

Electronic Formatting (Scannable Résumés)

Your job-search portfolio is not complete unless you have an electronic résumé (e-résumé). Some companies screen applicants as a first step by having them submit an e-résumé.

Here are tips for your e-résumé:

- Use a sans-serif font such as Arial, Calibri, or Helvetica, size 11 or 12 point.

- Use a maximum of 65 characters per line.

- Omit any kind of graphics, shading, italics, and underlines.

- Use all caps for headings.

- Do not use bullet points.

- Use "align left"; in other words, do not "right justify" text.

- Include a *keyword summary* at the top of the page and use *keywords* throughout.

- Adhere to parallel structure and end verbs in their -*ing* form, for example, *answering phone and e-mail messages.*

For an online application, send your electronic résumé attached to an e-mail or post it on the internet within personal web pages. Place the *keyword summary* that consists of 20 to 30 words at the top of the page after your name and contact information:

- Use words and phrases that highlight your education, experience, and accomplishments.

- Customize your summary with words taken directly from the job description.

- Use common industry terms to describe your skills and experience.

PAT VINCENT
109 Hillcrest Avenue,
Downers Grove, IL 60615
E-mail: pv@email.com
630-555-1212

KEYWORDS

direct youth services, client-focused, collaborative, diverse computer skills, multi-disciplinary team member, youth and senior advocate for community services, high caseload ability, leadership, communication and writing skills, college graduate

OBJECTIVE

A position in which I can use my case management, communication, and leadership skills to grow within a social service organization that has a client focus.

EDUCATION

MSW, Best University, degree in progress
BA, Sociology, State College, 2010
Related courses: social policy, research, group practice, communities and societies

Diploma, South Side High School, Downers Grove, Illinois
Graduated 2006

WORK EXPERIENCE

Case Manager, Department of Child Services, Chicago, Illinois, 2010 to present

Facilitating life skills group, maintaining a caseload of 20 families, creating behavior management plans, creating goals and objectives with clients, transporting clients to public aid appointments, recording daily and weekly case notes, providing crisis management to clients.

SKILLS

Word, Excel, PowerPoint, WordPerfect, Lotus Notes, Calendar Creator Plus, Outlook (e-mail), WordPress (online content management system)

On a traditional résumé, you describe your work experience in verb phrases that begin with strong action verbs (such as managed, supervised, processed). Instead, on an e-résumé, keyword summaries consist of noun and adjective phrases, such as "fluent in Spanish," "team-oriented," or "strong communication skills."

Employers report receiving thousands of résumés for jobs listed online. Unless the job advertisement calls for "apply by e-mail only," the best approach is to respond with a traditional résumé and cover letter.

Customize your keyword summary for each position for which you apply.

Though traditional résumés contain tabs and bolding for headers such as *Education* and *Experience*, e-résumés lack tabs and highlighting. Here's how to change your traditional résumé into an electronic one:

1   Remove all highlighting: bolding, underlining, and italics.

2   Eliminate bullets, and replace them with dashes, small o's, or asterisks.

3   Move all your text to the left.

4   Remove hard returns except for those separating major sections.

5   Use all capitals for headers.

6   Provide an additional line or two of spacing between sections.

7   Save the file in ASCII or Rich-Text Format.

To send your electronic résumé, start with a *subject line* that states the title of the job for which you are applying, such as "Research Assistant." Then copy and paste your cover letter followed by your résumé within an e-mail.

Employers are reluctant to open attachments from people they do not know, so check first before sending your traditionally formatted résumé as an attachment.

Recap

Finding a job is itself a job. By preparing your career portfolio now, you will be ready when the right opportunity arrives. You have worked hard to build your skills. Though searching for a job might feel daunting, the best response is to take action and stay active until you achieve your dreams. Do the work, and you will see the results.

> *Just remember, you can do anything you set your mind to, but it takes action, perseverance, and facing your fears.* – Gillian Anderson[6]

Job-Search Checklist:

- Write your career objective or personal mission statement.

- Create a personal business card.

- Collect samples of your written work.

- Compose a sample cover letter.

- Prepare your résumés: chronological and electronic format.

- Ask two to three contacts for a letter of reference.

- Prepare a list of networking opportunities.

Writing Workshop

Activity A. Writing a Self-Appraisal

Instructions: Write an honest self-appraisal; start with the following questions:

- *What are my strengths and best qualities?*

- *What are some recent accomplishments?*

- *What are my growing edges?*

Next, complete the following:

1 Write two or three goals, identify specific steps to achieve them, and include a time frame for each step. By including a time frame, you are creating an *action plan*.

2 Write yourself a letter of recommendation identifying your best qualities and highlighting your skills and abilities. Give yourself the same kinds of words of encouragement that you would give your best friend. Keep your letter and refer to it periodically.

Activity B: Researching Organizations

What are organizations that you can join now while you are a student or in the future as a professional? For example, expand your search beyond sociology to social work, criminology, psychology, research, and so on, depending on your interests. Research your community and also do an online search for professional organizations that could offer you the benefit of gaining experience and networking.

Activity C: Researching Careers in Sociology

What are some different types of positions that are available in sociology? Research opportunities by doing an internet search: go to www.careerbuilder. com and other sites.

- What positions are available?

- What qualities, skills, and types of experience are organizations seeking?

- What are some goals that you can set for yourself to become more marketable in finding your dream job?

Activity D: Writing a Thank-You Message

Thank-you messages are important job-search tools. By taking the time to send a thank-you note, your words of appreciation will be well-received—people are not used to receiving thank-you messages.

Who would you like to recognize for assisting you? *A networking contact? An interviewer? A friend or family member?* Compose a handwritten or typed note expressing thanks to the person for assisting you. Focus on what the person did: try to keep most sentences in the "you" viewpoint rather than the "I" viewpoint.

When a potential employer receives a thank-you note, it sets the applicant apart from the crowd.

References

1   Marcus Aurelius, Meditations, IV, 3.

2   Belli, G. (2017). How many jobs are found through networking, really? *PayScale*, April 6. Retrieved from https://www.payscale.com/career-news/2017/04/many-jobs-found-networking

3   Ibid.

4   Svehla, T., personal interview. Svehla recruits for major corporations, screening applicants and making job recommendations. www.managingthemosaic.com.

5   Gershon, I. (2017) "A friend of a friend" is no longer the best way to find a job. *Harvard Business Review*, June 2. Retrieved from https://hbr.org/2017/06/a-friend-of-a-friend-is-no-longer-the-best-way-to-find-a-job

6   Anderson, G. (1999). Foreword. In *Girl boss: Running the show like the big chicks*, by S. Kravetz. Girl Press.

Making a Presentation

PowerPoint—along with Prezi and other presentation tools—has the potential to be overused and misused, which is how the phrase "death by PowerPoint" became popular. Especially when information is complicated, presenters need to adapt to the needs of their audience.

By understanding the purpose of PowerPoint (and other options, such as Prezi), presenters can provide complicated information in an engaging way. Though this may take more work in planning and preparation, audiences deserve that respect. Doing the work up front is what it takes to achieve outstanding results.

Let no one underestimate the fear and anxiety that many people experience at the idea of presenting in front of a live audience. Most people go to great extremes to avoid being criticized, and that dynamic can lead to procrastination. By avoiding the inevitable, presenters lose the time that they need to learn their topic, simplify it, prepare supporting material, and develop creative ways to engage their audience.

When you have completed this chapter, you will be able to:

- Know the basics for creating engaging presentations.

- Understand how to select font style, color, and size.

- Design PowerPoint slides for readability.

- Select effective graphics.

- Be familiar with tips for making a professional presentation.

For ease of discussion, reference is made to PowerPoint throughout this chapter; however, the theory for developing a PowerPoint presentation applies to Prezi and other similar software.

Let's start with purpose and then walk through a process to help you *prepare, practice*, and *present*.

Respect the Purpose

PowerPoint slides are not meant to tell the whole story. That is the presenter's job. PowerPoint slides should also not be used to present complicated information; that is what additional handouts are for.

Every PowerPoint presentation should aim to engage the audience so that they interact with the information; otherwise, the presentation is a one-way communication. People do not learn well when information comes to them in a rapid-fire manner—this approach leads to information overload. Use PowerPoint slides to present key concepts and ideas. After you identify what you want your audience to remember afterward, use slides to engage them in a learning process about those key ideas.

By the way, professionals are often relieved when they learn that they will attend an event that does *not* involve a PowerPoint. By relying on flipcharts and whiteboards, you are using tools to support interacting with your audience. As a presenter, you would ask for audience input to generate information, writing it on the flipchart. Therefore, even when you present a PowerPoint, incorporate flipcharts, sticky notes, or whiteboards to ensure your presentation is *interactive*. Think of your presentation as a conversation—a dialogue between you and your audience.

The best use for PowerPoint is for short presentations that include large audiences. Even then, the presenter is the focus, not the slides: use slides only to highlight key ideas. When you learn your topic well enough to teach it in a simple way, your audience will walk away with something they can use, feeling satisfied for time well-spent. As Albert Einstein suggested, "Make the . . . basic elements as simple and as few as possible."[1]

Prepare

Prepare your presentation in a systematic manner similar to the way that you prepare other forms of communication. Keep in mind that preparing is not a linear, step-by-step process. Working on any part at any time will contribute to the success of the whole. Here are steps that must be completed for a presentation to be effective:

1 Determine the purpose

2 Identify the audience

3 Develop your topic: map it out

4 Choose a design for your slides

5 Sketch out your plan

6 Compose with text and graphics (do not overuse animated graphics)

7 Format each slide

8 For group presentations, put your initials on slides containing information you provided (to avoid plagiarism issues)

9 Edit text and graphics

10 Add citations on slides, as needed, and include a reference list at the end

11 Prepare your handouts

Remember that some people in the audience may be visually impaired so avoid using graphics such as flying balloons. After you have prepared meticulously, you will practice and present with ease.

Determine the Purpose

Start with your objectives: what do you want to achieve? What does your audience need to learn about your topic? In the beginning stages of preparing, all of your attention is on your topic because you are still learning it. As you teach a concept, you learn it at deeper levels.

Therefore, even if you are knowledgeable in an area, you are facing a learning curve that may feel uncomfortable: it is not your topic that is key—it is presenting the topic so that your audience has a learning experience, not just a listening experience. Ask yourself, "What ideas or principles would benefit the audience?"

Identify the Audience

Who are the members of your audience? How many will there be? What are their backgrounds? What are their *pain points*—what about the topic will help your audience solve some sort of problem? What do they already know about the topic?

- Regardless of the topic, keep it as simple as possible.

- Define your terms to create a common understanding of the topic.

- Avoid abbreviations, acronyms, and initialisms: even within organizations, jargon causes confusion.

- Respect cultural differences by using common words.

- Avoid slang, cultural terms, and idioms, which can cause audience members who do not understand the reference to feel left out.

By discussing your topic with others, you learn about their experiences, questions, and frustrations, further helping you to mold your topic to the needs of your audience.

Develop Your Topic: Map it Out

If needed, start by writing about the topic until you can identify your key points. As discussed in Chapter 2, "Process, Strategy, and Style," develop a mind map, a page map, or an outline, if you know your topic well enough.

If you are uncomfortable using PowerPoint or another presentation software, consider *storyboarding* to plan your slides. To storyboard, turn your paper horizontally so that its layout is landscape (sideways). Then draw a line down the middle, and put your text on one side of the sheet and a sketch of a graphic on the other. In planning your graphics, consider browsing for clip art; which could be used sparingly, depending on the audience. Your graphics should convey a message, not simply entertain. When selecting your graphics, consider the *tone* you wish to convey. For a more professional tone, you might use only photos; whereas for a lighter tone, you might use cartoons. However, if you do include humor, remember that it can backfire. Do it sparingly; and to show respect for your audience, do not reference anything political. When in doubt, stay conservative. In any case, jot down the image or the file name in your storyboard across from your text.

Choose a Design for your Slides

Part of planning the organization and content of your slides includes choosing a functional and attractive template. An almost infinite number of designs are available free online.

- Choose a simple theme that will complement your message, not compete with it.

- Select colors that contrast to enhance ease of reading.

- Use a *non-serif font* such as Arial or Calibri because their simplicity makes them easier to read from a distance. (For print, serif fonts such as Times New Roman are still the best choice.)

Sketch Your Plan

Transfer the information that you generate from your mind map, outline, or storyboard to slides. If an outline has been provided for an assignment, use the outline points for some of your headings.

- Decide on your *major headers*, which will each then be titles for individual slides.

- Create one slide for each major header.

- Divide each header into *sub-topics* or *second-level headers*.

Compose with Text and Graphics

Begin to build each slide with these outcomes in mind:

- As a general rule, limit the amount of your text to no more than *eight words per line* and *no more than eight lines per slide*; some guidelines recommend even fewer.

- Create a short introduction and a brief conclusion. (Write the introduction and conclusion last to make sure they are consistent with your presentation.)

- If needed, include *transitional slides* that introduce new sections or summarize what preceded them.

- For large groups, use fewer words and larger print.

Format Each Slide

As you format, add slides as needed so that your audience can read with ease.

- Set the size of the font so that those in the back of the room can read the slides (for example, use at least size 30 point in a large room).

- Break up information and add slides as needed to keep font size readable.

- Include *white space* around your text to improve readability.

- Limit the number of words, the size of your graphics, and the colors you use.

Keep in mind that light-colored fonts may look fine on your computer screen but can seem washed out and be difficult to read when projected on a large screen; dark backgrounds make some fonts/colors hard to read. Also, be wary of using too many *effects* or changing them too often. Having your words fly in from the left or having slides change like vertical blinds can work well, but mixing too many effects distracts your audience.

Edit Text and Graphics

As you edit, arrange your slides in a logical order, placing transitional slides appropriately.

- Check and cite your data.

- Edit each slide for accuracy, clarity, consistency, and conciseness.

- Cut unnecessary words and graphics: *When in doubt, cut it out—less is more.* Cutting is the painful part of editing, but your results are better.

- Use parallel structure: present your bullet points in the same grammatical form: noun for noun, verb for verb.

- Use active voice when feasible.

- Eliminate excess graphics.

If you are presenting with a group, include the initials of the person or people providing the data on each slide to avoid plagiarism. Finally, make sure that each slide presents information so that everyone in your room can read it easily, regardless of where they are sitting: when you present, you will discuss the information on each slide, *but you will not read your slides to your audience.* Your goal is to be concise, clear, consistent, and accurate, using your PowerPoint as a guide but not a crutch.

Prepare Your Handouts

Handouts are not only good tools for your audience, they provide a backup for you in case of any sort of system failure. When information becomes complicated, prepare it as a separate handout.

When you print your slides:

- Select the *Handout* option.

- Select the number of slides per page; three to six slides per page provides space for notes.

- Select the *Pure Black and White* option for a crisp, clear copy.

Practice

Regardless of whether your audience will consist of five people or 100, practice rehearsing—speaking your presentation aloud—until you feel confident.

The best way to practice is to record yourself. If you do not have access to video recording, recording only audio works well. (Most phones provide this option.) Listening to your own voice as you present your topic is the best way to notice subtleties so that you can fine-tune your words. Listening to yourself also helps you memorize your presentation, building your confidence. In contrast, if you present to a peer, you may find that you are interrupted at key moments, causing needless frustration. And frustration is the last thing you need. If you need to practice in front of someone, hire a professional coach who knows how and when to give feedback.

On the day of your presentation, ensure that all seating has good visual access to your presentation. If people cannot read your presentation, you will lose their attention. They will leave disappointed, even if you talk them through it.

Present

Reading out PowerPoint slides is no more effective than reading a typed speech. As you speak, consider eye contact and voice as well as your interaction with your slides and audience.

- In a room of 20 to 25 people, make eye contact with everyone at least once.

- With a large audience, look around as you speak and try to make contact with as many people as possible.

- Since the audience reads slides from left to right, you create a better flow by standing on the right side of the screen (from your audience's perspective).

- As you present, consider your *voice projection*, *pronunciation*, and *speed*.

  ○ Project your voice so that the people at the back of the room can hear it.

  ○ Practice pronouncing any words that you anticipate having difficulty saying.

  ○ Modulate your speed—speaking slowly at times and even pausing.

- Point to the slides and comment on individual terms.

- Interact with the audience by asking questions, even if you do not expect answers.

- Do not read your slides or "hide behind them": interact with your slides and audience, referring to your slides and elaborating on parts of each.

- Once again, speak slowly: the faster you speak, the more nervous you may feel.

If you feel confident, include a short activity in which you present the audience with a question; then give them a short time (not more than five minutes) to discuss with a partner or small group. However, if you are not confident or prepared enough, you may have difficulty regaining control and the presentation will feel chaotic.

Let it Flow

Prepare meticulously—do not let your fears hold you back. When you make a mistake, let it go quickly. Only you know what you had planned to say or do. Even if you have problems with logistics, stay confident and upbeat. Your audience will take your lead. As a wise mother once said, *act confident* and you will *feel confident*.

In the end, the only one who will give your mistakes a second thought is you—so do not spend any time after your presentation dwelling on what you should have done. If you make a mistake, appreciate the learning opportunity and move on. The key to doing a great job is preparing well and then going with the flow.

Use *Signal Anxiety* to Your Benefit

Signal anxiety is a healthy type of anxiety that tugs at your sleeve, gently reminding you to start working. However, rather than working on an unimportant task to relieve your feelings, take action on the task that you are avoiding, the one that has the impending deadline. You will feel instant relief and see immediate results.

As you take action, do not try to start from the beginning. Write about what you know first. Let what you already know lead you to fresh insights. In fact, once you start writing, you gain deeper insight, even when you are not thinking about your topic.

Writing forces you to make progress by pulling you to deeper levels of understanding. That is why writing sometimes feels painful: putting critical thoughts on paper takes energy and courage because you force yourself to take positions, make decisions, and think clearly. Writing is a problem-solving activity: writing is *thinking on paper*.

Writing Workshop

Develop a PowerPoint for Your Literature Review

Instructions: Develop a 10-minute PowerPoint presentation of your literature review. (See Chapter 4, "Literature Review," Writing Workshop, Step 7, page 110.) In your presentation, include the following:

1   Introduction that includes the thesis statement

2   Synthesis of your review

3   Conclusion

After your presentation, immediately write a reflection that includes new questions and insights for your final paper.

Note

Dr. Andrea Tamburro contributed to this chapter.

References

1   Einstein, A. (1934). On the method of theoretical physics. *Philosophy of Science*, 1, 163–169.

Keys to Activities

Part 2: Editing for Clarity

Chapter 7

Practice 7.1 Pronoun Point of View and Consistency

We begin to reason from the moment *we* wake up in the morning. *We* reason when *we* figure out what to eat for breakfast, what to wear, whether to make certain purchases, whether to go with this or that friend to lunch. *We* reason as we interpret the oncoming flow of traffic, when *we* react to the decisions of the other drivers, when *we* speed up or slow down. [*We*]can draw conclusions then, about everyday events or, really, about anything at all: about poems, microbes, people, numbers, historical events, social settings, psychological states, character traits, the past, the present, the future.[1]

Practice 7.2 Paragraphs and Information Flow

The key to the sociological perspective, which distinguishes it from other disciplines, is the search for common patterns in social relations. *The job of the sociologist* is to discover the ways that social relationships reveal order, consistency, and predictable change, even when change involves violence and volatility. *There is an underlying organization to all human affairs*—those of the past and present, those involving economic processes, those revolving around power and politics, and those involving people's personalities. *Each social science looks at a piece of social reality*, but only sociology and (at times) anthropology seek to put the pieces together.[2]

Chapter 8

Practice 8.1 Active Voice

1   Sean's manager asked him to lead the diversity team.

2   Phelps' coach gave him another chance to swim in the relay.

3   Our department hosted the holiday event last year.

4   Our president implemented a new policy on reimbursement for travel expenses.

5   The mayor cancelled the program due to lack of interest.

Practice 8.2 Passive Voice, the Tactful Voice

1   Meyers made an error in invoicing on your account last week. (passive is more tactful)

2   If you wanted to avoid an overdraft, you should have deposited your check before 4 p.m. (passive is more tactful)

3   You should have enclosed your receipt with your return item. (passive is more tactful)

4   We sent your order to the wrong address and apologize for our mistake. (active)

5   You needed to pay your invoice by the first of the month to avoid penalties. (passive is more tactful)

Practice 8.3 Nominals

1   Management implemented the policy in August.

2   Jane suggested that all new hires start on the first day of the month.

3   Our professor gave us information about that research.

4   At our last meeting, we discussed the new survey.

5   Our department chair announced the research grant before awarding
     the resources.

Chapter 9

Practice 9.1 Clauses

1   The control group will meet next week, and he suggested arriving early
     on Friday.

2   My research design needs input from the committee, and I will make
     suggestions for them.

3   Though I gave input, my department chair planned my schedule.

4   If I can adjust my schedule, I will take time off to complete my
     research.

5   My department chair approved the extra time, so now I must change
     my schedule.

Practice 9.2 Tenses

1   The message *was* not clear and *needed* to be changed. (Or: *is* and *needs*)

2   The project assistant *said* that their participation *was* inactive for some
     time now.

3   The new computers *arrived* today, so then I *had* to install them.

4   Yesterday my co-worker *told* me that I *was supposed* to attend the
     budget meeting.

5   First Mary *said* that she *wanted* the position then she *said* that she
     didn't.

Practice 9.3 Parallel lists

*   *Develop* questions for survey

*   *Identify* effective communication skills

*   *Compile* the requirements for the study

- *Resolve* conflict among the group

- *Recruit* and *retain* project leaders

- *Value* personality differences in committees

- *Assess* climate in change efforts

Practice 9.4 Correlative Conjunctions

1   My associate asked me *not only* to complete the report *but also* (to) present it at the meeting.

2   Milly (both) applied for the job and got it.

3   Our team *neither* focused on getting funding *nor* showed interest in the project.

4   The solution *not only* makes sense *but also* saves time.

5   My new project *neither* has been approved *nor* is being considered.

Chapter 10

Practice 10.1 Consistent Point of View (answers may vary)

1   *You* sometimes think another situation is better until *you* experience it.

2   *We* generally follow the rules unless *we* are told otherwise.

3   If *students are* conscientious, *they* will do well in their classes.

4   *We* do not always follow instructions, but *we* should. (Or: *People* . . . *they*)

5   *Everyone* must make *his or her* own reservations.

6   *John* went to the meeting with *Gary* to ensure that *Gary* gave a complete report.

Practice 10.2 Pronoun and Antecedent Agreement

1   When *employees call* in sick, *they* should give a reason.

2   When *sociologists* do not relate well to *their clients, they* need more training.

3   *Social workers are* going beyond *their job descriptions* when *they* assist a client's guests.

4   *Criminologists' jobs are* challenging because *they* work under difficult conditions.

5   When *customers do* not have a receipt, *they* may not be able to return an item.

6   *Charley* said that *John* should be on his team because *Charley* would be available during *John's* training.

Practice 10.3 Pronoun Consistency

I enjoy working on team projects because **I** learn so much from **my** teammates. **Team members need** to be helpful because they never know when they will need assistance from **their** colleagues. ~~When you are on a team, every~~ All members need to carry their weight. That is, teammates who do not do **their** share of the work can be a burden to the entire team and jeopardize their project.

Practice 10.4 Pronoun and Antecedent Agreement

1   When *pollsters do* not relate well to the public, they need more training.

2   *Servers are* going beyond their job descriptions when they prepare carry-out orders for customers.

3   *Pilots have* challenging *jobs* because they work long hours under difficult conditions.

4   When lab *assistants do* not turn in their work, they should expect negative feedback.

5   *Writers need* to submit their work in a timely manner.

Practice 10.5 Subjects and Objects

1   If you can't reach anyone else, feel free to call **me**.

2   The director told Catie and **me** to role play again.

3   Fred and **she** collected for the local food drive.

4   His manager and **he** have two more reports to complete.

5   That decision was made by Jim and **me**.

Practice 10.6 Pronouns Following *Between* and *Than*

1   Between you and **me**, who has more time?

2   Beatrice sings better than **I do**.

3   The decision is between Bob and **you**.

4   The Blue Jays are more competitive than **we are**.

5   You can split the work between Margaret and **me** so that it gets done on time.

Practice 10.7 Relative Pronouns: *Who, Whom,* and *That*

1   **Who** completed the monthly report?

2   **Whom** are you going to the meeting with?

3   Is Jim the person **who** spoke with you?

4   The doctor **who** saw you yesterday is not available.

5   Every person **who** arrives late will be turned away.

Practice 10.8 Indefinite Pronouns

1   Either one of the programs **works** perfectly.

2   Everyone who finished the project **is** free to go.

3   None of the employees **send** e-mail on Saturday.

4   Some of the assignments **need** to be distributed before noon today.

5   Everything **runs** much better when we are all on time.

Writing Workshop

Activity A. Pronoun Consistency: First Person Singular

I enjoy working on team projects because **I** learn so much from **my** teammates. **Team members need** to be helpful because they never know when they will need assistance from **their** colleagues. ~~When you are on a team, every~~ All members need to carry their weight. That is, teammates who do not do **their** share of the work can be a burden to the entire team and jeopardize their project.

Team members who stay motivated are more valuable to the team. I always strive to do my best because **I** never know when **I** will need to count on **my** team members.

Activity B. Pronoun Consistency: Third Person Plural

Working on team projects can be enjoyable because team members learn so much from each other. Team members need to be supportive because they never know when they will need assistance from their colleagues. When on a team, all members need to carry their weight. That is, if members would not do their share of the work, they can be a burden to the team and jeopardize their project.

If team members stay motivated, they are more valuable to the team. All members should always strive to do their best because they never know when they will need to count on their team members.

Chapter 11

Practice 11.1 Cut Redundant Modifiers

1   We hope ~~and trust~~ that you find our services ~~helpful and~~ worthwhile.

2   Our new ~~breakthrough in~~ design makes our laptop ~~even more perfect~~ better than it was before.

3   The ~~final~~ outcome of this project depends on ~~each individual~~ *participants* doing ~~his or her~~ their best.

4   We want you to be ~~absolutely~~ certain that you have not ordered multiple items that are ~~exactly~~ alike.

Practice 11.2 Remove Redundancy and Outdated Expressions

1   The papers that you requested are attached.

2   You have our confidence, and we value our client relationship.

3   As we discussed, the new policy should be reviewed this week.

4   You can eliminate any questions by sending your agenda in advance of the meeting.

5   Thank you for your support and assistance. (or simply "support")

Practice 11.3 Use Simple Language

1   We use that product, and the field supervisor is aware of our choice.

2   After the policy change, we tried to compromise as much as possible.

3   As you requested, we are omitting that information.

4   If the merger depends on our use of their facilities, we should try to change locations.

5   If you are aware of their objections, try to make respective changes.

Practice 11.4 Modify Sparingly

1   In my opinion, you should feel certain what the facts are before you sign the contract.

2   Can you confirm that they might back out of their agreement?

3   I would like for you to speak to the person who knows much about this topic.

Practice 11.5 Edit Out Background Thinking

Since the economy and tax laws have changed, we need fresh ideas to raise funds. What do you think about seeking input from our staff and major donors?

Practice 11.6 Leave Out Opinions and Beliefs

How about cutting our annual conference by one day this year? Generally our productivity goes down by the last day, and we could save about 20 percent of our costs.

Part 3 Proofreading for Credibility

Chapter 13

Practice 13.1 Rule 2: Conjunction (CONJ)

1   <u>Mark Mallory</u> <u>is</u> the new case manager, and <u>he</u> <u>starts</u> on Monday. CONJ

2   <u>Mark</u> <u>will be</u> an inspiration to our staff and an excellent spokesperson for our agency. (no commas)

3   <u>You</u> <u>can leave</u> him a message, but <u>he</u> <u>will</u> not <u>be</u> able to reply until next week. CONJ

4   The <u>office</u> in St. Louis also <u>has</u> a new case manager, and her <u>name</u> <u>is</u> Gia Rivera. CONJ

5   <u>You</u> <u>can mail</u> your information now and <u>expect</u> a reply within the next two weeks. (no commas)

Practice 13.2 Rule 3: Series (SER)

1   <u>We</u> <u>were</u> <u>assigned</u> Conference Rooms A and B on the first floor. (no commas)

2   (<u>You</u>) <u>Make</u> sure that you bring your laptop, cell phone, and client list to the meeting. SER

3   You should arrange the meeting, call your supervisor, and submit your
    housing assessment. SER

4   Mitchell, Helen, and Sally conducted the workshop on anger
    management. SER

5   They gave a workshop for Elaine, Arlene, Donald, and Joanne on
    preparing housing packets for the elderly. SER

Practice 13.3 Rule 4: Introductory (INTRO)

1   Because the proposal needed revision, we were not able to respond on
    time. INTRO

2   However, we were given an extension. INTRO

3   Although the extra time helped us, we still felt pressured for time.
    INTRO

4   To get another extension, George called their office. INTRO

5   Fortunately, the director was agreeable to our request. INTRO

Practice 13.4 Rule 5: Nonrestrictive (NR)

1   Our manager *who specializes in project grants* will assist you with this
    issue. (restrictive: no commas)

2   Tomas Phillips, *who works only on weekends,* will call you soon. NR

3   The therapist *who researched this case* is not available. (restrictive: no
    commas)

4   Nick Richards, *who is in a meeting until 3 p.m.,* can answer your
    question. NR

5   Your new contract, *which we mailed yesterday,* should arrive by Friday.
    NR

Practice 13.5 Rule 6: Parenthetical (PAR)

1   Clinical services, I believe, can best assist you with this issue. PAR

2   T. J., therefore, will work this weekend in my place. PAR

3   Our <u>invoice</u>, unfortunately, <u>was</u> <u>submitted</u> incorrectly. PAR

4   The new <u>contract</u>, in my opinion, <u>meets</u> specifications. PAR

5   <u>Social Research Corporation</u>, of course, <u>recommended</u> us to a vendor. PAR

Practice 13.6 Rule 7: Direct Address (DA)

1   (<u>You</u>) <u>Give</u> your report to the auditor by Friday, Marcel. DA

2   Jason, <u>do</u> <u>you</u> <u>have</u> tickets for the game? DA

3   Doctor, <u>I</u> <u>would</u> <u>like</u> to know the results of my tests. DA

4   <u>Would</u> <u>you</u> <u>like</u> to attend the banquet, Alice? DA

5   (I) <u>Thank</u> you for inviting me, George. DA

Practice 13.7 Rule 8: Appositive (AP)

1   <u>Jacob Seinfeld</u>, our associate director, <u>decided</u> to hire Williams. AP

2   My lab <u>partner</u>, Carol Glasco, <u>applied</u> for a job here. AP

3   <u>Jim Martinez</u>, the registrar, <u>approved</u> your request. AP

4   The <u>department chair</u>, Dr. George Schmidt, <u>did</u> not <u>receive</u> your transcript. AP

5   The <u>director</u> <u>asked</u> Claire, my sister, to join us for dinner. AP

Practice 13.8 Rule 9: Addresses and Dates (AD)

1   (<u>You</u>) <u>Send</u> your application by Friday, December 15, to my assistant. AD

2   <u>San Antonio</u>, Texas, <u>has</u> a River Walk and Conference Center. AD

3   <u>Would</u> <u>you</u> <u>prefer</u> to meet in Myrtle, Minnesota, or Des Moines, Iowa? AD

4   <u>Springfield</u>, Massachusetts, <u>continues</u> to be my selection. AD

5   <u>We</u> <u>arrived</u> in Chicago, Illinois, on May 22, 2011, to prepare for the event. AD

Practice 13.9 Rule 10: Word Omitted (WO)

1   The <u>president</u> <u>shared</u> two intriguing, confidential reports. WO

2   The <u>crew</u> <u>scheduled</u> filming on Tuesday at 5 p.m., on Wednesday at 6 p.m. WO

3   The <u>problem</u> <u>is</u>, some of the results are not yet known. WO

4   (<u>You</u>) <u>Leave</u> the materials with Alicia at the Westin, with Marcia at the Hilton. WO

5   <u>Silvana</u> <u>presented</u> a short, exciting PowerPoint on Italy. WO

Practice 13.10 Rule 11: Direct Quotation (DQ)

1   Patrick shouted "Get back" before we had a chance to see the falling debris. DQ

3   According to Tyler, "All children can learn if they find an interest in what is taught." DQ

4   My father warned me, "When you choose an insurance company, find one with good customer service." DQ

4   Sharon encouraged me by yelling "Go for the gold!" as I was starting the race. DQ

5   Lenny said to me, "Good luck on your exam," before I left this morning. DQ (OR: no commas because it is a short quote)

Practice 13.11 Rule 12: Contrasting Expression or Afterthought (CEA)

1   <u>You</u> <u>will find</u> the manuscript in John's office, not in Bob's. CEA

2   <u>Marcus</u> <u>secured</u> the contract, but only after negotiating for hours. CEA

3   (<u>You</u>) <u>Chair</u> the budget committee, if you prefer. CEA

4   <u>Lester</u>, rather than Dan, <u>received</u> the award. CEA

5   (<u>You</u>) <u>Work</u> to achieve your dreams, not to run away from your fears. CEA

Chapter 14

Practice 14.1 Rule 1: Semicolon No Conjunction (NC)

1   <u>Keri</u> <u>will</u> not <u>approve</u> our final report; <u>she</u> <u>needs</u> more documentation.

2   (<u>You</u>) <u>Ask</u> Bryan for the report; <u>he</u> <u>said</u> that it was completed yesterday.

3   (<u>You</u>) <u>Arrive</u> on time to tomorrow's meeting; (<u>you</u>) <u>bring</u> both of your reports.

4   A <u>laptop</u> <u>was</u> <u>left</u> in the conference room; <u>Johnny</u> <u>claimed</u> it as his.

5   (<u>You</u>) <u>Recognize</u> your mistakes; (<u>you</u>) <u>offer</u> apologies as needed.

Practice 14.2 Rule 2: Semicolon Bridge (BR)

1   <u>Carol</u> <u>suggested</u> the topic; fortunately, <u>Carlos</u> <u>agreed</u>.

2   The case management <u>team</u> <u>offered</u> assistance; however, their <u>time</u> <u>was</u> limited.

3   <u>Ken</u> <u>compiled</u> the data; therefore, <u>Mary</u> <u>crunched</u> it.

4   The <u>numbers</u> <u>turned out</u>* well; as a result, our new <u>budget</u> <u>was</u> <u>accepted</u>.

5   <u>Roger</u> <u>ran</u> in the marathon; unfortunately, <u>he</u> <u>was</u> unable to finish.

* "Turned out" is a verb phrase.

Practice 14.3 Rule 3: Semicolon Because of Commas (BC)

1   (<u>You</u>) Please <u>include</u> Rupert Adams, CEO; Madeline Story, COO; and Mark Coleman, executive president.

2   By next week <u>I</u> <u>will</u> <u>have</u> <u>traveled</u> to St. Louis, Missouri; Chicago, Illinois; and Burlington, Iowa.

3   <u>Mike</u> <u>applied</u> for jobs in Honolulu, Hawaii; Sacramento, California; and Santa Fe, New Mexico.

4   Your <u>application</u> <u>was</u> <u>received</u> yesterday; but when <u>I</u> <u>reviewed</u> it, <u>information</u> <u>was</u> missing.

5 <u>You</u> <u>can</u> <u>resubmit</u> your application today; and since my <u>office</u> <u>will</u> <u>review</u> it, <u>you</u> <u>can</u> <u>call</u> me tomorrow for the results.

Practice 14.4 The Colon

1 I have some exciting news for you: Jeremy proposed on Friday.

2 *Note*: The office is closed on Monday to honor the Martin Luther King holiday.

3 The supplies we need are as follows: markers, copy paper, and staplers.

4 Giorgio said that we need cereal, coconut milk, and bananas.

5 Here is what you should do: complete the inventory list and then work on the schedule. (Or: Complete . . .)

Practice 14.5 The Dash

1 Margie called on Friday—George is home!

2 Mike's parents are in town—he invited me to have dinner with them.

3 Helen Jones—the new CEO—asked me to join her team.

4 Call if you need anything—I'm always here to support you.

5 Give as much as you can to that charity—it's a good cause.

Chapter 15

Practice 15.1 Quotation Marks

1 My answer to your request is an enthusiastic "yes."

2 If you think that's a "good idea," so do I.

3 The code was "307A," not "370A."

4 All he wrote was, "Our dog can hunt."

5 If you call that "good timing," I don't know how to respond.

Chapter 16

Practice 16.1 Capitalization

Next year the president of my company will provide a financial incentive for all employees, and I plan to participate in it. Jack Edwards, vice president of finance, will administer the plan. Everyone in my department is looking forward to having the opportunity to save more. A pamphlet entitled, "Financial Incentives for Long-term Savings," will describe the plan and be distributed next week. If the pamphlet has not arrived by Friday, I will check with the vice president's office to find out the details.

Practice 16.2 Numbers

1   We are meeting on January 5 at 10 a.m. at our offices on Lake Street.

2   Call me on Monday at 407-555-1212.

3   Alex lists his address as 407 South Maple Street, Hobart, IN 46368.

4   We received hundreds of calls about the job opening but only five résumés.

5   Purchase 12 laptops but only seven new printers for our department.

Chapter 17

Practice 17.1 Apostrophes: Possessives and Contractions

1   My supervisor's report won't be ready until next week.

2   The weather report says it's going to rain later, but I don't believe it.

3   Though it's June's responsibility, it's in Jack's best interest to complete the task.

4   Dr. Jones's (or Dr. Jones') office isn't located down the hall; it's next to Dr. Raines' (office).

5   If you tell me it's Tess's (Tess') project, I'll adjust my expectations.

Practice 17.2 Possessives

1   the book's price

2   the report's cover

3   the team leader's influence

4   the professor's advice

5   the agency's reports

Practice 17.3 Singular and Plural Possessives

1	boss	my boss's office	both bosses' offices
2	waitress	this waitress's table	these waitresses' tables
3	year	this year's schedule	both years' schedules
4	secretary	my secretary's laptop	our secretaries' laptops
5	client	the client's needs	all clients' needs

Practice 17.4 More Possessives

1   *Ambra and Lucia's* instructor *refuses* to let them work together.

2   Either *Alexi's* report or *Basma's* will persuade the judge.

3   Milton suggested that we go to *Ditka's* for the meeting.

4   My *brother-in-law's* attorneys opened their office last week.

5   *Chandra and her partner's* office *needs* to be remodeled.

Practice 17.5 Hyphens

1   Your *first-class* treatment has impressed all of us.

2   Our budget is *one-half* spent.

3   The *short-* and *long-term* outlooks are quite different.

4   *Twenty-five* people attended the conference.

5   Do you have funding for your *30-* and *60-day* payment schedules?

Activity 1: Apostrophe Usage A

1   The women's comments were not taken as they were meant.

2   Paul and Mary's file was in the wrong cabinet.

   Or: Paul's and Mary's files were in the wrong cabinet.

3   Our agency's mission is to assist young people.

4   I have taken several classes in sociology this year.

5   Her assistant's response was that he could not do the work.

6   The men's and women's responses were recorded by the assistant.

7   The speaker's remark sparked the audience's laughter.

8   It's all in a day's work!

Activity 2: Apostrophe Usage B

1   Amanda Wittfield, director of marketing, will lead this week's meeting.

2   Amanda will complete her Bachelor of Arts in Sociology this fall.

3   The children's toys were scattered around the play room.

4   He recommended reading the book *How to Find a Job in 30 Days*.

5   When you receive your master's degree in social work, you can put MSW after your name.

6   Mary received her bachelor's degree last year and is now working on her master's.

7   Every time that I tried to assist Barb's client, she refused my help.

8   This week's activities were challenging.

Chapter 18

Activity 1: Similar Word Pretest

1   Will that decision ~~effect~~ you in a positive way? *affect*

2   The ~~principle~~ on my loan is due on the 1st of the month. *principal*

3 My ~~advise~~ is for you to get a job before you buy that new car. *advice*

4 Please ~~ensure~~ my manager that I will return in one-half hour. *assure*

5 ~~Its~~ been a challenging day, but things are getting better. *It's*

6 ~~Their~~ are a few issues that we need to discuss. *There*

7 The agency gave ~~are~~ report a new title. *our*

8 Pat lives ~~further~~ from work than I do. *farther*

9 You can have a meeting ~~everyday~~, if you prefer. *every day*

10 ~~Whose~~ going to the ballgame? *Who's*

11 I enjoy movies more ~~then~~ I enjoy plays. *than*

12 Megan ~~assured~~ that the project would be successful. *ensured*

13 It's ~~alright~~ for you to contact the manager directly. *all right*

14 I didn't mean to ~~infer~~ that you were late on purpose. *imply*

15 Try ~~and~~ be on time for the next meeting. *to*

Activity 2: Gender-Neutral and Unbiased Language Exercise

Outdated	Revised or Alternative
1 Policeman	police officer
2 Waiter/waitress	wait staff or server
3 Fireman	fire fighter
4 Mailman	mail carrier
5 Salesman	sales person
6 TV anchorman	TV anchor
7 Mankind	humankind
8 Chairman	chairperson
9 Oriental	Asian
10 Afro-American	African American
11 Man a project	staff a project

12 challenged	people who have challenges
13 wheelchair-bound	uses a wheelchair
14 AIDS victims	people with AIDS
15 high-risk groups	high-risk behavior
16 nonwhite	*state what the population prefers to be called*
17 minority	*state what the population prefers to be called*
18 the disabled or the handicapped	people with disabilities
19 the lower class	people who are poor
20 the blind	people who are blind

Activity 3: Similar Word Posttest

1 The ~~affect~~ of that decision is not yet known. *effect*

2 When you know the ~~principle~~ on your loan, let me know. *principal*

3 Her ~~advise~~ was that you take the other part-time job. *advice*

4 Can you ~~assure~~ the quality of your work? *ensure*

5 The dog chased ~~it's~~ tail, amusing several children. *its*

6 ~~They~~ are a few issues that we need to discuss. *There*

7 Is that ~~are~~ new computer? *our*

8 You are ~~farther~~ along on the project than I am. *further*

9 We meet ~~everyday~~ at 3 p.m. *every day*

10 ~~Who's~~ book is that? *Whose*

11 Sue was taller ~~then~~ Mary last year. *than*

12 Melanie ~~ensured~~ me that we would be finished by Friday. *assured*

13 ~~Its alright~~ for you to contact the manager directly. *It is* or *It's all right*

14 I'm not trying to ~~infer~~ that you were late on purpose. *imply*

References

1   Elder, L., & Paul, R. (2016). *The thinker's guide to analytic thinking*. Tomales, CA: Foundation for Critical Thinking Press, p. 6.

2   Turner, J. H. (2006). *Sociology*. Upper Saddle River, NJ: Pearson Education, p. 26.

Glossary

abstract

A short, written statement that gives an overview of a report, study, or proposal; usually associated with scientific studies but equivalent to an executive summary or a synopsis.

academic writing

A formal style of writing that stresses the third person viewpoint; for papers, a thesis statement is used to develop the introduction, body, and conclusion; it characterizes research papers, arguments, essays, and creative writing. Also known as *scholarly writing. Compare* **professional writing.**

acronym

An abbreviation pronounced as a word (for example, AARP, SADD).

action plan

A detailed plan for achieving a goal; includes action steps, deadlines for completing them, and a list of any obstacles and ways to overcome them.

action step

In an action plan, an identified task along with who will complete it when it is due.

action verb

A verb that transfers action from a subject to an object; in English, all verbs except 11 linking verbs. Also see **state-of-being verb.**

active listening

A listening skill that involves focusing on the meaning, intent, and feelings of the person who is speaking to gain a clear understanding of the message.

active voice

As applied to verbs, a term indicating that the subject performs the action of the verb (for example, "Bob *wrote* the report"). *Compare* **passive voice.**

adjective
A word that modifies a noun or pronoun.

adverbial conjunction
A word or phrase (for example, *however, therefore, thus*) that serves as a transition between sentences or paragraphs; shows the relationship between ideas, and plays a significant role in punctuation.

antecedent
The word or words to which a pronoun refers.

appositive
A restatement; a brief explanation that identifies the noun or pronoun preceding it. *See also* **essential appositive**.

background thinking
A person's thoughts about how he or she arrived at a conclusion or how readers will interpret that conclusion; a type of meta-discourse that should be eliminated from writing.

bar chart
A graphics tool that displays information in vertical or horizontal bars; enables the reader to compare and contrast different items.

base form
The original state of a verb. *See also* **infinitive.**

bibliography
A comprehensive list of the sources cited in a document (and sometimes of sources consulted but not cited); follows a standard format, including author, title of work, and publication or other identifying data for each work.

bidialectual
Fluid in speaking two dialects of the same language; for example, the ability to speak Edited American English and a community dialect.

bilingual
Ability to speak two languages.

boundary
A hypothetical construct that defines the border that separates the system from its suprasystem; for example, personal boundaries and generational boundaries.

career portfolio
A collection of relevant job-search information and documents, including résumé, sample cover and contact letters, network contacts, among others.

central idea

A thesis statement that expresses the main point of a paper.

chronological format

For résumés, a traditional structure that emphasizes job history; lists education, positions, and accomplishments in order, starting with the most recent and working backward in order of occurrence.

closing

(1) The last paragraph of a letter, stating action the recipient needs to take; (2) a complimentary sign-off (for example, for letters, *Sincerely*; for e-mail, *Best regards* or *All the best*).

coherent

A term referring to a paragraph that presents a logical flow of ideas, developing a topic in a consistent, rational way. One idea leads to another.

cohesive

A term referring to a paragraph that presents one main topic along with details to support that topic, demonstrating connectedness among the ideas it contains. All ideas adhere together for a common purpose.

colloquial

Informal, conversational language patterns which include slang and nonstandard English. Also called *idiomatic*.

colloquialism

A saying that is not taken literally; expresses an idea unique to specific time and location; for example, "That dog can't hunt."

community dialect (CD)

Any language pattern which differs from Edited American English (Standard English); informally known as "home talk" or "talkin' country." Most people shift codes depending on context, speaking less formally when with family and friends.

coordinating conjunction

A word that joins items of equal grammatical structure, such as independent clauses or items in a series. The seven coordinating conjunctions are *and, but, or, nor, for, yet, so.*

correlative conjunction

A pair of conjunctions (for example, *not only . . . but also*) that compares or contrasts ideas. The information presented after each conjunction must be presented in the same grammatical form (parallel construction).

cover e-mail

For online job searches, an e-mail message that indicates an electronic résumé is attached, summarizing the sender's interest in a company and requesting an interview. Also see *cover letter* and *cover message*.

cover letter

(1) Enclosed with a proposal, a letter summarizing key points in the proposal; (2) enclosed with a résumé, a letter that summarizes the sender's interest in a company, highlights accomplishments, and requests an interview. Also called *application letter*. Also see *cover e-mail*.

cover message

For sending documents as attachments via e-mail, a message that fulfils the same function as a *cover letter*.

credibility

Believability; equates to trust, a critical element in all relationships.

critic's block

A barrier to writing that is caused by being too critical of one's ability to write well or improve writing skills.

cultural sensitivity

The dynamics of communication that relate to diversity, such as cultural, generational, gender, and personality differences.

dash

A substitute for the comma, semicolon, period, or colon, used to emphasize the information that follows it; appropriate in both formal and informal documents.

dependent clause

A group of words that has a subject and verb but does not express a complete thought; cannot stand alone as a sentence.

Edited American English (EAE)

The type of written and spoken language that, for the most part, follows the standard rules of English usage; used by formal media programs (such as newscasts) and academia. Another term for EAE is Standard American English or Standard English.

editor's block

Being overly concerned with product at the expense of process.

ellipsis marks

Three spaced periods used to indicate the omission of a word or words from a quotation. (Add a fourth period if the ellipsis [plural *ellipses*] occurs at the end of a sentence.)

e-memo

An electronic memo sent on a company's intranet to its own employees; formatted like a traditional memo created by means of a template.

emphatic

An adjective or adverb used to place emphasis on the word it describes; can detract from the message rather than place emphasis on it, so should be used sparingly (for example, *very, really, incredible*).

empty information

Irrelevant or redundant information that adds nothing of value for your reader.

e-résumé

A résumé specifically formatted for electronic transmittal; at the top, summarizes work skills and experience in keywords that are scanned by employers for matches with their needs.

evidence

Proof of an assertion or research finding; typically consists of objective data, such as facts and figures, thereby eliminating bias.

external due date

A project completion date specified by the person or agency commissioning the project. *Compare* **internal due date**.

filler

An empty word that adds no value to a message (for example, *just, like*).

flowchart

A graphic representation of information that depicts progression through a procedure or system.

font

The style of type face, such as Times or Arial. Fonts number in the hundreds, and each word processing program includes its own series of fonts. *See also* **serif** and **sans serif**.

fragment

A phrase or dependent clause that is incorrectly punctuated as a complete sentence.

functional format

For résumés, a nontraditional structure that highlights experience and accomplishments in each area of expertise; lists skills and education before work experience.

gender bias

In writing, the exclusion of one gender by using only masculine or feminine pronouns in contexts that apply to both genders. Plural pronouns and the phrase *he or she* are gender-neutral.

gerund

The *ing* form of a verb (for example, such as *seeing, going, following*); functions as a noun.

gerund phrase

A gerund followed by a preposition, noun, and any modifiers (for example, *going to the meeting, being on time*); functions as a noun.

global communication

Communication across language and cultural borders.

grammatical subject

A subject that generally precedes the verb but may or may not be the actor or agent that performs the action of the verb; in an active-voice sentence, the same as the real subject. *Compare* **real subject**.

groupthink

A phenomenon in which everyone "goes along to get along," agreeing with decisions regardless of quality; occurs when a need for approval (or a fear of disapproval) exists among members.

hard copy

A paper copy of a document (as compared to an electronic copy). *Compare* **soft copy**.

hypothesis

An explanation that can be tested.

idiom

An expression peculiar to a language, not readily analyzable from its grammatical construction or from the meaning of its component parts; for example, "to put up with" translates to "tolerate or endure." *See* **colloquial**.

independent clause

A clause that has a subject and verb and expresses a complete thought; can stand alone as a sentence.

infinitive

The base form of the verb preceded by *to* (for example, *to be, to see, to speak*); functions as a noun, adjective, or adverb.

infinitive phrase

An infinitive along with an object and any modifiers (for example, *to go to the store, to see the latest book reviews*); functions as a noun, adjective, or adverb.

information flow

In writing, the transition between ideas. Presenting old information that leads to new information creates smooth transitions and ensures that messages are cohesive and coherent.

initialism

An abbreviation pronounced letter by letter (for example, *IBM, NYPD*).

input

All of the resources that are required by a social system to accomplish its purposes, including people and money.

internal due dates

A project completion date that group members set among themselves to ensure they will meet external requirements. *Compare* **external due date**.

irregular verb

A verb that forms its past and past participle in an irregular way (for example, *fly, flew, flown; sink, sank, sunk*).

jargon

using initials, abbreviations, technical, or occupational terminology as a sort of verbal shorthand.

logic modeling

A tool for applying critical thinking skills to identify an underlying system of reasoning as the means of explanation.

macro

A large social system such as a formal organization or community.

memorandum (memo)

An internal communication tool used to inform or make announcements to peers, subordinates, and supervisors within an organization; in hard-copy form, sent via interoffice mail or posted on boards. *See also* **e-memo**.

meta discourse

As coined by Joseph Williams, author of *Style*, a term that refers to the language a writer uses to describe his or her own thinking process; usually consists of unnecessary information.

method

The "how, when, where, and who" of accomplishing a project.

micro

A small social system such as a social group or family.

mirroring

Paraphrasing what the speaker said to ensure the message was received clearly.

networking

Engaging in social and professional activities that facilitate interaction with people who can provide assistance with one's career or problem-solving endeavors

new information

Unfamiliar information; information that extends the reader's understanding.

nominal

A noun that originated as a verb; often formed by adding *tion* or *ment* to the base form of the verb (for example, *development* from the verb *develop*).

nonverbal behavior

Body language that communicates feelings and thus can affect the meaning of a verbal message.

nonverbal cues

Hand gestures, eye contact, and other types of body language that affect communication.

null hypothesis

A hypothesis that is negated so that statistical analysis can be used to disprove it, thus showing the likelihood that the original hypothesis is valid.

objective

A narrow, precise statement of a specific and measurable intended action.

objective case

The form of pronouns that function as objects of verbs or prepositions (for example, *me, him, her, them*).

old information

Familiar information; information that is obvious or that the reader already knows; creates a context for new information.

outcomes

The results a project will produce and how people affected by the project will change or grow.

output

The status of signal/task and maintenance inputs following a conversion cycle of a social system.

paraphrase

Putting someone else's ideas or words into one's own words; requires a citation to the original source. Incorrect paraphrasing (making a few changes in word order, leaving out a word or two, or substituting similar words) is a form of plagiarism.

passive voice

As applied to verbs, a term indicating that the subject does not perform the action of the verb (for example, "The report *was written* by Bob"— the subject, *report,* did not perform the action, *was written*). *Compare* **active voice.**

pie charts

A graphics tool that displays information as "slices" of a circle; enables the reader to easily see both the relationship of one item to another and the relationships of all parts to the whole.

plagiarism

The use of another's ideas or words without crediting the source; constitutes a form of stealing. (The term is derived from the Latin *plagiarius*, "an abductor" or "thief.")

portfolio

For a job search, a collection of pertinent documents and information (for example, purpose statement, résumés, work samples, reference letters, networking contacts, business cards).

practice

The process of providing professional assistance to clients so that they make planned changes to move to a state of well-being.

professional writing

A direct style of writing characterized by use of the active voice, simple words, personal pronouns (for example, *I, you, we*), and at times contractions (for example, *can't* for *cannot*); used in most business communications.

pronoun

A word (for example, *I, you, he, she, it, we, they*) that is used in place of a noun or another pronoun; must agree with its antecedent in number, person, and gender.

pronoun viewpoint

The point of view that emanates from the number, person, and gender of a subjective case pronoun (for example, the "I" or "you" viewpoint); should be consistent within sentences, paragraphs, and at times documents.

protocols

Formalities and rules of order and etiquette; play an important role in global business, governing interactions such as introductions, greetings and written communications.

qualitative research

Research that involves collecting narrative data to gain insight into phenomena of interest; often done by administering surveys and questionnaires.

quantify

Express numerically; a way to describe an achievement or goal (for example, as a percentage, length of time, or amount of money) that shows its contribution to the bottom line.

quantitative research

Research that involves collecting numerical data to explain, predict, and/or control phenomena of interest; often done by applying the scientific method, with experimental and control groups.

random sampling

A research technique in which the researcher surveys a group of people who are chosen at random and thus believed to be representative of the broader population; reduces bias and enables calculation of a margin of error.

real subject

The actor or agent that performs the action of the verb but may or may not appear in the sentence; in an active sentence, the same as the grammatical subject. *Compare* **grammatical subject**.

reflexive case

The form of pronouns that reflect back to subjective case pronouns (for example, *myself, yourself, ourselves*). Also called *intensive case*.

reliability

In research, consistency of measure; for example, if the same study is repeated several times and the outcomes are the same, then it is *reliable*.

research

The process of investigating, inquiring, and examining; involves seeking answers in a methodical, objective manner that includes an established line of thought and credible experience.

resistance

A barrier consisting of beliefs, attitudes, and behaviors that keep people from moving forward with a decision, can stem from tangible sources (for example, lack of resources) or from intangible sources (for example, lack of trust) and from valid or invalid concerns.

run-on sentence

A sentence that contains inadequate punctuation to support its grammatical structure, such as two or more independent clauses that fuse together for lack of punctuation.

salutation

The opening greeting of a letter or e-mail message.

sans-serif

A nonserif font; a font in which the top and bottom of the letters are uniform in thickness and look flat; literally, "without the line." *Compare* **serif**.

scannable résumés

A hard-copy résumé that summarizes work skills and experience in keywords that are scanned by employers for matches with their needs. *See also* **e-résumé**.

scholastic writing

Also known as academic writing, a formal style of writing in which the third person viewpoint is stressed; for papers, a thesis statement is used to develop the introduction, body, and conclusion; it characterizes research papers, arguments, essays, and creative writing. *See* **academic writing**.

scientific method

A rigorous process used to identify predictability of hypotheses in quantitative research, including a control group and an experimental group.

screening interview

A preliminary interview for the purpose of developing a pool of qualified candidates; may occur over the telephone, online, or in person.

sentence

> A group of words that has a subject and a verb and expresses a complete thought; an independent clause.

serif

> A font in which the edges of the letters end in short lines, creating a pointed or sharp look (for example, Times New Roman). *Compare* **sans-serif**.

slang

> Informal, nonconventional language (for example, jargon, colloquialisms) that reflect a dialect rather than standard English; not acceptable in multicultural communication exchanges.

social system

> A social entity possessing functionally interdependent relationships with each other, for example a family, agency, or community.

social systems perspective

> A set of assumptions on which social systems theory is based.

social systems theory

> A set of assumptions and concepts that seeks to explain behaviors exhibited in the functioning of social systems and how such systems achieve well-being.

soft copy

> An electronic version of a document. *Compare* **hard copy**.

Standard American English

> The type of language that follows the standard rules of English usage; used in most books, in classrooms, and in public and professional forums. *See also* **Edited American English**.

storyboarding

> A technique for planning presentation slides; involves depicting the ideas by dividing a horizontal sheet of paper into two columns and putting text in one and a sketch or a graphic in the other.

strategy

> An approach to solving problems or accomplishing a vision that consists of developing goals, objectives, and action plans.

strengths perspective

> An approach that focuses on the strengths and capacities of people and their organizations to achieve a sense of well-being.

stress interview

An interview characterized by intense questioning and quick subject changes; intended to test an applicant's response to pressure.

subjective case

The form of pronouns that function as subjects of verbs. Subject pronouns must be followed by a verb (either real or implied). Also called *nominative case*.

subordinating conjunctions

A word or phrase (for example, *if, when, as, although, because, as soon as, before)* used to connect a dependent clause to an independent clause; defines the relationship between the ideas in the clauses.

subsystem

A component element of focal system that displays all the attributes of a system, but can be located within a larger designate system; for example, a married couple functions as a system and is a subsystem of the total family unit.

suprasystem

A part of the social environment to which a subject system is functionally linked; for example, birth families are relevant parts of a family's suprasystem.

survey

A research tool in which a questionnaire is administered to a number of people; designed to elicit responses about a specific topic being studied.

synergy

The energy created in team dynamics that leads to the whole becoming more than the sum of its parts.

synopsis

A short, written statement that gives and an overview of a report, study, or proposal; used in academic writing but equivalent to an abstract or executive summary.

syntax

The orderly arrangements of words. Also called *grammar*.

table

A graphics tool that displays data in columns and rows.

team

Two or more people who come together to work on a common goal.

theory

A logically derived set of assumptions and concepts used to explain something; for example, social systems theory.

thesis statement

a one- or two-sentence summary of the problem being discussed or argument being made in a paper.

topic sentence

A broad, general sentence that gives an overview of the paragraph.

topic string

A series of sentences that develop the specific idea presented in a topic sentence.

transferable skills

Qualities, skills, and expertise that characterize a person regardless of his or her job description or profession and thus transfer with the person from one job to another.

validity

In research, whether a study examines what it is intended to examine.

value

A belief pertaining to what is right and good, comprising the normative structure of a social system; for example, values form the foundation on which social systems develop.

visual persuasion

Incorporating special features such as bold, underline, italics, numbering, and bullet points so that key points are instantly visible for the reader.

"we" viewpoint

In written messages, a pronoun point of view that expresses teamwork and indicates that the ideas are those of the company or collective as well as the writer; frequently used in business today.

"you" viewpoint

In written messages, a pronoun point of view that helps the writer connect with the reader and focus on the reader's needs. Contrast with the "I" viewpoint.

Index